MULTIMEDIA COMPUTING

Case Studies from MIT Project Athena

MULTIMEDIA COMPUTING

Case Studies from MIT Project Athena

Matthew E. Hodges
Russell M. Sasnett

with members and associates
of the Visual Computing Group
at MIT Project Athena

ADDISON-WESLEY PUBLISHING COMPANY

Reading, Massachusetts • Menlo Park, California • New York
Don Mills, Ontario • Wokingham, England • Amsterdam • Bonn
Sydney • Singapore • Tokyo • Madrid • San Juan • Milan • Paris

This book was acquired, developed, and produced by
Manning Publications Co., 3 Lewis Street, Greenwich, CT 06830

Copyediting: Vivian Wheeler
Design: A. Christopher Simon
Page layout: Mary K. Piergies

Library of Congress Cataloging-in-Publication Data
Multimedia computing: case studies from MIT Project Athena/
[edited by] Matthew E. Hodges, Russell M. Sasnett.
          p. cm.
Includes bibliographical references and index.
ISBN 0-201-52029-X
1. Hypertext systems.   2. MIT Project Athena.   I. Hodges, Matthew E.   II. Sasnett, Russell M.
QA76.76.H94M83   1993
006.6--dc20
                                                                92-3687
                                                                CIP

2 3 4 5 6 7 8 9 10-MA-9594

Contents

Preface

In the excitement of developing a new technology, such as multimedia computing, one can lose sight of the historical context in which the work takes place. It is easy to forget that the ideas we implement were foreseen and enabled by others, who (like us) could implement only a part of what they could imagine. At the same time, we are subject to another form of myopia that comes with day-to-day routine—a sense of "ordinariness" overtakes us, and the genuine novelty and significance of what we do is lost. The efforts described in this book take place amidst sweeping technical and social change—the technology of communication is undergoing a fundamental transformation. The work described here is not ordinary; it represents genuine innovation in both technique and content in the field of multimedia computing.

MIT Project Athena was the context for this research. Project Athena was a concentrated effort to provide ubiquitous computing resources for MIT undergraduates. It was a large project with major support from Digital Equipment Corporation and IBM. Over eight years the total investment in the program approached $100 million. With a goal of supporting thousands of workstations and tens of thousands of users, the core of the work centered on rethinking the architecture and system resources needed for the foundations of a large-scale networked computing environment. The results include the X Window System, the Kerberos authentication system, and other key operations and maintenance tools.

The Visual Computing Group (VCG) was launched as a research initiative within the broader scope of Project Athena. Its purpose was to support a budding interest in multimedia technology growing among the MIT faculty. Five years ago the components needed to create a multimedia workstation were just starting to find their way to market. One of the first achievements of the VCG was to take the still-raw technology for digitizing video and couple it with the X Window display system. "Video-in-a-Window" brought still and motion imagery into the workstation world. Today it is hard to imagine the excitement this generated among interactive video and visual database enthusiasts: it was the first time users could view many video images simultaneously, on the same screen, alongside other applications.

This basic technical capability was far from the vision motivating the MIT faculty. Students could watch televised newscasts (or cartoons) in one window and complete their homework assignments in another. But the teachers wanted to construct simulated trips to Paris and Bogotá, to open the MIT image libraries for exploration via the campus network, and to guide students on virtual tours of the cortical brain stem. The Visual Computing Group was driven by these and similar target applications.

Where technology grows with one application in view it tends toward a rigid solution to that one problem. Where it grows with no application in view (as is often the case) it tends to offer somewhat greater flexibility but serves no useful purpose. The Visual Computing Group was favored with a good set of problems—diverse yet attainable. These are the circumstances where ideas of general utility can emerge and be tried.

This book is meant to describe the ideas that came out of this four-year research effort. These span a range from implementation technology to content design. They represent an unusual view of multimedia computing—this can be understood in terms of the ingredients that went into the effort. The technology base was unusual, growing on a network of high-resolution color workstations rather than stand-alone personal computers. The skills in the development team were unusual, with a core of members trained in the humanities: graphic arts, film, video, education, psychology, archaeology, and literature. Similarly, the clients of the project were unusual, starting with some of the most creative teachers at MIT and expanding to include great cultural centers such as the Smithsonian Institution, the Musée d'Orsay, and CERN (the European Center for Research in Particle Physics).

The tangible results of the project include the multimedia workstation (now an antique), the AthenaMuse authoring system (with yet-untapped potentials), and approximately 35 multimedia applications (which push the idea of "electronic document" far beyond its normal role as "automated paper"). A number of these applications have been used extensively at MIT; one has been in continuous use in the visitor's center at CERN for several years; still others have been used to spark the thinking at GTE, Digital, and other private companies. The research itself continues at MIT with the Center for Educational Computing Initiatives. This group formed the AthenaMuse Software Consortium, sponsored by industry and university partners who are interested in seeing the work advance.

Concerning the intangible results of the project—the ideas and observations—we hope that the best will be found in these pages. On the technical topics, we have tried to extract general observations which will have utility beyond their specific implementations. With content, our intent has been to reflect some of the diversity we have discovered, and to convey some of the ways of thinking we found useful in the design and implementation of various forms of multimedia documents.

In our roles as co-architects of AthenaMuse, we felt privileged to play a central part in a most unusual research effort, surrounded by talented individuals in an exhilarating environment. Now, as writers and editors describing this work, we hope that through our efforts and those of our colleagues, some portion of the excitement and the potential we feel for multimedia computing will be transferred through these pages.

MATTHEW E. HODGES

RUSSELL M. SASNETT

Acknowledgments

It has been our privilege to edit the work of our colleagues in the preparation of this manuscript. We thank our co-authors for their enthusiasm and desire to share their ideas in this format: Daniel Applebaum, Ben Davis, José Diaz-Gonzalez, Brian Michon, Evelyn Schlusselberg, and Michael Webster.

We thank Marjan Bace of Manning Publications, for his inspiration and assistance; as well as Vivian Wheeler, for copyediting and clarifying our text; and Mary Piergies, for her skills in design and production. We appreciate their patience and good humor in bringing about this book over the past two years.

We thank our reviewers for their helpful comments and suggestions: Rosalyn Gerstein of The Public Works, Inc.; Bernard Hahn of Siemens-Nixdorf Information Systems; Jennifer Lund of Digital Equipment Corporation; and Michael Trask of Computer Vision Research.

The work described in this book represents the talents of many creative people under the auspices of the Visual Computing Group at MIT Project Athena, including members from diverse backgrounds and institutional affiliations: Mark Ackerman, MIT Project Athena; Lynn Bolduc, MIT Project Athena; Paul Boutin, MIT Project Athena; Roman Budzianowski, MIT Project Athena; David Carver, Digital Equipment Corporation; Ben Davis, MIT Project Athena; Robert French, MIT Project Athena; Rus Gant, MIT Project Athena; Matthew

Grebner, MIT Project Athena; V. Judson Harward, MIT Project Athena; Solange Karsenty, Digital Equipment Corporation Europe; Joel Kehle, MIT Undergraduate Research Assistant; Mark Levine, MIT Project Athena; Robert McKie, IBM; Brian Michon, Digital Equipment Corporation; Evelyn Schlusselberg, MIT Project Athena; Dorothy Shamonsky, MIT Project Athena; Mark Sirota, MIT Project Athena; Michael Webster, MIT Project Athena.

We would like to give special recognition to Ben Davis, whose leadership and vision as manager of the VCG guided the efforts of the group through four years of research. He saw the potential of collaborating with other institutions who owned large collections of visual material, such as the Smithsonian and the Musée d'Orsay, and worked hard to bring about these relationships. Ben was also ultimately responsible for designing and producing over twelve videodiscs for faculty projects that formed the core content base for our explorations.

Several Athena administrators lent key support to the establishment of the VCG, including Steven Lerman, former director of Project Athena and current Director of the Center for Educational Computing Initiatives at MIT (CECI); Earll Murman, former director of Project Athena; and Jacqueline Stewart, Manager of Application Development and User Services.

We extend our appreciation to our corporate sponsors: Jean Bonney, Deidre Brophy-Moore, George Champine, and John McCredie from Digital Equipment Corporation; and Gerald Jones, William Griffin, and David Decker from GTE Laboratories Incorporated.

We owe thanks also to Catherine Avril, Janet Daley, and Kenneth Goldman, all Directors of the Athena Visitors Center, who demonstrated and described this work to approximately three thousand visitors each year.

Key technical contributions were made by a number of highly talented engineers: Daniel Applebaum, MIT Media Lab, video device control; Todd Brunhoff, Tektronix, video extensions for X; David Carver, Digital Equipment Corporation, video extensions for X; Bob Goodwin, Parallax Graphics, Inc., video X server; Mark Levine, MIT Project Athena, video X server; Lester Ludwig, BellCore, video X server; Marty Picco, Parallax Graphics, Inc., video X server; Ben Rubin, MIT Media Lab, non-linear video editing.

In addition, many people contributed their ideas and efforts to the applications developed on this foundation. To the members of the MIT faculty, who lent their support and graciously allowed us to experiment within the context of their own research and teaching, we owe our deepest gratitude: Lois Craig, Associate Dean of Architecture; Glorianna Davenport, Assistant Professor, Media Arts and Technology; Herbert Einstein, Professor, Civil and Environmental Engineering; Gilberte Furstenberg, Senior Lecturer, Foreign Language and Literature; Douglas Morganstern, Senior Lecturer, Foreign Language and Literature; Janet Murray, Senior Research Scientist, Foreign Language and Literature; Charles Oman, Senior Research Engineer, Aeronautics and Astronomics; Sheldon Penman, Professor, Biology; Merrill Smith, Associate Librarian, Rotch Visual Collection; Steven Wertheim, Instructor of Neuropathology, Harvard Medical School; David Wilson, Professor, Mechanical Engineering; Muriel Cooper, Professor, Media Arts and Technology.

We thank the Visiting Associates to the VCG, whose focused efforts on developing new and unusual applications continually brought us new ways of seeing: Beth Adelson, Rutgers University, *Love and the Search for a Cheap Flat;* Constantinos Doukas, Columbia University; Jennifer Lawson, Harvard University, *Film Analysis: Citizen Kane;* Wendy Mackay, Digital Equipment Corporation, *EVA;* Linn Marks, Columbia University, *Visual Poetry;* Girish Muzumdar, Bibliothèque de France; Michael Spencer, Blacksmith and Media Technologist, *Blacksmithing;* Pierre van Berkel, MonteVideo, University of Amsterdam.

In addition, a number of people from collaborating institutions worked on specific projects: *Bibliothèque de France*—Alain Giffard; CERN *Diorama*—Jean-Pierre Vialle, Eric Gerelle, Hervé Platteaux, Julia Geer, Greg Grajew, Werner Kienzle; *Chronoscope,* Musée d'Orsay—Françoise LeCoz, Fabrice LeMessier; *Dans le Quartier St. Gervais*—Ayshe Farman-Farmarian, Michael Roper; *Navigation*—John Borden, John Spencer, Thomas Arnold, Joanna Hattery; *Smithsonian Institution*—Janet Gomon, Kim Nielsen, Jacqueline Hess; *Harvard Scientific Instruments Collection*—Will Andrewes; GTE *Real Estate*—José Diaz-Gonzalez, Vincent Phuah, Steven Gutfreund; GTE *VideoLine*—Robert Virzi; GTE *FAIRS*—S.C. Chang, Horace Dedieu.

Authors

Matthew Hodges and **Russell Sasnett** are experts in multimedia and communication-oriented computing. They worked together as Visiting Scientists at MIT Project Athena from 1987 to 1991. During this time they designed and implemented the *AthenaMuse* multimedia authoring system and much of the application software described in this volume. They subsequently returned to their sponsoring corporations, Matthew Hodges to Digital Equipment Corporation and Russell Sasnett to GTE Laboratories. They continued their research in distributed multimedia business applications, design practices based on Quality Function Deployment (QFD), rapid prototyping, and case study methods.

In 1992 Matthew Hodges left Digital to form Hodges Associates, a consulting firm specializing in technology innovation management. He works with businesses to improve their communications through process analysis, technology innovation, and user-centered design methods.

Russell Sasnett is a Senior Member of the Technical Staff at GTE Laboratories in the Distributed Multimedia Applications Project. He designs advanced distributed applications and authoring services in the context of a high-speed network computing environment.

Matthew Hodges and Russell Sasnett can be reached by electronic mail at *hodges@world.std.com* and *rsasnett@world.std.com* respectively.

Daniel I. Applebaum is a software engineer at Vicor Incorporated in Incline Village, Nevada, developing multimedia communications systems for business applications. He created the Galatea Network Video Device Control System at the MIT Media Laboratory with funding from Project Athena. Galatea is a server-based solution to the problem of building distributed video applications. Galatea is a core component of many research projects throughout the world, and has become the basis for several commercial products.

Ben Davis is the Manager of the AthenaMuse Software Consortium and a Research Associate at the MIT Center for Educational Computing Initiatives. While he was Manager of the Athena Visual Computing Group (1986–1991), he also taught in the Visual Language Workshop at the MIT Media Laboratory, in the MIT Visual Arts Program, and in the Department of Computing, Communications, and Technology at Teachers College, Columbia University. He was also a Fellow at the MIT Center for Advanced Visual Studies (1983–1984).

Dr. José Diaz-Gonzalez is the President of OpenWare Incorporated in Santo Domingo, Dominican Republic, where he provides consulting and system integration services. From 1988 to 1992, he was the Principal Investigator of the Distributed Multimedia Applications project at GTE Laboratories. He holds a Ph.D. in Computer Science from the University of Southwestern Louisiana.

Brian Michon is a Visiting Scientist at the Georgia Institute of Technology, where he manages the Multimedia Database Technologies project for Digital Equipment Corporation, working with industrial partners to develop applications in telecommunications, health care, and manufacturing. His interests include the design of highly iconic user interfaces, the integration of temporal media into computational environments, and technology transfer.

Evelyn Schlusselberg is a Research Associate at the MIT Center for Educational Computing Initiatives, where she prototypes and develops multimedia applications, conducts formative evaluation studies on interface design, and is part of the core AthenaMuse-2 development team. Her research interests concern effective ways of structuring multimedia information to allow multiple approaches for accessing material and flexible presentations that adapt to users' information needs.

Michael Webster is a Research Associate at the MIT Center for Educational Computing Initiatives, where he focuses on cross-platform application development and the design of graphical editors for AthenaMuse-2. His interests include the human factors of multimedia and its uses in large audience settings such as classrooms, theatres, and interactive television.

Part 1

FOUNDATIONS

1. A New Literacy

The computer is the chameleon of the communication world—a versatile implement that can take on any color. In its earlier days it was a device for processing numbers. Some felt that only a few of these "giant brains" would be needed because there was little demand for large-scale numeric analysis. The computer developed as a tool for information processing. But now word processing, spreadsheets, and desktop publishing have taken a primary role in computing; *communication* is the role of the computer today. The evolution of computing has been a steady expansion of instruments for the communication and expression of ideas.

What we call multimedia computing—the subject of this book—takes one more step in extending the power of the computer as a communication medium. This expansion is based largely on the addition of new media, especially of sound and image. Why are these changes taking place today? The primary cause is a hundred-fold jump in desktop processing power, from 1 to 100 MIPs, with similar gains in storage and transmission capacities.

But "multimedia" involves more than the simple addition of new data types—simultaneous *integration* of a wide range of symbolic modes into a coherent framework is taking place. Media integration means "compound documents" in a broad sense. It is the combination of different representations or symbolic modes. The technical requirements

There is some quibbling on exactly what is and what is not "multimedia." Here the term is used simply to refer to widespread use of sound and image data.

One "MIP" means one million instructions per second.

underlying this integration have spurred a rethinking of what goes into a computer, spawning hundreds of "multimedia add-ons" and new generations of "multimedia workstations." Much further work is needed, however, before the present mixture of technology is blended into a fluid medium of expression.

This book is a waystation on a long path of evolution. Earlier books on multimedia were "visionary" or research oriented—descriptions of isolated experiments or ideas about what might be. Here, the aim is to move toward coherent treatment of a large body of work. The discussion is based primarily on four years at MIT Project Athena, which entailed the development of a multimedia workstation, a multimedia document architecture, an authoring environment, and approximately thirty-five applications built on this foundation. The book does not describe all of the work at Project Athena, nor all of the media-technology research at MIT.

LITERACY AND TECHNOLOGY

On the evolution of the written record in England, see M. T. Clanchy, *From Memory to Written Record: England, 1066–1307*, Harvard University Press, Cambridge MA, 1979.

Consider the development of computing as the emergence of a new communication technology. Compare it with similar changes in history. One of these is especially relevant: the change from oral tradition to written record, when the basic methods for using written documents for record-keeping were developed (the eleventh to thirteenth centuries in England). Some of the problems that had to be overcome at that time are curiously parallel to those we face today. With multimedia computing we are preparing, after more than half a millennium, to readopt the oral record (through video and audio recordings).

Among the first (and most impressive) efforts to commit a nation to written record was William the Conquerer's *Domesday Book*, completed in 1086. *Domesday* was intended to make a complete inventory of William's domain after twenty years of rule—it was the first time that any comparable undertaking had been conceived and implemented on such a scale.

In terms of information gathering, the project was remarkable. In seven months the king's agents produced documentation on thirty-four English counties. The detail was so fine that according to the Anglo-Saxon Chronicle of that period, "there was no single hide nor a yard of land, nor indeed (it is a shame to relate but it seemed no shame to him [the king] to do) one ox nor one cow nor one pig which was there left out, and not put down in his record."

In the end, though, *Domesday* played more of a symbolic role than a practical one. It was not frequently referenced in the activities of the court after its completion. The machinery of written record was still too new—the mentality of accessing written documents had not yet developed, nor had the techniques for organizing them. *Domesday* had no consistent functional role, but stood to mark the beginning of profound change that would transpire over roughly two hundred years. The use of written records grew slowly, and it was not until the time of the *quo warranto* proceedings at the end of the thirteenth century that systematic attempts were made to *require* written records in legal proceedings.

Some of the issues faced during that two-hundred-year period are quite interesting. Sophisticated techniques for database management, such as alphabetical sorting, had not been introduced to the official archive. People were experimenting with graphical icons as a user-interface device for mapping cross-references. For example, the Exchequer *Liber A* in 1294 used an icon showing a man bearing a lance and sword as a reference for documents pertaining to Scotland (these documents were stored in "Coffer T"). People realized that although the database existed (and would play an increasingly important role), the administration could not cope with the influx of documents and there was no reliable way to retrieve information from the archive. For this reason the twelfth century has become known as the "golden age of forgery."

E. L. G. Stone, "The Appeal to History in Anglo-Scottish Relations," *Archives*, Vol. IX, 1969, p. 11.

Will it take two hundred years to solve the information management problems of multimedia? It has taken nearly fifty years to get started. In 1945 Vannevar Bush proposed the "Memex"—his vision of a computer system that would allow a reader to build and follow chains of cross-references through large databases of text and images. This idea percolated for about forty years before the technology matured enough to support the first commercial "hypertext" systems, the first (partial) implementations of Bush's vision.

V. Bush, "As We May Think," *Atlantic Monthly*, July 1945, pp. 101–108.

Our focus in this book is only on the next five years—not the next hundred fifty; but it is useful to have a broader perspective. The next section discusses the nature of computer documents as a key to understanding the changes in multimedia that may occur over this time frame.

Document Architecture

Having mastered the transition from memory to written record, we live today in an age dominated by paper documents. The trends in computing, especially the development of multimedia, suggest that we may be at the beginning of a fundamental transition in which the technology of documentation will undergo another radical shift. One of the indications of this transition is "document architecture," a recent expression used to discuss the internal structure of a document as represented on a computer. The very combination of the two words—implying a fundamental scrutiny of what a document is—says something about the nature of the changes taking place.

A. Dengel, R. Bleisinger, R. Hoch, F. Fein, and F. Hores, "From Paper to Office Document Standard Representation," *Computer*, Vol. 25, No. 7, July 1992, pp. 63–67.

One of the first document architecture standards was the Office Document Architecture (ODA) developed by the International Standards Organization (ISO). This "architecture" defines a range of possible forms that a document's contents may take. The early versions of this and related proposals were closely modeled on paper documents. They described various levels of subdivision and formatting that could be applied to a sequential stream of text. Over the past years, ODA and other efforts have struggled to cope with the explosion of graphic and image formats, and more recently with time-structured information such as video, audio, and animation.

The very notion of what constitutes a multimedia document has undergone radical change. New document architecture committees and prestandard committees are working to standardize each incremental extension to the idea of a multimedia document, working as energetically as if the ideas they promote had already been shown to be useful (the current trend is toward "anticipatory" standardization).

Current changes in the architecture of documents can be understood in terms of two fundamental trends. One is the return to "nonliterate" forms of communication, especially video and audio. The second is toward new ways of representing or expressing ideas that the computer offers—advanced "visualization" techniques and simulation.

The Return to Nonliterate Communication

Film, television, radio, and telephone have had an enormous impact on the way we communicate. All are based on nonwritten communication. All offer certain advantages over paper, primarily *fluency* (less effort for most people to talk than to write) and *richness* (subtleties of intonation, oral language, and gesture).

The main problem with nonwritten forms is their poor fit with the machinery of recordkeeping. So far, audio and video are not handled well as records. Broadcasting companies maintain huge archives of tape; the image of medieval bureaucrats rummaging through bins of parchment "rolls" is too close a parallel to what we see among the racks of modern video and audio archives.

Multimedia allows the record-keeping power of the computer to be applied to nonwritten forms of communication. It is for this reason that one can anticipate the resurgence of these forms. Recording and storage technologies have been available with film, video and audio recording, and now with digital video and audio. The addition of computers to these technologies brings the organizational aspects needed to transform raw recordings into an effective system of documentation.

A modern *Domesday* survey was completed in England in 1986—nine hundred years after the original. This version, implemented as a multimedia document, contains some 50,000 photographs, 250,000 pages of text, and 60 minutes of motion video. Like its predecessor, the modern *Domesday* is a marvel of information gathering (it was produced with contributions by over a million people). But again, the mentality for access and application of this type of information is still too new. And like its namesake, the modern *Domesday* plays a symbolic role rather than a truly functional one. Like its precursor, it marks the beginning of a passage in human communication, this time with "nonliterate" forms in the ascendancy.

The next chapter describes a prototype system developed to record design decision processes directly in audio and video, using the computer for retrieval, editing, and presentation.

New Modes of Expression

The basic models for computer documents will be borrowed from earlier media—from paper, film, telephone, and radio. But the computer offers fundamentally new techniques for expressing ideas that have not been available via these earlier media. In order to understand the direction that computer communication will take over time, one should look not only at the prior media that can be assimilated to the computer domain and how these media will change as a result, but at the unique characteristics of the computer itself, in an effort to comprehend its potential role in human communication.

One of the unique strengths of the computer, for example, is its ability to model processes of change—something that is quite difficult to achieve on paper. With film or video it is possible to depict change, but these images are still much more restrictive than a computer simulation, in which one can explore complex phenomena by manipulating many parameters and rendering the result through real-time three-dimensional animation, for example.

A simulation is a form of communication. People try to express ideas about how things work—economic systems, biological systems, weather systems. The models they create are the expressions of their ideas. A simulation is not normally thought of as a document; the idea of combining a simulation with a body of text and sending it as an electronic mail message is still relatively new.

This trend can be seen, however, in the recent uses of spreadsheet models (which can be viewed as a form of simulation). At first, the spreadsheet was used in isolation—the reams of tabular output were appended to paper documents by hand. Later, one could cut and paste directly on the computer, and even have the spreadsheet tables automatically "cleaned up" by a smart word processor.

Now one can begin to carry along the *dynamics* of the spreadsheet through "dynamic data exchange," where a change in a spreadsheet model is automatically propagated into text documents that have been bound to it, or by directly inserting a functional sheet as a "region" in a compound document. Here is the beginning of an idea with much broader implications—the spreadsheet still a relatively humble species of computer simulation. One can anticipate the possibilities as more powerful simulation techniques are merged into the communication domain.

THE LOCI OF CHANGE

These two trends—the return to nonliterate forms of documents and the development of simulation and visualization as fundamental forms of expression—constitute the underlying currents in the growth of multimedia. They define the long-term direction and fundamental motives; with this background one can assess some of the short-term movements and technology advances that are currently under way.

Growth at the local level is occurring on two different fronts—two loci of change. One is technical, looking at multimedia as a fusion of different *data types* on the computer and specifying the technical requirements for combining and managing text, graphics, audio, and video. From this perspective there are a number of interesting issues relative to hardware and software, (synchronization, distribution, and so on).

The other perspective is human. Here multimedia is a fusion of different *modes of expression*. One can clothe a message or represent an idea in text, images, sound. The issues deal with human symbolic capacities—how people use symbol systems, the implications of combining them, and perhaps most important, what tools will make it possible to draw upon the full range of expressive possibilities with a minimum of confusion and specialized skill.

The following sections outline the main threads of these developments. The aim is not to give an in-depth analysis, but rather to give a sense of the complexity and interdependence of the factors involved in multimedia computing. A number of these issues are taken up in more detail in later sections of this book.

Technical Issues

On the technical side, there are many issues that affect the implementation of a multimedia system. In various stages of solution, they can be grouped roughly in terms of (a) display, (b) transmission, and (c) storage—corresponding to the principal components of a multimedia system.

Display

Display refers to the technology needed to render imagery on a screen or to play audio over a speaker. Much of the work centers on the devices that actually process the data (digitize video, for example) and write it on the display device (the computer screen or audio amplifier). Video is one case where display hardware has gone through a number of generations over the past ten years. The earliest systems dealt with video in the analog domain; today most systems take analog video as input but digitize it into a display frame buffer. The trend is toward all-digital video, with the first custom hardware products already on the market. CPU speeds already are reaching the point where simple video applications can be implemented without using any custom display hardware.

At the same time, fundamental changes are taking place with video technology in and of itself. High-definition television (HDTV), initiated by the consumer electronics community with an eye to improving the conventional uses of television, is advancing rapidly. The first HDTV designs were analog. The computer community is moving directly to digital HDTV (or to a hybrid broadcast format), where a "device-independent" or "scaleable" video format could be developed.

In parallel, the accessibility to consumer video has grown dramatically. There are many new possibilities for video documentation and other "video-as-data" applications which do not require high production values.

It is important to remember too that graphics display technology is moving ahead quickly. The limitations have centered on the time it takes to create and render images. Real-time three-dimensional animation is possible in limited contexts (30 frames per second with a model of 20,000 polygons, for example).

The cost of graphics technology has been dropping to the point that reasonably sophisticated systems for data visualization and 3D imaging applications are entering the desktop market. Until now, graphics and video have remained separate. But there are possibilities for combining them. One example is the depth-cued camera, which measures the distance of objects from the camera, thus making it possible to derive the partial geometry of a scene.

Along with the problems of displaying different types of information is the difficulty of synchronizing them. Some forms of information, such as audio and video, require close coupling. This is possible on single-user systems, but becomes more difficult when a network or multiprocessing operating system is involved. The problem of synchronization is discussed further in Chapter 16.

Transmission

For the most part, network distribution is viewed as critical technology for multimedia, since communication is the primary objective. But multimedia data stretch the state of the art in network technology. One problem is the limitation of network bandwidth. Networks are growing from a data rate of roughly 10 megabits per second up to 100 or 1000 megabits per second. There are a number of approaches to achieving this expansion, which have significant differences other than the raw bandwidth. In particular, the protocols that actually send and receive data can have quite different characteristics. These, and other issues pertaining to network distribution, are discussed in more detail in Chapter 20.

Image compression is another technology closely related to transmission (and to storage as well). Reducing the data that must be transmitted has a direct impact on the potential uses of a distribution and storage system.

A number of different compression schemes are under development. The ISO standards JPEG (from the Joint Photographic Experts Group) and MPEG (Motion Picture Experts Group) are two current examples. JPEG was developed originally for still images but can be used for motion (30 frames per second) as well. The difference between the two is that the JPEG method stores complete information for each frame, whereas the MPEG approach stores differences from one frame to the next.

As an example of how the various issues can interact, the JPEG and MPEG compression standards have been drafted with no provision for network distribution; they were conceived from the perspective of storage and the need to read data quickly from storage devices. They assume that the packets of data will always be delivered in proper sequence, as they would be from a storage device. This is not always the case on a network, however, so the compression standards or the network protocol standards must change to take into account that possibility.

Storage

Finally, there are significant issues concerning storage in a multimedia system. The data in a multimedia environment have a diversity that conventional data management systems are not prepared to handle. The data objects can span an enormous range of size and of format; new models of data management systems are needed.

Also, because the multimedia database contains a mixture of structured data (relations with fixed fields) and of unstructured data (text and images), the definition and access facilities must be more diverse than a conventional database. These should provide the typical join and union operations for structured data queries, but also support unstructured text queries and eventually some form of query for image and sound. The indexing facilities should support retrieval of partial objects as well, which becomes important with large video and audio archives.

Multimedia systems are generally built using an object paradigm. In terms of managing object-oriented data, important issues of version control and dependency mapping need to be addressed by the database management system. A general communication environment must allow people to create multiple versions of objects over time without burdening the storage resources. If an object is deleted or modified in some way, the object manager must access the other objects that are dependent on that object; in other words, it must be possible to trace dependencies through the database. These technologies are in various stages of research or product offering at this point. None is fully developed or well-understood.

Human Issues

More interesting than technical issues!

Beyond these technical matters, specifically human issues are involved in the development of multimedia. These have to do with how people create and use documents of various forms and in various settings. Issues of this kind are addressed through the design of software tools that allow people to do efficiently what they want to do. They are often overshadowed by the technical issues, which are more tangible and seem to have more immediacy. But the human issues should not be ignored, for they have just as much bearing on the success or failure of multimedia technology. Some of the principal topics concern (a) authoring, (b) information retrieval, and (c) distribution.

Authoring

Creating multimedia documents is closely allied to the design of document architecture, which determines what types of documents it is possible to create. Authoring deals as well with the steps one must go through to create these documents. The architecture itself is a difficult issue. It is partly a chicken-and-egg situation in which people have not yet had enough experience with multimedia documents to understand the possibilities and know what it is they want.

Document architectures will move from strictly paper-based models to those accommodating time-based material such as video and audio, and then to forms that admit more complex forms of simulation and dynamic interaction. Authoring is a central topic of this book, and many of the principal issues are addressed in the following chapters. Chapter 5 discusses the relationship between authoring and document architecture in more detail.

Information Retrieval

Think for a minute about data retrieval in an image-rich communication environment. Currently there is no equivalent to text searching for image and audio data; one cannot use a direct sample of a visual style as the basis of a query—the search is always mediated through linguistic descriptors. What does this mean in terms of access to the desired information? All reference to image and audio data is currently based on linguistic channels—text descriptors of content. The trend here will be to incorporate more of the content-based retrieval techniques (neural nets and the like), image analysis, and voice recognition. Most of these techniques are of limited practical use at present, finding their place in relatively specialized niches and research environments.

Information filtering is another topic that becomes more important as the volume of computer-based communication increases. The trend is toward more intelligent messaging systems, which attach descriptive information to documents so that they can be processed automatically (filed, sorted, thrown away, and so on). Similarly, present research efforts aim at automatically indexing or otherwise building content-based linkages within a set of documents.

As the use of time-based documents increases, the need for filtering gains new significance. Video and audio cannot be scanned as easily as text; it takes time to extract their meaning. One of the examples in the next chapter discusses some tools that can help to isolate the useful segments of time-based information.

Distribution

Most communication takes place between groups, many of which are widely separated in space and time. Distribution of information in such contexts presents a variety of issues:

- Security and access, both for multimedia mail and for distributed information archives;
- Social interaction over video-mediated communication links and "collaborative" software applications;
- "Graceful degradation" of services over heterogeneous delivery systems;
- Support for multilingual applications.

Each of these issues has become the subject of research in academic and industrial settings; each presents substantial challenges, and each is important in developing the potential of multimedia.

SUMMARY

This brief survey is meant to give a feeling for the complexity and scope of multimedia—there are many issues that interact in complex ways. It is often difficult to maintain perspective in this situation; people tend to become absorbed in one or two of these topics and want to shrink the subject to their own field of view. Without understanding the larger context, multimedia becomes mysterious and seems to take on a life of its own.

Our aim here is not to survey all the issues mentioned above; the focus is on the nature of multimedia applications, the central problems of authoring and design, and a variety of related technical topics. The presentation is meant to be of immediate practical value for those who want to produce or evaluate applications and at the same time provide a fundamental grasp of the broader view of multimedia as a transformation of communication technology.

The book is divided into three parts. The first presents an overview of multimedia in business and education, and reviews some of the major conceptual issues in the design and implementation of multimedia applications. The second part dissects a number of applications using a case-study approach. The cases have been chosen to cover the principal approaches to multimedia design, from simulation to information access, and to represent a range of content domains. The case studies show something of the design, the overall structure, and the unique implementation details of these applications. The third part covers a number of technical matters. These include timing and synchronization, distributed device control, and various aspects of data integration and tool design.

2.   Multimedia in Business

Like the quest for the Holy Grail, people are seeking a "core applica-tion" for multimedia in business and industry—an application to set the market on fire. Some see training; some, presentation; some, docu-mentation; some, conferencing. But so far, no such core application is clearly evident; indeed, no large market exists for *any* multimedia application.

In fact, there may never be a core application for multimedia (like the spreadsheet); that dream may belong to the world of information processing. There, individuals could buy a shrink-wrapped package and build powerful spreadsheet models in the privacy of their own home.

Multimedia belongs much more to the world of communication. The core *function* of multimedia in business is to improve communica-tion—to capture higher-quality information and move it with less resis-tance through an organization. Effective communication is a collective enterprise that takes many forms and touches many points of an orga-nization.

One might think then of a *multimedia mail* system as a candidate application (and many companies do). But a mail system alone, even one with voice annotations or pictures, does not have the right impact on an organization to be called a "core application"—it does not moti-vate organizations to make large-scale investments.

Multimedia may instead find its place in business organizations through a variety of applications, all working together. The combined impact of several applications that will generate a higher quality of information access throughout an organization—this is the benefit that will make the multimedia technology pay for itself.

The aim of this chapter is to construct a picture of what such a communication infrastructure might look like. We will look at various aspects of business activity that incorporate multimedia. Five areas are included in this scenario: (a) gathering and retrieving information, (b) sharing information through conferencing, (c) documenting design decisions, (d) constructing prototypes, and (e) documentation, training, and presentation.

All of the examples presented here were developed using the AthenaMuse authoring system, developed by the Visual Computing Group of MIT's Project Athena. Accordingly, there is a coherence that runs *across* applications—communication is the driving need, and it is not met with a hodgepodge of "point solutions." These applications do, however, deal with different problems and contents, and therefore the picture is bound to have something of a "cubist" quality. But our purpose is only to explore directions and not to proclaim solutions.

CATALOGING RESOURCES

The scenario begins with gathering and organizing information relevant to a business problem. Much of this information is multimedia in nature—patent literature, design information, customer requirement data, vendor or subcontractor services, sales information, and so on. The first application, then, is a multimedia archiving facility that allows people to store and retrieve these kinds of information. Our example deals with a real estate database.

This application was developed at GTE Laboratories by members of the Distributed Multimedia Applications project.

The object of the *Real Estate* application was to let potential customers explore listings in a real estate database, modeling a relocation bureau whose function is to help corporate employees find housing in a new community. An employee might begin by browsing through the multiple listings. The first step, therefore, is to construct a query that will initiate a database search.

In the prototype version of the application, a query "builder" helps novice users construct SQL queries for requests such as "houses in Cambridge with more that 2,500 square feet"; the interface is shown in

Figure 2.1. In addition to traditional Boolean query, there is support for a free-form input construct as used in information retrieval systems (where one simply types a sequence of words and the system uses built-in assumptions about logic and importance to formulate a query).

The system accesses two databases over the network: one of them is *SyBase*; the other is an information retrieval system called *FAIRS*, developed at GTE. *SyBase* contains structured records with fixed fields for each entry. The *FAIRS* database contains free text descriptions of the different houses. As an example, one could ask for a green house with four bedrooms on a cul-de-sac near a pond for less than $250,000. The system will try to match the color, the pond, and the location in *FAIRS*, and the number of bedrooms and price information through *SyBase*.

The two databases are designed to deal with radically different information, stored in different forms, and searched with different query constructs. The user knows only that one form must be filled out; AthenaMuse gathers the query information through a single interface but generates separate queries to the two databases. It then receives the results from both queries and merges them to produce an integrated response in the form of a customized "listing booklet" which is constructed dynamically based on the return of the queries.

The book appears as a separate document on the screen, as shown in Figures 2.2 and 2.3. It has the complete record for each house, including information from both databases, pictures, and in some cases video tours of the properties. The pictures and video are stored as references in the database. AthenaMuse uses the Galatea video server to access the remote video source (see Chapter 19). A remote Galatea server locates the video material and delivers it to the local workstation through a switched broadband digital video network (based on SONET at OC1 rates). The images are displayed on the user's screen, scaled and positioned to fit on the page. Any of the images can be enlarged to full-screen size for more detail.

These custom listing booklets can be saved and can be called up independently—in fact, they are self-sufficient AthenaMuse documents. A user can call up the results of a previous query to make comparisons. The system provides editing capabilities as well, so the user can copy any record and append it to a separate "stack of cards" document in which the pages can be pulled out and viewed side by side.

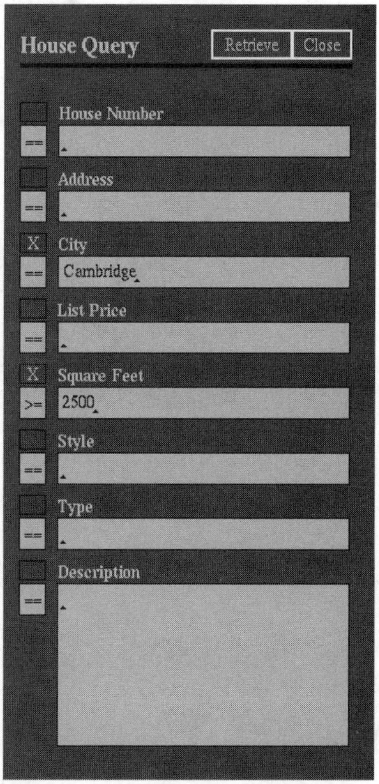

SQL refers to the Structured Query Language format for Boolean combinations of keyword search descriptors.

FAIRS works on inverted text files, prioritizing output based on the order of terms in a query string.

Figure 2.1 Interface for the query builder in the real estate archive

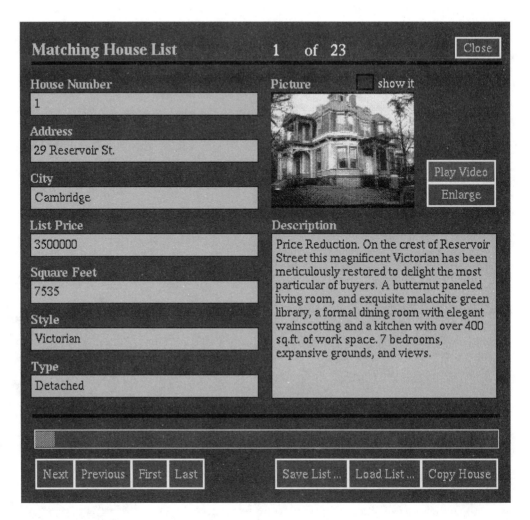

Figure 2.2 Returns from the database queries are used to fabricate a customized listing booklet as shown above.

If a house in the database has a video tour, a button opens a motion video window where the tour is displayed; other information could be included in the same way (plot plans, blueprints, a slide show, or even a full surrogate travel model of the property).

The motion video can also be delivered through the switched network. Galatea can serve a large number of users for still images, but motion video requires one video device for each user, so it becomes equipment intensive to deliver this service with analog devices. With digital video there is less difficulty with resource sharing—many users

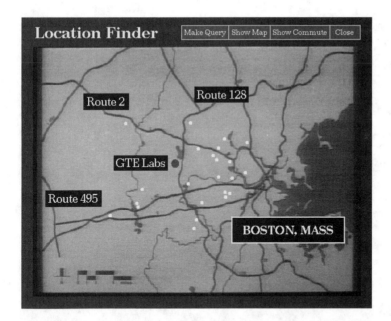

Figure 2.3 As part of the listings booklet, a map shows the location of all properties selected. The user can request information by clicking on the map.

can access the same image file. The difficulty in this situation is with network bandwidth; it is inefficient to have a single fixed connection per user. This is the argument for having an ATM cell or packet switched network; otherwise this sort of application does not scale well. The real estate application shows a multimedia information archive in action. The description of this application continues in the next section, but first two important points should be noted.

1 The real estate archive represents a set of basic features that can be used in many other business settings, including resource directories such as yellow pages; archives of customer interviews for requirements definition; sales, bidding, or marketing "catalogs"; patent information; engineering drawings; and design documentation.

2 The application is constructed as an AthenaMuse "document" and all of its products are AthenaMuse documents—these can be carried forward in a much broader communication environment because they are built on a consistent architecture.

Figure 2.4   A two-way video conference allows the Realtor and buyer to discuss properties in the listing booklet as they appear on the screen.

CONFERENCING

To continue, suppose that you as a user have reviewed the real estate database and selected a small number of houses. Your next questions might concern demographics and geographics—commuting times, neighborhood resources, and the like. The most efficient way to elicit this information is to talk to a Realtor in the remote town. This leads to the next major application—conferencing.

A button in the interface for each house says *Call the Realtor.* A business card appears on the screen for the Realtor when this button is pressed. An option menu also appears, which lets you set the parameters of the call: voice only; voice and video; or voice, video, and shared graphics and data. As you set the parameters, a data field tells you the estimated price of the call according to the amount of bandwidth you want to reserve. You push a button on the screen and the call is made. At first the call is voice only—your phone rings and the Realtor's phone rings.

Once the connection is established and the call proceeds, you may switch to the shared-data mode. The AthenaMuse application then sends a copy of the records you have selected to the Realtor's workstation; the same booklet appears on his or her screen (with the video illustrations). Either of you may turn pages: sometimes the Realtor will drive the application; sometimes you will drive it.

This is what is meant by shared data. The Realtor has a spreadsheet calculator, to make financial projections. As each house is reviewed, the Realtor can load the figures for that property into the spreadsheet, figures which appear on the screen of both the Realtor and the client.

The real estate prototype described here was produced in four weeks at GTE Laboratories. It uses AthenaMuse, *FAIRS, SyBase, sc* (a public domain spreadsheet calculator), and *DOM* (an interoperability tool for managing heterogeneous object-oriented data developed at GTE Laboratories).

DOCUMENTING DESIGN DECISIONS

We became interested in documenting the design decisions we were making in the development of the AthenaMuse authoring language. Because of frequent staff turnover due to the academic environment, only three people of fifteen were continuously involved in the project from start to finish. It was desirable to reduce the time spent in meetings and in writing documentation. We were aware that much important information was lost as the project progressed, and difficult questions had to be reexamined each time a new person started.

As we spoke with corporate visitors, we found that the issues of internal communication within a design team are regarded as extremely expensive matters, both in terms of direct cost (education of a new group member is estimated to be anywhere from three to six months), and in terms of product quality. We undertook some preliminary design documentation efforts to explore the use of video in recording design decisions. This usage represents a third class of multimedia application related to decision-making processes within an organization.

Our aim was to generate materials that could be later used to develop (a) customized training materials; (b) documentation for software support staff once the project was handed off; and (c) presentation materials for "marketing" and technology transfer. The hope was that multimedia documentation could reduce the "communication overhead" in the design group and at the same time provide a means to achieve a more cohesive design.

Data Acquisition

We tested three techniques for gathering the information: (a) personal presentation, (b) peer focus group sessions, and (c) design review meetings. All the video was recorded with an 8-mm camera. The process of data collection proved to be an interesting experience itself; the three techniques yielded quite different results.

For the personal presentation, the camera was focused on an illustration board. The engineer prepared simple block diagrams and explained them briefly. This type of documentation was used in cases where a design feature had implications across different aspects of the system—in explaining the mechanics of a complex timing system used to control the display of annotated video material, for example. Where the implementation is distributed across different points of the system, there is no single place where a comment can be added to make the whole design clear. Cases of this kind are where the normal documentation practices tend to break down, yet they are the points where documentation is most needed.

The peer focus group sessions showed one engineer asking another questions about some portion of a design. This technique yielded the best results overall in that it drew out information quickly, yet required no scripting or preparation. Some parts of the material were better than others; these portions were selected for storage in the archive, the rest were discarded.

The third approach, the design review meeting, was effective only in the summary portions of the meeting. That is, when proposals had been discussed and decisions made, one person stood to summarize the main points of the discussion and the results. Otherwise, the material was too diffuse, and people were sometimes uncomfortable expressing themselves before a camera. On the other hand, watching a meeting through the camera lens proved to be an educational experience in terms of how much repetition and irrelevant discussion can occur in a design meeting.

The Meeting Analyzer

The problem with collecting large amounts of video data is that most of it is not of great interest—the main points of a meeting or a design discussion can be summarized succinctly. For video recordings to work effectively, a powerful set of editing tools needs to begin filtering the information immediately. The whole premise is that this approach should be faster and easier than writing.

The Meeting Analyzer is a prototype developed to process video data recorded in this way. It was conceived as a tool to be used in the context of a design review meeting, a focus group research session, or a customer interview. It could be used post hoc as well, for annotating and filtering video data. The interface is shown in Figure 2.5. The video plays in one window of the screen, surrounded by controls and text input fields. The video can come either from a camera as it is recorded, or from a tape of a previous session. The tools were designed to speed up annotation of the video so that it could be done in real time. Our goal was to do as much annotation as possible during the meeting to reduce the time spent in post hoc analysis.

On the left in Figure 2.5 is a free text input field that allows the annotator to write comments and have them automatically attached to a time duration in the video. There is also a set of predefined keywords that can be applied to the video with a click of the mouse. In our prototype these included a list of the attendees, a list of actions they might take in a meeting (make a proposal, object, summarize), and a list of topics expected to be discussed. The keywords were arranged in three columns so that simple descriptive phrases could be constructed with a click in each column. These statements would serve as a semiformal coding of the time spent in the meeting that could be searched later— for example, "Show me all the things that Evelyn said during the meeting," or "Show me the arguments offered against my proposal."

There were also "salience" buttons to mark the relative importance of the various moments of the meeting. These could be used later to automatically edit the material onto an archive tape, separating out the most important sections.

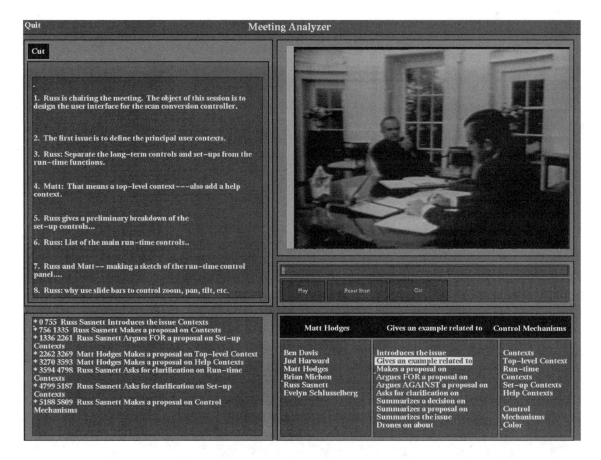

Figure 2.5 **The Meeting Analyzer is intended for use by a secretary or researcher in the context of a meeting. The video is displayed as it is being recorded. Alternatively, prerecorded tapes can be used.**

The documents produced with the Meeting Analyzer would be accessed through a repository like the resource directory in the real estate example. These materials could be automatically indexed according to the keyword descriptors.

 The Meeting Analyzer never became an active part of the development process with AthenaMuse. Nonetheless, the prototype convincingly demonstrated the value of design documentation of this kind.

BUILDING PROTOTYPES

During the design phase of a product development cycle, prototypes can play an extremely valuable role in clarifying or formalizing the design ideas of the development team or in conducting formative research. Again, the multimedia computing environment can make a significant contribution.

The VideoLine Controller

Researchers at GTE Laboratories were interested in designing an interface to a movie selection service for home viewers. The idea called for a form of remote control unit that would interact with a "movie catalog" displayed on the television screen. As part of the project, a "high-fidelity" model of the system was produced, complete with infrared sensors, a functional control panel, and videodisc players to display the films.

VideoLine was a research prototype developed at GTE Laboratories, not a commercial service.

As an alternative approach, an AthenaMuse prototype was constructed (Figure 2.6). The simulated control unit is on the right and the viewer's television display on the left. The buttons on the controller can be used to scroll through the library of available movies with all of the display shown on the viewer's television. This prototype models the interaction that is needed to select and display a film.

The AthenaMuse-based prototype does not capture many of the details built into the high-fidelity version of the system. Still, it can be used to determine visual characteristics such as colors and button placement, and to simulate the interactive behavior of the service. In addition, it was completed in a few days at no real expense, and it can be packaged and sent as a mail message, should there be a need for remote presentation.

The prototype was implemented as an AthenaMuse document. One of the design objectives for AthenaMuse was to erase the boundaries between interactive applications such as these and the more conventional document formats such as the meeting notes or real estate booklets. In this way, prototypes can be brought into the communication environment and used, for example, as figures or illustrations in a functional specification or presentation document.

as long as everyone agrees the prototype's purpose!

Figure 2.6 The *VideoLine* control unit is simulated on the right side of the screen, and the home viewer's television screen is shown on the left.

DISTRIBUTION CHANNELS

The premise underlying this series of examples is that multimedia in business must be regarded as a communication vehicle, and that to be effective it must be thoroughly integrated into the fiber of the business operation. There are many points where such integration is possible, and the selection of applications will of course vary in different situations. The examples presented above are the "deep" components of such a system, where the information is gathered and stored.

The information archive described with the real estate service is the backbone application for storage and retrieval. The design documentation and prototyping applications produce business-related information. There are other applications that have to do with the *distribution* of this information. Examples include training, documentation, business presentation materials, and related mail and messaging systems.

Part 2 of this book presents a wide range of examples of presentation materials. In most cases the contents pertain to university course materials or museum presentations, but the same formats can and have been used to produce business-related documents, such as interactive annual reports, technical training materials, and interactive documentation. Chapters 11 and 12 give examples of some of these materials, including experiments with the on-line AthenaMuse documentation and the customized training materials on mechanical bearings. These are only some of the possibilities of distribution formats for business information.

As to the distribution itself, the conferencing model has already been described. Electronic mail is another vehicle, where the goal is to package and send these forms of documents over a network as mail messages.

One of the experiments with AthenaMuse was to produce a front end to the UNIX mail handler *mh* that would send AthenaMuse documents as well as conventional text messages. Given the name of an AthenaMuse document to be sent, a custom utility identified and packaged all of the associated resources into one file. This package could then be sent as a mail message and "opened" and run on the recipient's terminal.

There are significant issues with multimedia mail systems. One difficulty is the distribution of the video data, which depends on having the network bandwidth and storage capacity at both ends of the connection. A second problem is security; the mail message is a program that can seriously affect the reader's environment, and some provision must be made for the reader's protection. A third issue is that of distributing multimedia messages over heterogeneous environments, where the message should be able to adapt reasonably well to an environment with greater or lesser resources than the environment it was sent from.

like current mail products

SUMMARY

The examples presented here are not put forth as *solutions* for multimedia in business, but as *directions*—multimedia will play a role in the communication infrastructure of a business organization and therefore will appear as many applications dispersed throughout the organization.

AthenaMuse was produced as a development system for educational materials, not as a general-purpose communication environment for business. We have chosen to structure our presentation around AthenaMuse applications in order to underscore our fundamental premise: communication in business means a flow of information through an organization, which can best occur when the document format is flexible enough to take on the many shapes that are required in such an environment.

Production, transformation, and distribution of business information touches an organization in many places. The liquidity of this information depends on the coherence of the environment in which it exists. Every format-interchange transformation, every inconsistent user interface, every ten-second delay, every shift in conceptual model from one application to another adds resistance to the line—dissipates energy—and reduces the impact of the communication system in a business environment. These many small points of resistance quickly result in a net loss of energy and the system founders. Multimedia in business will depend on a coherent system of applications that can produce, transform, and distribute meaningful business information across an organization without this energy dissipation.

3. New Views of Education

Education and multimedia computing have a symbiotic relationship; education is shaping the development of multimedia, and multimedia is opening new possibilities in education. Education has been one of the first and best clients of multimedia computing systems. Educators have supplied a stream of application ideas that range across all levels of technical sophistication. This process has been important to multimedia technology in terms of understanding applications and the tools and technology necessary to support them. For its part, multimedia is bringing about a number of significant changes in education.

This chapter focuses on four such areas—ways in which multimedia offers something new to education. More than simple administrative or labor-saving strategies, these areas have to do with how ideas are represented and how students explore them. They are discussed in the following sections, with examples drawn from our experience:

1 Learning environments
2 Constructivist learning materials
3 Customization and small-scale projects
4 Collaborative learning

This list, although not exhaustive, encompasses the principal new directions in educational computing. Computers have been regarded by some educators as a panacea, by others as a fraud. In this chapter we review the major areas where multimedia computing offers substantive contributions and thereby provides a framework for understanding the forces that educators will be exerting in the development of multimedia.

LEARNING ENVIRONMENTS

If you want to learn French, it helps if you can spend time in Paris. To learn to navigate a boat, it helps to get out on the water. In many cases the best way to learn something is by seeing and doing it. But the best way is not always the most practical. One of the attractions of the computer for educators is that it enables students to experience, at least partially, situations they would not otherwise have a chance to encounter. Although the simulations generally fall far short of reality, even a limited experience can be better than none at all.

One way in which a computer simulation can compensate for its shortcomings is by offering to explain itself—something that real situations never seem to do. This combination of explanation and experience is what in this book will be called a "learning environment."

Computers in education have evolved along two principal lines: one line emphasizes the theoretical and discursive aspects of knowledge; the other focuses on the experiential. Computer-based instruction tradition (CBI) heads the list on the theoretical side. Here the computer is used to present packaged information in the form of tutorial lessons. This model of educational computing dates back many years and has produced a wide literature, ranging from the design of instructional material to the design of artificially intelligent tutors.

More recently there has been interest in something closer to a "reference" model of educational materials, where students are provided with databases of information to explore as reference resources. These range from the loosely structured nonlinear formats promoted by the "hypermedia" community to more highly structured reference materials accessed through conventional databases.

Both forms of reference materials, as well as the tutorial lessons, emphasize *explanations*—the discursive, theoretical aspects of knowledge. On the other side of the picture is computer simulation, where the emphasis is on *experience*—a fundamentally different aspect of knowledge. For the most part, the different approaches have remained separate. Tutorials and reference materials rarely include an experiential component, and most simulations do not explain themselves. The result is that students learn theory they cannot transfer to real situations, or they have experiences they cannot explain or generalize.

Why not put the two together? One of the difficulties is that specialized tools have built up around these various approaches and it is not easy to combine the products. One of the first objectives for the AthenaMuse authoring system was to combine the different forms of materials common in educational computing; in particular to combine simulation with tutorial and reference materials. An example of this direction is the *Navigation Visual Learning Environment* (described in Chapter 7), a combination of simulation, tutorial, and reference material designed to teach coastal navigation and piloting.

Briefly, the simulation is a model environment where students can practice navigation. The setting is an area of two square miles off the coast of Maine. Students can see a 90-degree view of their surroundings on the screen. They have a control whereby they can look in any direction. They also have controls to steer the "boat" and to speed up or slow down. The simulation is built on a database of images and landmarks, so that as they move through the simulated space, their view changes. If they crash into a rock, the system will detect the collision and display a short film of a sinking ship. The simulation also provides basic tools for navigation—compass, binoculars, depth finder, and so on.

But this simulation is not written as a conventional computer program; it is not written with a specialized simulation language. In the AthenaMuse authoring system the boat, the environment, and the tools are all written as electronic documents. The use of the word "documents" implies that they share some of the same fundamental structure as text documents or video documents. They are all implemented as AthenaMuse "packages." They all contain the same basic kinds of display elements. They all have "dimensions." The main difference is that while the supporting documents generally have one or two dimensions, the simulation has seven.

This similarity in structure is important for two reasons. First, for the author, the simulation of a text or of a video document are not much different—all the basic components and the tools for manipulating them are the same. The whole program is therefore much easier to produce. Second, because it has essentially the same form, the simula-

"Simulation" is a notoriously difficult term. Here it is meant to be contrasted with discursive forms of reference in its approximation of experience. But to define precisely what is simulation is a wrong-headed pursuit, and even to decide when something is functioning as a simulation—when it is exemplifying some aspect of a possible experience—is beyond the scope or purpose of this book.

Chapter 21 describes the AthenaMuse document architecture.

tion can be linked to other documents in the environment by means of the standard tools for cross-referencing provided by AthenaMuse. The tutorial and reference materials can be keyed to specific locations or states in the simulation without using special-purpose tools or protocols.

Within a single authoring environment, the producer can write the sailing simulation, the tutorial lessons on how to use it, and the reference materials (such as nautical charts and guide books), then link them together using a single method of cross-referencing. The result for the student is a *learning environment,* in which the theory and the experience can be explored simultaneously. This approach of combining theory with experience does not bring anything fundamentally new to the science of pedagogy—teachers have always taught both aspects of knowledge. What is new is the packaging, which holds the potential for a major advance in students' interaction with ideas.

CONSTRUCTIVIST LEARNING MATERIALS

Consider next the role of the student as creator. For the most part, computer-based materials—whether in the form of tutorial or simulation—have been prepared as fixed packages. Recent projects are making an effort to give students a creative role; the assignments are not simply to react to prepared materials, but to create new ones.

This shift builds on a long tradition in education, promoted by John Dewey and Alfred Whitehead and carried to educational computing by Seymour Papert and others seeking to apply Jean Piaget's genetic epistemology. The basic concept, somewhat simplified, is that the enactive role is central to the learning process; students learn by being creative. Although the computer is perhaps not the best way to let students create, it does offer some very interesting possibilities.

One example is a project at MIT prepared by the Athena Language Learning Project, called *Dans le Quartier St. Gervais.* Students of French are given a simulated reproduction of a historic neighborhood in Paris (described in Chapter 8). They can move up and down streets, enter shops, and listen to residents of the neighborhood discuss a variety of topics. (This is another example of a learning environment where reference materials are woven into the fabric of the simulation.)

Rather than moving freely through the simulation, discovering what they will, the students are assigned the task of producing a guidebook,

or in some cases a set of postcards, of the neighborhood. They begin
with a book of empty pages. As they move through the neighborhood,
they have a simulated camera with which they can take snapshots. The
photos are put in the book, where they can be positioned and scaled.
The students then add text describing the points of interest; in the
case of the postcards, they compose short messages on the "reverse"
side of the cards. The materials they produce can be made available to
others visiting the neighborhood. In this way the students are extending what was given at the start by adding their own personal creations.

The assignments
described here have
been developed by
Gilberte Furstenberg.

In order to make such a book, the students need a set of tools that
lets them rearrange pages, cut and paste images, write text, add color,
change layouts, and so on. The issue for the developer is how to provide editing tools that are customized to the application. In the present example, the editing tools for the postcard assignment are different from those used to make the guidebook. Both are produced specifically for the given application—general-purpose editors are too complex and too distracting to achieve the purpose of the assignments.

This problem led us to the notion of "plastic editors"—document
editors that can easily be reshaped to meet the needs of a particular
application. If every piece of educational software that lets students
create or manipulate information needs customized editing tools, then
the editors themselves ought to be as flexible as the material they create. The approach we have explored (see Chapter 13) for this issue is
to handle the document editors themselves as another form of document.

CUSTOMIZED LEARNING MATERIALS

On a larger scale, the kind of flexibility shown in the creation of these
custom-made editors will have a much broader impact on educational
computing in general. Historically, it has been so difficult to produce
multimedia learning materials that the field has developed under a
"publishing" model that focuses on singular titles of high-quality materials intended for broad distribution. The advent of more powerful
authoring tools, along with the rapid advances in computer and video
technology, are making it more feasible to produce custom materials
for small-scale education and training needs. The stage is set for something analogous to the desktop publishing phenomenon, whereby it
will be possible to consider developing small-scale or localized educa-

The standard rule
of thumb a few years
ago was 200 hours of
development time for
each hour of finished
material.

tional materials in addition to the more conventional large-scale software.

Customized materials open a broad range of possibilities in education. These materials can be produced in two ways. One way is by changing an existing body of information. If the students studying French with the St. Gervais materials can produce a customized guidebook, the teacher can certainly do the same. With modifications of this kind, the same material can serve a multitude of purposes.

The process can lead to interesting results. The CERN *Diorama*, described in Chapter 10, was initially produced as an exhibition for non-technical visitors. Some interesting discussions with the technical staff have followed, however, about reusing the material for general safety training of the staff or for training researchers new to the facility. In this case the exploration resources that the application provides would remain intact, but the commentary would have a quite different character.

Another way to produce custom material is to build it from scratch. In many situations, especially in business and industry, small-scale custom training materials can be extremely effective. Consider any group that works over a substantial period of time on a project of any sort: there is a history and direction to the project that need to be communicated every time a new person joins the group, and every time the group communicates its results outside through technology transfer, documentation, marketing, or support activities. In this and in many other situations, the number of people involved is small; but at the group level the cost is relatively high, in terms of both time spent on this kind of activity and the quality of the outcome.

Desktop training, based on low-cost video technology and highly efficient authoring tools, offers a way to reduce some of these costs. This approach was discussed in the previous chapter, which reviews some applications of multimedia in business and industry.

COLLABORATIVE LEARNING

Educators find the concept of students collaborating and learning together to be particularly appealing. The possibilities for crossing language and cultural barriers are enormous; and with the ability to participate in large-scale scientific and social inquiry, the learner will find the world expanding by quantum measures. Already widespread programs are in place for information exchange even at primary and secondary grade levels. For the most part, these programs rely on electronic mail to transmit information, such as weather or ecological data, from one participant to another. This model is based on asynchronous communication.

The *Telescience* project, sponsored by the Manned Vehicle Research Laboratory, gives a picture of synchronous collaboration with a relatively broad communication channel. The system was established to allow scientists in diverse locations (in this case, the Kennedy Space Center and MIT), to collaborate on complex scientific experiments. The locations were linked by video, voice, and data channels. The video was transmitted in analog form via satellite. Four cameras at the experimental site had a switcher and a quad-split multiplexer under the researcher's control. The voice connections and eight channels of streaming binary data were carried over ground-based telephone lines. The objective of this program was to explore the feasibility and practical limits of close collaboration on a demanding technical activity over great distance, in this case an earth-based researcher working with a colleague in space.

Remote conferencing is one of the primary applications for multimedia in which users are interested. Thus it is likely that there will be adequate pressure to develop the necessary technology. Because this area has not yet matured, the first widespread implementations will have a highly restricted information bandwidth compared to the *Telescience* project. However, there will be plenty of opportunity in the future for distance learning supported by both synchronous and asynchronous communications.

A further step in collaborative learning is specially designed software. Our first experiments have been with the *Navigation* project, described above and in Chapter 7. Because the application is accessible over the network, *individuals need not work alone*. Students, each with a copy of the "world," can explore independently. If they prefer to explore as a group, they can link the worlds together over the network and move in unison. A teacher could take a class on a "field trip" along the coast of Maine, letting the students wander about independently, but on finding some object of interest call them together for discussion. Students and teacher need not be in the same physical location. Interpersonal communication would take place first with a text-based "intercom" system and later through video or audio conferencing.

LOOKING AHEAD

Many teachers are waiting for the time when they can offer their students access to large bodies of real data—especially at the university level, where students are being trained to undertake research and analysis. The development of large information resources, today only beginning, awaits the development of extensive network technology and new storage technologies.

Project Athena at MIT was one of the first to put the infrastructure for such a system in place on a large scale. Currently, over a thousand workstations are available to undergraduate students at MIT. The system is used by several thousand students each day, primarily for word processing and electronic communication, but also for educational programs such as the ones described in this book.

Some critics feel that the system has had a minimal impact on education at MIT. In fact, the educational potential of the system has not yet begun to unfold. The large-scale information resources and the tools for exploring them are not yet available. Some of the most profound changes in education will take place in this area, but the changes are only beginning.

Indeed, it appears that major research efforts in computer science over the next five years will focus on the problems of distributed access to large-scale information resources such as libraries, visualization databases, and other data resources. At the same time, it is important to bear in mind that the technical elements of scale and distribution are in many ways orthogonal to the issues of how people will interact with such systems.

The computer is a tool that can present knowledge to students in ways that have not previously been possible. In part, this is a matter of logistics and scale. But the computer—in particular the multimedia computer—offers new ways in which ideas can be *represented* to students and new models of interaction. These changes may take quite some time to realize fully, but they can be anticipated as genuine contributions to education.

At the same time, it is important to understand that in the end, the computer is only a tool, just as the book and the pencil are tools. In education tools can be used with positive or negative results. Education is, after all, one of the subtlest of human activities. And whether the potential benefits that the computer seems to offer are actually achieved depends largely on the teachers who use it.

For this reason, our aim has been to present some of these potentials to teachers in ways that will stimulate their creativity, and through effective tools to allow them to develop their ideas with a minimum of resistance and delay.

4. Design for the New Medium

Every communication medium is unique. Each has its own language—its own effective ways of communicating ideas. The multimedia workstation is a communication medium; in this case a combination of video, audio, text, and graphics, sharing the potentials of all these media. Each of the four is familiar; each has a well-developed design tradition. To a certain extent the conventions from these domains can be carried over to the computer. But the combination of media that we have today is more than the sum of its parts, and design for this new medium is challenging.

Just in terms of scope, a skillful designer must be conversant with all the base media that are combined in a multimedia environment. Challenge enough—but compounding this requirement, some of the wisdom from other domains is modified or reversed in the transition to the computer. This sort of difficulty was experienced some years ago by filmmakers who shifted to video; similar problems arise now in moving from linear to interactive video.

There are, however, completely new design issues as well—design problems that arise from the combination of media. For many important issues in multimedia design, there simply are no well-developed conventions.

This chapter presents a framework for discussing interface design in interactive multimedia. There are already whole books devoted to the subject. This chapter proposes a theoretical foundation for the discussion and offers a few general observations and examples. It is not meant to be a "cookbook," with specific rules and recipes for good design. Also, the emphasis in what follows will be on issues that are unique to multimedia computing. Many important design issues in multimedia are common to other disciplines, such as film or typography, and in general are better studied elsewhere.

We are in the early phases of multimedia communication. With every new medium, a new design aesthetic must evolve. The frustrated cry for better user interfaces is heard frequently today. At the same time, we need to appreciate the design aesthetic that is evolving in the wake of our advancing technology.

GOOD DESIGN

Nelson Goodman,
Languages of Art,
Hackett Publishing,
Indianapolis IN, 1976.

Deriving from the philosopher Nelson Goodman's observations on art, the proper question should not be *what* is good design, but *when* is good design. For our purposes we can define good design as effective communication. When a message is communicated effectively, then there is good design. This simple polarity will be useful later, but at face value it says little. The design of an interface depends entirely on what it will be used for.

Every computer trade show or technology journal contains pictures of computer screens with bright colors and images of rockets, cover girls, or, for some reason, the face of a mandrill. The control interfaces on these screens either resemble something from a Boeing 747 or are nonexistent. Such screens are advertising concoctions, designed to entice the glazed eye on the trade show floor. Are they badly designed? They may be, but they should not be so judged for their visual clamor alone; their main purpose is to attract attention and communicate an air of excitement. For this we may say their design is excellent (especially those with the mandrill)—quality of design must be judged in the context of its use.

As it happens, the first interfaces designed for any multimedia system are designed precisely for this kind of use—marketing-oriented demonstrations. Since they are not designed for extended practical use, visual intensity is emphasized.

Unfortunately, the stylistic conventions of computer interface design seem to propagate in the same way as fashions in clothing (to the chagrin of human-factor professionals advocating a more scientific approach). The result is that most of the multimedia interface designs today seem too "hot" for everyday use; they almost always trace their ancestry to a program designed for demonstration or marketing.

This pervasive tendency is one of the greatest obstacles to good design in multimedia applications. We have struggled with the issue in our own work, in the course of building many applications of different sizes and for different purposes. In some instances we have built two versions of an interface—one for presentation and demonstration, one for actual use.

We begin now with a discussion of some fundamental design issues. The focus is on the most superficial aspect of interface design, namely, the appearance of the material on the screen. The deeper aspects of any interface that have to do with its conceptual and functional foundations are treated elsewhere. Our objective is to create a framework for discussing issues of visual design for multimedia in a coherent way.

A THEORETICAL FRAMEWORK

In film analysis, theorists traditionally divide their subject into two major components, *mise-en-scène* and *montage*. Mise-en-scène treats the construction of individual scenes—what objects are included, how they are framed and composed. Montage treats the combination of scenes—which are chosen, how they are sequenced, the transition from one to the next.

Multimedia design rests on a very similar dichotomy. There are parts of an interface that correspond roughly to the scene; these are groupings of information resources (text, graphics, video) and the controls needed to manipulate them. Configurations of this kind usually act as independent *contexts* that appear and disappear as units. A video document, for example, normally displays some body of visual material but has associated control buttons (to play forward, reverse, or stop) as well as slidebar, title, and so on. This equipment normally behaves as a unit, a single *context* to the user.

A number of these contexts may share the screen at any one time; they may be nested within one another in a hierarchy, or they may appear and disappear in sequence. The *combination* of contexts—how they share the screen or how the transitions are made from one to another—corresponds to montage in film theory.

In terms of interface design, each context will have its own internal design considerations. Because often more than one context is involved in an application, there will also be design considerations governing the combination of these components.

Mise-en-Scène

In terms of multimedia computing, the context becomes the equivalent of a scene in film. A context is a set of information resources and any control mechanisms associated with them. The discussion in this section focuses on the "internal" design issues—those having to do with the selection and arrangement of parts that make up a self-contained context. The intent is not to offer an exhaustive treatment, for that would be subject enough for a separate book. We touch on three design topics that are especially relevant or unique to multimedia.

The first is a discussion of the general principles of *composition* that apply where the aim is (a) to emphasize certain information for communication, or (b) to create a work environment, as opposed to something intended to function as art. Second is a consideration of *dynamic elements* in a composition and how they affect the overall design. This area becomes quite significant in multimedia design with the introduction of video and graphic animation. The third topic is the *controls and actions* available to the viewer, and how these are organized and represented. Here again is an issue of special relevance to computer-based communication environments.

Composition and Balance

Design for communication imposes some constraints different from design for artistic expression, although there is a considerable overlap. In fact, multimedia design involves these two primary design motives, sometimes in opposition to each other. The first motive is to achieve a good information balance in the composition; the other is to achieve satisfactory visual balance.

The central goal of communication is to lead the viewer's eye through the composition to the action that needs to be taken first or the information that needs to be seen first. This means giving visual weight to the important information on the screen and deemphasizing the less important material. We call this information balance; the eye is led to the important information.

However, this motive is often orthogonal and sometimes opposed to the tenets of visual balance. From the standpoint of information alone, the tendency moves sometimes toward an isolationist, or "island" design, where bits of information float on a tractless visual space, as in Figure 4.2. The critical information is there, but the visual space might be addressed more coherently.

Sometimes the visual design takes over to the point that the information is completely lost. Figure 4.1 shows three variations on a small database display panel. The versions are arranged from top to bottom to show different stages in the design of this interface.

From the top to the middle image, notice that the general layout is reversed. In version *a*, the large text window holds a more prominent position than it does in version *b*. The text is not the focal point of the display and is made less prominent by moving it to the right-hand side. The data image and the descriptor fields become more prominent as the eye first explores this display.

Second, in the top two images the data descriptors are displayed in white horizontal bars. The text between the bars labels these fields. The idea is that the actual data are much more important than the labels, so they are placed in the visually dominant white bars. These bars are so commanding, however, that they overshadow *all* of the text— not only the labels, but their own contents as well. In the bottom version they are eliminated altogether. The relative importance of the data is conveyed through the color of the text—the data are displayed in a lighter tone and the labels in a more subdued one.

There are no hard and fast rules for achieving proper balance in any given situation; this problem-solving domain is highly dependent on context. The critical content must be allowed to be the center of interest on the screen. If a flow of ideas must be communicated, the eye should follow them in the proper sequence, the most important being weighted most heavily.

Note in particular that the window borders and the nonfunctional areas of the screen should not be designed so that they draw attention from the meaningful content of the screen. In screen design it is easy to create thick black

Figure 4.1 Three stages in the design of a database display panel. The later stages attempt to create a better information balance by manipulating the visual design of the panel.

lines and brick-patterned backgrounds around a critical but visually dull block of text (the same effect as the white bars in Figure 4.1). Furthermore, the design of one context is usually not possible in isolation. In most cases it must be done with consideration to the other contexts with which it will share the screen.

Dynamic Elements in Composition

Video, and anything else that moves, acts as a visual "super attractor." It takes a great deal of strength, visually speaking, to balance a dynamic element of a composition.

Balancing video in a display depends on its use. Consider three types of material: decorative displays; displays with primary focus on the video content; and utilitarian displays, where video is handled as data. The handling of the video will be different in all three cases.

Decorative Displays Often video serves no purpose other than to offer an attractive display. It is not highly important that the viewer remember the content; the overall intent is to elicit an affective response. Sometimes the video is shown alone, sometimes it is built into a composition with other materials.

The CERN *Diorama* is an AthenaMuse application that allows visitors to explore the particle accelerators at the European Center for Research in Particle Physics near Geneva. The project is described in detail in Chapter 10.

An example is the entry sequence of the CERN *Diorama* project. The sequence is built on a full-screen aerial photograph of Geneva and the surrounding area, where the accelerator is located. This aerial photo is used as the access path to various locations at CERN; visitors click on the image at the point they want to visit. With the first click, a close-up view of the site is overlaid on the full-screen aerial view; part of the larger image remains exposed, so the visitors never lose the context. The close-up functions as a title screen to the site. A title and brief explanation appear along with it, and instructions for the visitors to backtrack if they have made a mistake.

The next click starts the actual site visit, which begins with an aerial approach filmed from a helicopter. This motion video sequence is laid directly into the close-up aerial photo. The result is shown in Figures 4.6 and 10.1. The helicopter approach does not contain a discursive message; it functions as an establishing shot to create an enticing entry to the application. As visual imagery, it is not as commanding as the aerial photographs that surround it; however, it moves—its visual weight is increased to the point that it balances quite well when placed directly on these larger images.

A different example and different solution comes from the *Bibliothèque de France* project. This demonstration was designed to show

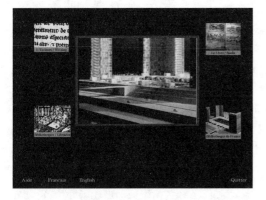

Figure 4.2 **Two stages in the interface design for the** *Bibliothèque de France* **project. In the second version, the motion video is removed to a separate context and visual emphasis is placed on the four primary options available.**

how multimedia services might be used by the French national library being built in Paris.

The idea for the introduction to the application called for a motion video sequence. In the first version, the video was centered on a black field surrounded by small still images functioning as the main menu of the application (Figure 4.2). This layout is an example of "island" design, with one dominant item in the center surrounded by weaker ones and nothing at the edges. It is the weaker floating elements that are most important.

The design was changed, but instead of trying to strengthen the menu items and the periphery, the motion video was separated out and given the full screen. A mouse click on the video stopped it and brought up the main menu, this time with the menu items taking center stage.

Video Content When the viewer is intended to focus completely on the video, in order to extract and remember its content, the video should not compete with other materials on the screen.

The solution for the CERN project—embedding the video in a highly active visual framework—is not acceptable for this application. Attention is divided between the video and its surroundings. The opposite approach—isolating the video—often is not appropriate either, because of its effect on orientation and viewer context.

One procedure we have used is *zoom*—a technique whereby the user can zoom in on the video to let it fill the screen. It is dependent on the capabilities of the video display system; some systems are able to expand the motion video in this way. If the user understands the zoom (either causes it or sees it occur explicitly), orientation can be preserved and the user can focus fully on the video.

Video Data Handling Aside from the decorative or communicative roles that video may play, it is also frequently encountered in more mundane circumstances as data being edited or manipulated. Here its relative importance can vary according to how the developer is using it at any point in time. Sometimes it becomes the sole focus of attention; sometimes the important action is happening at some other point in the display.

One of the AthenaMuse applications is a control interface to a video editing system. This application displays the output of the source and record decks on the workstation screen, with a complete model of the edit interface appearing below (Figure 4.3). The system allows the operator to carry out all the functions of video editing—selecting in and

Figure 4.3   Screen layout for the video edit controller. The user can instantly zoom in to concentrate on either the source or record video. The small scrollbar and "play" arrow below the left image remain accessible in the zoomed-in state.

out points, and performing edits on the video. The application controls the source and record decks, where the actual edits are made. In addition, the application keeps track of all the edits in a database. The user can log any video segment with annotations for later use.

The interface to the editor allows the operator to zoom in on either of the two video windows in order to focus on the video without the distraction of the rest of the interface. A small strip of controls remains visible at the bottom of the window so the deck can be controlled without having to zoom out each time.

These three examples show video in different roles that call for different treatments. One needs to decide how the video is functioning and how much competition it should have.

Controls and Actions

The third aspect of mise-en-scène concerns representing actions to the user. The overriding objective is clarity—helping the user know what to do when the context appears. The primary responsibility for clarity resides with the design of the information architecture. If the actions are not well thought out at that level, no amount of tinkering at the level of the screen design will be able to salvage the application. There are a number of interesting issues.

Consistency The first is consistency, which seems to float to the top of every discussion of interface design. Consistency has become a problematic term; a precise meaning is elusive. Basically there should be a *sameness* in how the actions are presented across the application, and indeed across all applications, if possible. If names or organizations of similar actions are not consistent from one context to another, the user will have difficulty comprehending the interface.

The trick with consistency is to know when is enough. All applications cannot use a single interface; all hardware and software platforms cannot support identical interfaces. Therefore, sameness always has limits. Abandoning consistency, either for ease of use or for clarity, is often far more important than maintaining it. Consistent design extends beyond the presentation of actions, of course; a good document design shows consistency through every aspect of its visual and auditory presentation. It is mentioned here because of its pressing importance with respect to how users understand the actions they can employ to control the material.

Relative Importance A second issue is that of conveying the relative importance of actions. Actions must be presented clearly (and consistently), but they must take their proper place in the overall hierarchy. It is easy to call too much attention to buttons, for example, or to hide meaningful actions deep in an incomprehensible menu.

Especially challenging are cases comprising a large number of actions. Here again the conceptual organization is more important than the appearance. Complex systems need to be organized so that users can find the actions they need; it is crucial to build a framework or model of expectation so they will know what they are looking for. The UNIX operating system is a counterexample, where there are 800 or 1,000 actions with only the barest framework to help imagine what is available or how to find it.

In terms of the presentation of action, it is vital to follow the rule "form follows function." The layout of actions in a user context must take into account the efficiency of their use as well as their appear-

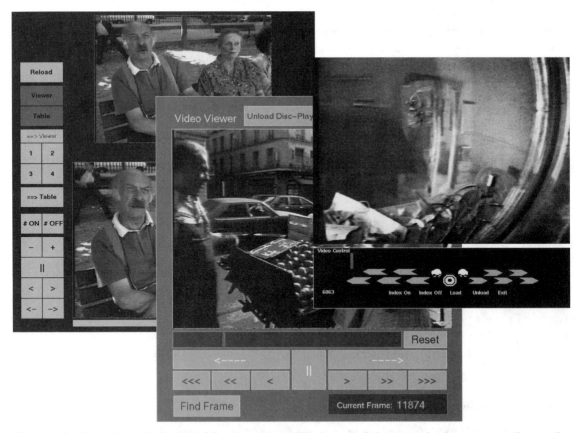

Figure 4.4   Control panels for the video documents. The layout of the controls changes according to the needs of the application.

ance. For example, consider the layout of a control panel for a videodisc viewer. This is the typical first exercise in AthenaMuse, and control panels have been made to suit every taste. But the optimal layout depends as much on performance characteristics as on visual appeal. Controllers where the aim is to stop on a particular frame are somewhat different from those where the need for precision is less (Figure 4.4).

Transient Actions Dynamic controls—those of short or intermittent duration—present a special problem. These resources appear and disappear, depending on the context as a whole. Sometimes they are simply not seen by the user because of where they are placed. The tendency is to reserve a special area (consistency) for information or intermittent controls. This area may be in a position that commands attention when the user first scans the context, but is not especially close to the visual action at the time the information or control is presented. The result is that the new control or information is not noticed at all.

Magical illusion works on the same principle: let the right hand take the audience's attention with a grand gesture while the left hand is reaching into a pocket. Let the control button or error message appear in a corner while the user is looking at some other part of the screen—where big things happened (or should have happened).

Montage

Montage deals with the transition from one scene to the next, and the combination of scenes. In multimedia design it refers to the combination of contexts in space and time. *In space* means the arrangement of more than one context on the screen. *In time* speaks to the transition from one context to another in sequence. In this section three topics are addressed: balance, articulation, and transition.

Balance

Attaining balance across a combination of contexts that appear together is closely related to the problem of achieving a balanced composition *within* a single context, and many of the same principles apply. If more than one context at a time is visible on the screen, the eye needs to take the appropriate path among them, so they should be given appropriate visual weight. The principles that have already been discussed or referenced can be applied to avoid dividing or misdirecting the viewer's attention. In the case of montage—here meaning

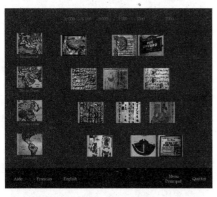

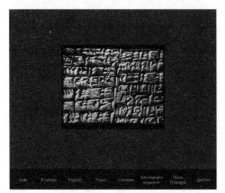

Figure 4.5 Context transitions in the *Bibliothèque de France* project. The strip along the bottom merges controls from global and local contexts.

that contexts appear simultaneously—it is inevitable that the visual complexity increases, and the first question should be "Why is this necessary?" More than one context almost always results in a complex design problem.

There are generally two reasons for showing contexts simultaneously (Figure 4.5). The first relates to the content—a need to make direct comparisons from one set of materials to another, for example. One may wish to compare two pages of a book, two film segments, or two code samples, and therefore need to see more than one context at once. Similarly, information may be transferred from one context to another, as when cutting film segments from one document and placing them in another. In all such cases, multiple contexts are needed at the same time.

Multiple contexts are also needed for managing orientation and control in the application. If the application is organized with hierarchical levels, it is often necessary to provide access to controls at higher-level contexts, or simply to have them visible to maintain the user's orientation within the application.

In a montage of simultaneous contexts, it is important to understand *why* they are appearing together and then to determine *how long* they need to appear together. The goal is to avoid having useless information occupy screen real estate, especially since it may have much more damaging effects than simply wasting space. In terms of *how long* items should appear together, space should not be allocated permanently based on a need for brief comparison or transfer.

Hiding Information Even when there is a need to provide access to a higher-level context for application control, it is sometimes necessary to hide that information in order that another context may function properly. For example, graphic drawing programs such as MacDraw usually divide the screen into a drawing area and a control area. Often it is not possible to hide the control interface, so the drawing must always be viewed next to or surrounded by a field of buttons, icons, and patterns. These always exert a strong visual

field of buttons, icons, and patterns. These always exert a strong visual influence, and in some cases it is simply not possible to evaluate the subtleties of balance or color interaction. In contrast, the Targa/TIPS program (another graphic drawing package) uses an interface that lets the user hide the control menus completely, so that the artwork can be viewed without interference.

When it is important to keep the higher-level context visible in order to maintain user orientation, it is possible sometimes to weaken it when not in use. On the *Navigation* project, some of the contexts use a *fade-out* technique. For example, the top-level context with title and "Exit" button is always visible, but it is programmed to decrease its luminance after the operator begins using other parts of the application; it lights up again if the mouse moves into its range. The same is possible with some of the other contexts that are visible but infrequently used.

Navigation is described in Chapter 7.

Articulation

Articulation has to do with the visual separation of contexts on the screen. It can happen that four or five control contexts are visible at a time, and the user can lose track of what scope any action may have. Keeping the actions clear to the user is one of the primary objectives of articulating contexts. Another is to maintain separation between content material.

In some instances contexts are woven together seamlessly and there is no articulation. When it is needed, articulation is achieved in one of three ways. The first is by *proximity*, where the contexts are separated spatially from one another. The second is by some form of visual *containment*, where a boundary (such as a border line or a change of color) is used to delimit a context. This is the customary strategy in windowing environments, where the various windows are marked off by border lines and background colors. The third technique is *attribute grouping*, where parts of a context share some common attribute. All the controls for a video document, for instance, could be made blue and those for a neighboring text document, green.

Transition

In complex documents with many contexts, it is rare that the viewer sees them all at once. More often, there are transitions where contexts disappear and new ones take their place. Changes of this kind raise a number of design considerations: maintaining continuity and orientation; making the best use of screen space; and the significance of different visual styles of transition.

Continuity and Orientation   "Out of sight, out of mind" is the best description of what happens when the scene changes in a multimedia information landscape. In real space, people build mental models of places and use them to navigate even when only part of the space is visible. Unfortunately, this powerful ability does not seem to transfer well to information systems.

Maintaining continuity and orientation through a transition becomes a critical design consideration. This is not only a matter of screen design; the bulk of the problem rests at the architectural levels of the application. But even the visual design of transitions can make or break an application.

Much of the problem can be related to the *percentage of information change;* in general, the more information that remains on the screen through a transition, the easier it will be to follow. If 100 percent of the information is changed at once, continuity will be minimal.

The CERN *Diorama* sequence described earlier shows a stack of contexts, where part of each higher level in the hierarchy remains visible to the viewer. This design is based on the metaphor of a stack of cards—the viewer can get to any point in the stack by clicking on it. At least 10 to 15 percent of each context remains on the screen through each transition (Figure 4.6).

In an earlier design of the interface, clicking on the top-level aerial photograph caused a 100-percent scene change to the location indicated. Although a button was provided to return to the previous level, the button was a small part of a 100-percent screen change and it did little to preserve orientation. The application was designed for the general public, so good orientation was extremely important. The solution was to retain more information on the screen through the transition.

Use of Screen Space   Another way to look at transition is in terms of space on the screen. When reading the *New York Times,* you have about 80,000 characters before your eyes on a double-page spread; a 1280 × 1024 computer display holds about 10,000. Screen real estate becomes a critical resource, and context transition is the principal method of recycling this commodity. From this perspective, the higher the percentage of information change, the more screen space be-

Figure 4.6 The transition sequence used to move from global to local contexts in the CERN *Diorama* project

comes available. Because screen real estate is so valuable, one's inclination is to recycle as much as possible.

This tendency runs directly counter to the issue of continuity; one would prefer not to leave any space merely for the sake of orientation. So the tradeoff must be decided on a case-by-case basis, taking into account the requirements of the audience, the need for the space, and any alternative techniques that may be available. This type of design question can benefit from even a small amount of formative research with the target audience.

Visual Styles of Transition   Much can be said in the details of a transition—in how it appears visually. In film editing, a "cut" within a scene usually implies exact continuity in time and location; a "dissolve," on the other hand, is often associated with a change of time or location. The analogy cannot be carried too far—indeed, the effects may be reversed—but different styles of context transition in multimedia interfaces also say something about the content of the different materials involved.

Primarily, transitions involving a high percentage of change suggest a semantic change of magnitude. They free the largest amount of screen area for new material, but they suggest a discontinuity between contexts. Piece-by-piece transitions have the opposite characteristics: they give up less space but suggest a closer relationship between contexts and generally preserve the viewer's orientation.

SUMMARY

The examples offered in this chapter are not intended to be a complete treatment of multimedia design, but instead to show how such issues can be considered within an organizing framework. Here that framework is based on an approach common in film analysis, which divides the subject into mise-en-scène and montage.

In the multimedia interpretation, mise-en-scène is concerned with the arrangement of the components of an individual user context, a set of information resources and any interface controls associated with them. Montage encompasses the issues of transition and concurrent display of contexts.

Within each of these domains are many design issues. The focus in this chapter has been on some of the main elements that are more or less peculiar to multimedia computing. In terms of mise-en-scène, the problems of composition (especially with moving design elements such as video or animation) and the presentation of actions to the user were the main topics. In terms of montage, the topics included balance across contexts, articulation, and various aspects of transition.

The design of these multimedia interfaces is complex, requiring a balance of visual information delivery and functional requirements. There are no well-developed conventions for handling these problems, a situation that is normal for a new communication medium. The aesthetic and the skill for coping with multimedia design will come with experience; the field is new, and the evolution of design is only beginning to unfold.

5. Ways of Worldmaking

Computers are tools now capable of building worlds. "Worldmaking" is meant to evoke the philosophical notion that a world is defined by the symbols used to represent it. The computer is a premier symbol-manipulating machine, and our goal is to build worlds of information with it.

See Ernst Cassirer, *Language and Myth*, Dover Press, New York NY, 1946; also Nelson Goodman, *Ways of Worldmaking*, Hackett Publishing, Indianapolis IN, 1978.

This chapter discusses the sorts of tools needed for worldbuilding. It reviews the uses of the term "authoring" and some of the tools that have been offered under that rubric. Our overall objective is to provide some basis for evaluating what tools are needed to create an effective environment for communication-oriented computing.

We are assessing "authoring" at a time when the nature of computing is undergoing a radical shift; from its roots in information processing, it is becoming a broad-based medium for communication. As a result, the requirements for authoring are changing radically.

This topic will be extremely important over the next few years, as the market will be flooded with every species of software claiming to provide multimedia authoring capability. We aim here to give some perspective on the broader issues of authoring and to offer a framework by which different approaches can be evaluated.

There are three main questions to consider in evaluating an authoring system: (a) what does it let you author? (b) how much work is involved? and (c) what can be done with the results?

HUMAN REPRESENTATIONS:
WHAT DOES AN AUTHORING SYSTEM PRODUCE?

Authoring means using the computer to express ideas. As the role of computing shifts more to communication, and especially with the evolution of multimedia communication, the types of expressions that people want to produce are changing rapidly. Currently, there is a substantial gap between the possibilities envisioned for the technology and the authoring tools available to express them.

In communication-oriented computing, people want to create *messages*. The messages usually contain a variety of parts—video, text, simulation, audio, and so on. The author has three fundamental problems in creating a message on a computer:

1 Describing what the pieces of the message are.
This means specifying the content data for each component and its presentation format—what text or video to display and how to present it, for example.

2 Defining the relationships among the various components.
Sometimes relationships are *logical*: "A user looking at component x should be able to move to component y or z." Sometimes they are *physical*: "Button x should appear below and to the left of button y." Relationships of both types transform a set of individual elements into an *information structure*.

3 Specifying processes of change within the information structure.
In all but the simplest of computer-based messages, there is some dynamic aspect that must be exactly specified by the author.

These descriptive problems are quite different, and different tools are appropriate for them. A powerful authoring system should provide a proper range of tools with enough coherence so that people can learn how to apply them effectively.

"Tools" here does not refer simply to "point-and-click" interface details but to the underlying cognitive frameworks that people use to conceive and define information structures and processes of change. Several are described in the following section.

Defining Structure and Change

Worlds are defined in terms of structure and change. The tools of expression are the techniques for defining these attributes. *Structure* refers to logical and physical relationships among the many components that make up a multimedia document—buttons, video, windows, audio, and so on. *Processes of change* refer to the flow and sequence that unfold among these components when they are in use.

AthenaMuse provides five fundamental approaches for defining the information structure and processes of change in a document:

1 Directed graph structures (linked networks)

2 Text markup

3 Spatial frameworks

4 Declarative constraints

5 Procedural code.

Networks   In many cases, document architectures are defined exclusively in terms of networks. In a network, the document is modeled as a set of *nodes*, each representing some component of the document. The *linkages* among these nodes define the relationships among the components. The network, or graph, has a long tradition as a device for representing structural relations. Examples can be found dating back at least several thousand years. The use of networks was formalized as a mathematical discipline (graph theory) starting with Léonard Euler's project to find a pathway over the seven bridges in the city of Königsberg in the middle of the 18th century.

In computer documents, networks can be used in many different ways and in many different forms. They can be organized as trees, lists, or interconnected webs. They can be used to represent *physical* or *logical* relationships—placement of items on the screen or pathways of movement through a "state transition," "semantic," or "data flow" network. Hypertext and hypermedia systems are all based on network structures. In these systems, documents or their components are defined as nodes. Cross-references from one to another are encoded as linkages. The essential point is that a simple system of nodes and links makes a powerful conceptual tool for describing many different structures of information. What is vital in multimedia authoring systems is that the user have the ability to create arbitrary networks of documents or their components.

The AthenaMuse architecture provides basic support for network structures by allowing authors to create "packages" of information as independent nodes (refer to Chapter 21). These can then be tied together into arbitrary networks through simple methods of cross-referencing (Figure 5.1). One of the weaknesses of the AthenaMuse architecture is that these linkages were never handled as data as they normally are in a hypermedia system, where they can be searched or manipulated collectively.

Text Markup   Text markup is another technique for describing an information structure. As its name implies, this approach is closely related to the notational format of *text*.

The Standard Generalized Markup Language (SGML) is an example of such a system.

Text is encoded on a computer as a sequential stream of characters. The "markup" is where special characters or keywords are embedded in this stream to indicate structural features of the document, such as paragraph and section boundaries, indentations, and the like. The essential form of the document remains a bytestream of characters, with the structural markers interspersed in the text.

Text markup can be quite an efficient technique for defining an information structure when a paper-like format is needed. Accordingly, it is best at representing hierarchical tree structures with a sequential

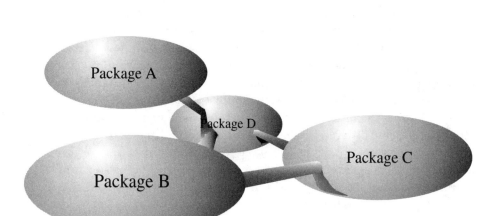

Figure 5.1   Packages become the network nodes in AthenaMuse. They can be linked to form networks of various kinds.

order at each level. It is not particularly effective at describing arbitrary networks or spatial configurations.

Efforts have been made to extend this approach to multimedia, by embedding markers for multimedia data objects such as audio or video into the bytestream along with the text. In general, the embedded entities are treated as chunks, as if they were single characters in the bytestream. There is little or no support for defining or accessing any internal structure within these materials. This style of authoring is used in both Macintosh and NeXT text processing utilities; numerous other systems use it as well.

With the AthenaMuse architecture, text markup is included in the form of a modified Scribe previewer, which allows the author to insert references to AthenaMuse packages directly into the text in the same way he or she would insert an illustration. The result is that the screen-based previewer formats the text into pages and inserts the appropriate material into the text. Because the insert is an AthenaMuse package, it has complete interactive capabilities, including motion video and a full complement of control and cross-referencing capabilities—a substantial enhancement over the typical picture on a page. Furthermore, in this implementation these marked-up text objects are themselves AthenaMuse objects, so they can be included as components of still larger AthenaMuse structures.

This technique is described in Chapter 11, Electronic Books.

Space   A third method for defining information structure is the spatial framework. Space as an organizing principle is as old as graphic notation itself. It has played a central role in the history of computing; virtually every higher-level computer language provides a mechanism for using dimensioned arrays to define and manipulate data structures in terms of space.

The use of space as a notational device has not been carried forward effectively in most multimedia authoring systems. Generally, the only vestige is a dimensionality associated with the x and y coordinates of the screen—or, more recently, with the use of *time* as an organizing dimension for temporal documents. Otherwise, the only spatial construct is found in the procedural programming aspects of these systems. Using spatial frameworks to describe information structure proves to be a powerful tool for much more complicated formats. Authoring becomes a matter of defining a spatial framework, filling it with information, then manipulating the view simply by "moving around" in that space.

The timeline is a simple case: the author defines a span of time, fills it with video or audio information, and then moves forward or back-

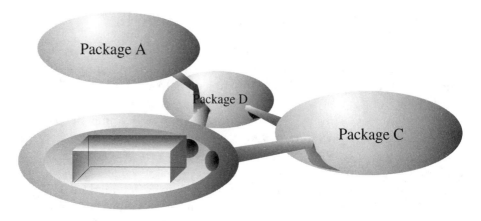

Figure 5.2   Each AthenaMuse package has an internal space. Cross-references can connect a region of one package's space to a region of another package's space.

ward to view the material. The frame rate is determined by how fast the user is moving in time. Other documents can make reference to this dimension of time through general communication facilities. An immediate handle is thereby provided for cross-references or data binding to specific points in time.

Imagine that the problem is not simply to reference a point in time within a video sequence, but to pick out a particular region of an image at a given point in time, or to track an object over time. A single dimension of time is no longer sufficient. Two more dimensions must be added to model the width and height of the image. With this three-dimensional framework, a reference can specify x, y, and t values to select any region of any frame of the video sequence at any point in time.

AthenaMuse is equipped with a "spatial" architecture that permits many layers of fine-grained cross-referencing into a temporal sequence of images or into the spatial structure of an image. The video, therefore, can be much more closely coupled with other information in the document. The same process of adding dimensions to a document is extended in this architecture to support much more complex information structures and cross-referencing schemes.

In the AthenaMuse architecture, every package can have a spatial structure defined by the author, with as many dimensions as needed. These documents can then be connected via the network model (Figure 5.2). They can be embedded within one another using either the text markup facilities or the spatial constructs themselves.

The important point is that many tools are available to the author to define information structure. The tools can be freely combined so that

The problems of achieving rich integration of different types of data are a major theme of this book. Chapter 17 discusses further the problems of integrating video as a form of data. Chapter 18 discusses strategies for integrating graphics. See also Chapter 7 for an example of integrating simulation with other document types in the *Navigation* project.

the most appropriate one can be used to define each part of the total message content.

Procedures and Constraints

With an information structure, some of the dynamic interaction that an author needs in a message can be achieved quite easily. Often all that is needed is the ability to move through the structure in different ways. In a hypertext system built on the network model, the primary activity is traversing links from one node to another. In a video document, based on a one-dimensional spatial model, the primary activity is moving forward or backward in time. In a text document, the primary activity is moving forward or backward through the bytestream of characters.

With a combination of approaches available to an author, a large range of interactions can be described in terms of simple movements. For many interactive messages the author need do no more than sprinkle action specifications through the document. In AthenaMuse, sixteen basic actions can be used in this way without leaving the data specification context. In other cases the document depends on more complex or customized dynamics. These more complicated interactions can be defined in a number of ways. Two such techniques are *procedures* and *constraints*. Procedures and constraints need little explanation. Procedural definitions are the core of conventional programming languages—step-by-step descriptions of complex processes. Here are found all the traditional difficulties of managing procedural logic and data integrity. With procedural programming, authoring moves into the realm of the specialist.

See Chapter 21 for more details.

Constraints are declarative relationships between different entities, often expressed as mathematical relations. Spreadsheet calculators depend on constraints. Each of the formulas that goes into a spreadsheet cell declares the relationship between that cell and others it may reference. As their values change, that change is propagated to the target cell. As a way of specifying processes of change, simple constraints can be much more accessible than procedural programming (taking the spreadsheet as the primary example). On the other hand, this more restrictive approach is not appropriate in every situation.

Most authoring systems offer some mechanism for defining processes of change. Support for procedural definition is quite common; indeed, the earliest authoring systems grew out of procedural programming languages, and many retain this character. Constraints are less common, except as they appear in systems similar to spreadsheets.

See Chapter 22 for
an overview of
EventScript.

AthenaMuse includes support for both approaches. Procedural definition is provided through an interpreted object-oriented language called *EventScript*. This language lets users define procedural scripts that can be associated with the packages defined in the data specification component—the objects that define the bulk of the information structure. Constraints are also provided in limited forms: one-way constraints are used to control dynamic graphic objects, and two-way constraints can be attached to the scrollbar controllers. These uses of constraints in AthenaMuse are discussed in more detail in Chapter 18 on Dynamic Graphics.

Strength in Diversity

To summarize, the first and most important step in evaluating an authoring system is to determine which expressive tools the system provides. These tools directly determine the overall power of the system. (In specialized domains of authoring, of course, a more limited tool may be perfectly adequate.)

Consider a case where the same application was developed with two different systems, AthenaMuse and HyperCard. The application was a set of foreign-language teaching materials for the Athena Language Learning Project.

HyperCard provided a *network* structure with a *procedural* extension (HyperTalk). For most of the application this structure was perfectly adequate. But when the teachers wanted text subtitles synchronized to the video at a phrase-by-phrase level, the network model showed its weakness. The only way to describe this information structure with a network was to cut the video into bite-sized pieces and make a huge network of phrases. It was not practicable to undertake the task by hand—a special program had to be written to generate automatically the many "cards" needed to implement this feature of the application. The authoring system failed to provide adequate expressive tools.

Apple's
QuickTime
extension ad-
dresses some of
these problems.

For this problem, AthenaMuse showed the advantage of having a broader repertoire of expressive tools. The *spatial* construct it provided is more appropriate for describing the relations between a number of subtitles and a stream of video: the author works on a timeline model, where the location of the subtitles is expressed by "painting" them over an appropriate span of time. The network aspects of the AthenaMuse document architecture supported the bulk of the application in the same way that HyperCard did.

Fundamentally, it is the document architecture that determines what sorts of things an authoring system can produce. The document architecture defines the internal structure of a document with the precision needed to implement it on a computer.

In many cases an application calls for a well-defined and limited form of document, and a simple document architecture will suffice. When evaluating a system, however, we need to consider the potential for growth. If simple paper-like documents with video or graphic appendages appear to be sufficient for today's users, what directions will they want to take tomorrow, and what will be the implications of changing?

How Much Work?

There are a hundred ways to describe anything on a computer; what is important is the time required and the level of experience or skill needed. If we assume that an authoring system can produce the right sorts of documents, we must ask "at what cost?" The design of an authoring system is a process of abstraction, whereby certain tasks or operations considered important by the designer are optimized. Accordingly, it becomes quite efficient to do certain things that fall within the "target" domain. We saw in the preceding example of subtitles that in one system it is quite easy and in another quite difficult.

Let us consider another example. HyperCard (network with procedural scripts) makes it very easy to make a Rolodex index, since that was its initial target application; while MacroMind Director (timeline and procedural scripts) makes it easy to create time-based business presentations. Reversing the tasks—making a card file with Director and a time-synchronized business presentation with HyperCard—immediately reveals significant boundaries of both systems.

In general, high-level authoring tools trade flexibility for efficiency. The aim is to produce a particular type of material very quickly. Speed always comes at the expense of flexibility; such tools often have a narrow *scope* and it may be difficult or impossible to deviate from the target domain. The solution is to provide a layered architecture, where the "higher" layers provide the efficiency and the "lower" layers the flexibility.

AthenaMuse, HyperCard, and Director all follow this strategy; Figure 5.3 shows the model as implemented in AthenaMuse. At the top level, "workbenches" provide highly customized authoring tools for producing standard forms of material. These equate roughly to the two hundred or so "course-authoring" systems on the market today, designed to produce industrial training material or other material of

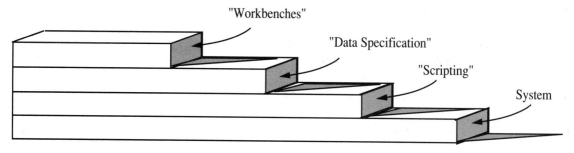

Figure 5.3   Layered development tools in AthenaMuse

well-defined structure. With AthenaMuse this level has received the least amount of attention to date, but the MuseBuilder (described in Chapters 13 and 14) suggests how such materials will be produced.

At the next level is the PackageSpec data-specification environment, which permits development of a class of applications using only data-specification techniques. In such cases the entire application is represented as a structure of information objects that are defined in terms of their attributes and relations. All the information is coded as data (*what* is to be produced, as opposed to the procedural approach that emphasizes *how* the material is to be produced).

An important extension at this level in AthenaMuse is the addition of constraint declaration and a set of sixteen fundamental operations that can be coded as data. A large range of dynamics can then be expressed at this level, and a greater portion of the application can be handled without going to the next level.

The third level is EventScript, which lets one customize the application when the standard components in the PackageSpec library fall short. EventScript is an object-oriented language, which uses an event-driven message-passing scheme. EventScript provides access to the lowest layer of the pyramid, the compiled program space. At this level any compiled module linked to the image is accessible to EventScript. External computing and database resources on the system can therefore be used.

The Difficulty Gradient

If we assume that the authoring system provides a reasonable solution to the flexibility issue (that is, high-level efficiency can be combined with flexibility in some way), then we can consider the "difficulty gradient." The difficulty gradient asks how far one can go before calling

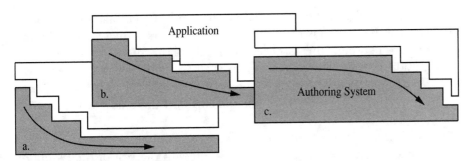

Figure 5.4 **In terms of difficulty, (c) shows the goal, where the bulk of the application is produced with higher-level tools; (a) and (b) show more of the application depending on lower-level tools.**

in a specialist (remember that authoring is an activity of nonprogrammers). In other words, it is not enough to say that an authoring system has so many layers or so much flexibility—one must also ask how much can be accomplished at each layer, and how big the steps are in terms of difficulty from one layer to the next (Figure 5.4).

In many systems, the data-specification layer is quite narrow. One can define basic display materials—texts, video, and so on—but to define even the simplest flow of control means dropping into the procedural domain, which involves substantial penalty. With AthenaMuse we found that the most common actions (movement through the information structure) could be handled at the data-specification layer, and a broader range of applications can be implemented without stepping down into the procedural domain.

One of the weaknesses of AthenaMuse is that the procedural portion (EventScript) is separate from the data-specification portion (PackageSpec); see Figure 5.5. This schism is fairly common; the same

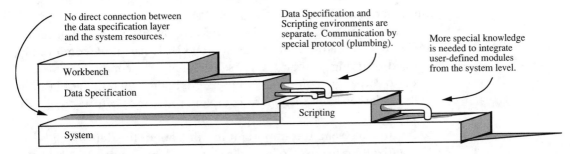

Figure 5.5 **In AthenaMuse, there is a special communication protocol between the data-description environment and the scripting layer.**

division is found between HyperCard and HyperTalk, for example. One of the results is that it is difficult for users to make a conceptual bridge between the procedural model and the data-specification paradigm(s). With this fundamental division there is no graceful way to introduce the procedural aspects of the system. It would be easier to do so if there were a closer relationship with the data-specification aspects.

In effect, a sort of "plumbing" is used to connect the two parts—specialized messages that are not consistent with the rest of the system or evident to the user. This plumbing is not a good feature of any authoring system, in that it makes the system much more difficult to learn. Plumbing must be introduced when the original system architecture has not anticipated some important feature. In evaluating an authoring system, one should always try to locate the plumbing.

Simplicity, Boredom, and Debugging

A few final points relative to how well or how poorly an authoring system measures up have to do with the simplicity/boredom trade-off and the debugging or environment support. Simplicity is a highly valued feature of any authoring system, because it means that the tool can be used by a wider audience, with less training. But if the system imposes repetitive tasks, it may quickly become boring, which means it will not be accepted by users.

Therefore, it is important to consider how the authoring system can handle the scaling of a simple operation. For one or two repetitions, the point-and-click interface can be quite appealing—simple to understand, easy to use. But if the task involves hundreds or thousands of repetitions (for instance, making subtitles in HyperCard), there must be a way to scale the operation efficiently. This scaling normally means describing a process, and hence moving up the difficulty curve. "Templates," object "cloning," and "plastic editors" show promise in this regard (refer to Chapters 13 and 14).

The best authoring system is not necessarily the simplest, but rather the one that helps its users grow in experience most comfortably. Instead of trying to hide (or worse, to eliminate) complexity, we may need to reveal the complexity to users gradually; when the application calls for larger scale or greater complexity, the user can respond productively.

In the same vein, it is important to think about the debugging facilities and other features of the development environment. While the idea of treating different aspects of the document or application with different tools or programming paradigms has some clear advantages, it also has the result that the program becomes divided, and it can be more difficult to locate problems or to understand the functioning of the whole. No solution is yet evident, but a good authoring system certainly must support users in this critical area.

WHAT CAN BE DONE WITH THE RESULT?

Having produced a document, hopefully by the least objectionable means, one should consider what can be done with it. There are important differences in the products of various authoring systems. The following is a short list of questions meant to raise some of the important issues:

1 *Can the reader manipulate the document?* Many authoring systems make a fundamental distinction between authoring and reading. The author works in a development environment and the reader works in a presentation or "playback" environment, where the document has been compiled.

It is normal in most cases for the author to have a richer toolset than the reader; however, if the system treats authoring and reading as two separate worlds, then the ability to modify or manipulate the document will be severely impaired. This may be an important consideration depending on the nature of the documents being produced; most of the materials described in this book depend on some editing activity on the part of the reader, so a hard distinction is not acceptable.

These issues are treated in more detail in Chapter 13.

2 *Can one document be included in another?* Inclusion is certainly one of the most useful features of a multimedia document. It is seen frequently in the examples throughout this book, typically where an editor or some part of an interactive controller is inserted into another document.

See Chapter 15 for further discussion of compound documents.

3 *Can the documents be searched for content?* The only material that can be searched effectively today is text, and even then there are substantial difficulties. Searching images and audio for specific content can be achieved only in extremely narrow domains. Searching dynamic systems for possible states poses an even greater challenge. Ultimately one would like to be able to extract content from interactive documents, no matter what form of representations they may contain. But even in the case of text retrieval, the document architectures used by an authoring system require specialized search algorithms.

4 *Does the document fit into a communications setting? Can it be mailed or distributed?* Mailing interactive documents introduces a number of interesting problems in security, since the document executes as a program with access to destructive system utilities such as *rm* that can remove or damage the user's files.

5 *Does the authoring system provide any special support for multiple languages?* Changing language in a document can be assisted by the authoring system. Language typically pervades a multimedia document—occurring not only in the text, but also in audio, video, and graphic segments. Providing support for multiple languages means that the document architecture offers some means of coding different language versions of the component elements. The effort needed to distribute the document across language boundaries is thereby greatly reduced.

6 *What level of security is provided?* In many applications the security requirements extend to the level of the individual document or even to part of a document. Locking readers out of an entire information domain is too coarse a level of security. In many cases it will be important for the authoring system to enforce access rights at the object level.

SUMMARY

In this chapter we have raised some of the important issues in evaluating a multimedia authoring system. The focus of the discussion has not been on the superficial aspects of the interface or on "feature lists," but on the fundamental modes of expression provided for defining structure and processes of change. If these are not present, and provided in good measure, then no human interface—not even a 3D virtual reality with goggles and gloves—will render the system useful.

The aim of authoring is to move document development out of the domain of programming, yet still provide a rich communication environment that takes advantage of the unique expressive powers of the computer. Achieving this goal means finding ways of defining structure and change through data-specification techniques rather than procedural definition, even if the procedural definition is clothed in a visually attractive interface. An authoring system should be measured by how broad a scope of applications, or documents, can be produced and to what degree they can be implemented with the various data-specification techniques available.

As discussed in Chapter 2, many of the applications of the technology will be concerned with communication. This outlook implies a high degree of dependence on interactive documents that can be distributed, edited dynamically, secured, transformed linguistically, searched, and displayed across a variety of platforms.

The principal point to emerge from this discussion is that a general-purpose authoring system that meets these objectives is complex and difficult to produce. Efforts to date are in their infancy. One of the difficulties we face is that of generating and supporting a literature of multimedia documents through this period when the effective techniques of authoring are changing rapidly. In effect, with multimedia authoring we cope with the dilemma that is so familiar to advancing technology in general—some of what we build today will be lost tomorrow, but we cannot afford to wait until tomorrow.

Part 2

SAMPLE APPLICATIONS

Introduction

In this second part of the book, the focus is on applications, and in particular, how multimedia applications are conceived and implemented. Ten projects are described in the following chapters. These represent approximately one fourth of the total number developed by the Visual Computing Group and its successor, the AthenaMuse Software Consortium.

Our design philosophy rested on the idea that applications should drive technology. With this in mind, we aimed for a broad range of applications, preferring those of modest size but which introduced innovative ideas in content, interaction, or interface design.

The list below includes most of these projects. The titles are loosely grouped into different classes of applications.

Virtual Museums

Chronoscope (Musée d'Orsay)
Smithsonian Image Collection System
Harvard Scientific Instrument
   Collection
Man Ray Paris Portraits
Seeds of Change

Simulations

CERN Diorama
Dans le Quartier St. Gervais
A la Rencontre de Philippe
Navigation Visual Learning
   Environment
No Recuerdo

Analysis Tools

Film Analysis with Alfred
  Hitchcock
Environmental Literacy
Women's Roles in Developing
  Countries
Film Analysis with Citizen Kane
Project DOC Edgerton
Media Literacy Curriculum
Boston Suburbs

Editors

Color Palette
Font Editor
Attribute Editor
Video Editor
MuseBuilder
Subtitle Editor
Object Browser
Action Editor
Pixmap Editor

Information Management

GTE Real Estate Project
AthenaMuse Mail Agents
The Meeting Analyzer
Quality Design Toolkit

Electronic Books

Neuroanatomy Learning
  Environment
Engineering Geology Educator
Mechanical Bearings
Biology
Bibliothèque de France
AthenaMuse On-Line
  Documentation

All of these applications were created with AthenaMuse. Readers may find it helpful to refer to Chapters 21 and 22 to get an overview of the resources available to application authors. Many of the core concepts and features of AthenaMuse are encountered in this section, with examples demonstrating their use in practical situations.

6. The *ChronoScope:* Impressionist Art, 1848–1914

The *ChronoScope,* a timeline interface for images, was developed as an interface for a collection of impressionist art dating from 1848 to 1914. These works belong to the Musée d'Orsay in Paris. The museum is interested in providing on-line access to its collection; it began by offering one of the first distributed image display systems for public use. The *ChronoScope* is one of several prototypes developed to help the museum enable its visitors to explore the museum's assets more effectively.

The idea was to see an artist's work spread out on a timeline and be able to zoom in on any region or look at any specific work in detail. Another goal was to allow side-by-side comparison of different artists' work by displaying their timelines concurrently.

In the present chapter, we describe how this application was developed, from a general conception to a functioning prototype of the system—a process that took five days. We show the application as an organic, evolutionary development and suggest some of the major phases it passes through. This example is not offered as an equivalent to, or replacement for, the more formalized development processes that take place on large-scale software engineering projects. The process here is more relevant to a communication or prototyping environment, where the materials are smaller in scale and produced in the spirit of documents.

CONCEPTIONS

Certain initial conceptions shape the development of every application. Sometimes there is an overriding message that needs to be conveyed, sometimes there is a central activity the user will engage in, sometimes there is a particular way of structuring information.

The driving conception for the *ChronoScope* was the timeline display of an artist's work. The virtual space capabilities of AthenaMuse (described below) seemed to offer a way to implement such an interface with little effort. The initial concept was to create a linear space which could be scrolled left and right, and then put images on it. In the course of implementation, many variations and extensions suggested themselves. Some of these were added to the application, others will be added later.

Conceptions to Contexts

The first step in moving from a general conception to a working prototype is to define the principal *contexts* with which the user will interact. These contexts are, in effect, the "sketch" of the application—they are refined and articulated as the development proceeds and detail is filled in.

For the *ChronoScope*, the timeline is one of the major contexts—in fact, it was the starting point for developing the application. The broad idea mentioned above was elaborated by allocating separate strips to each artist, which could be placed on the timeline independently. The user can select a small number of artists to compare and bring up a display of their work into the context of the timeline (Figure 6.1).

A second major function of the system is to allow users to look at individual paintings and their details. Users should be able to point to a painting on the timeline and have it appear full size, perhaps even full screen. For purposes of comparison, we decided to have the paintings appear in a notecard-like format that would let users move them around on the screen and look at more than one at a time. The cards would be the second principal context a user would see—each card would provide essentially the same format and be considered a separate context.

Finally, in order to select the artists to be put on the timeline, a general catalog is needed, listing the artists' names along with descriptions

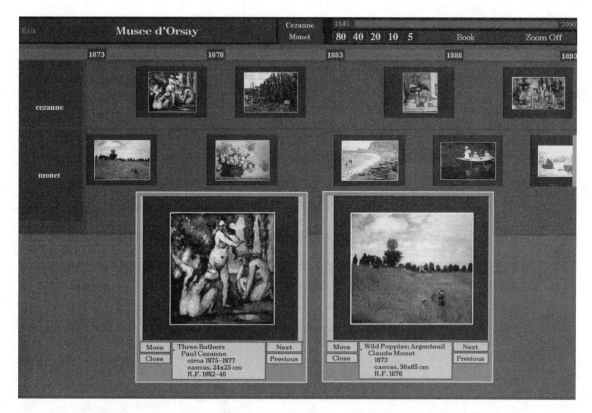

Figure 6.1   The *ChronoScope* timeline allocates a separate horizontal band for each artist's work. This example compares paintings by Cézanne and Monet.

and examples of their work. This catalog would offer searching capabilities and possibly be connected to an external database. The catalog would be the third major user context.

The timeline, the notecards, and the catalog are the core of the application. Several other contexts are needed as well: a title screen and introduction, a context for looking at biographical information on the artists, and a way for users to "collect" their own materials. This last idea suggested a small book that would let users select images, add text, and keep cross-reference linkages to the paintings or timeline entries.

In all, then, the application was conceived in terms of six primary contexts, as shown in Figure 6.2. In this chapter the focus will be on the three key contexts mentioned above.

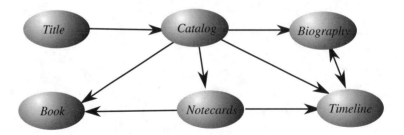

Figure 6.2 The six major contexts of the *ChronoScope* and how they relate to one another

How the Work Unfolds

One of the tendencies that sometimes overtakes designers (including artists, writers, and multimedia producers) is to fill in the last degree of detail in one area and leave the rest of the paper blank. One needs, instead, to know how to unfold the work gradually through an iterative process. The key is to set intermediate goals across the various parts, then not become involved in further detail in any one area until these objectives have been met.

Because the "timeline" context carries the essence of the *Chrono-Scope* application, it was the natural starting point. The intermediate goal for the timeline was to put a set of images on a virtual space and get them to scroll properly. Many other details, such as the zooming functions and screen management, were postponed.

The second context to develop was the "notecard"—here the intermediate goal was to get a click on a timeline image to trigger the creation of a notecard for that image.

The last of the three major contexts was the "catalog," technically the simplest to implement. The intermediate catalog was merely a few buttons that would send a message to the timeline calling for a particular artist's work.

These objectives yielded a skeletal version of the prototype, with the principal interactions defined. The second round of development focused on the *functional* characteristics of each context—zooming on the timeline, enlarging the notecard image to full screen, and so on. The present "final" stage focuses on the details of *appearance* and *control* interface; by this time, the decisions are based on at least a minimal amount of practical experience.

The timeline itself was conceived in terms of the virtual space capabilities of AthenaMuse. The following section gives a brief overview of virtual space and how it provides the foundation for the timeline.

Virtual Space—The Fabric of the Timeline

There is "screen space" and there is "virtual space." Screen space is real: it is measured in terms of pixels on the monitor screen—1,280 × 1,024, for example. Something positioned in screen space will always appear in the same place and be the same size. Virtual space (by definition) is not real. Used to escape the rigidity of screen space, it has a flexible connection to the boundaries of the screen. Virtual space can be squeezed or stretched with respect to screen space. If the virtual space is large compared to the screen space, then the screen becomes a viewport that shows one portion of what is painted on the virtual space. The viewport can be moved around to show different regions of the virtual space; it can be scaled up or down to show more or less of the underlying terrain.

In the *ChronoScope* timeline, the screen (or a window on it), becomes a viewport onto a virtual space whose width represents a long span of time (Figure 6.3). The images of artworks are placed in the virtual space according to their date.

This viewport can be moved to the left or right over the virtual space—or, seen the other way around, the virtual space can be slid left or right "under" the viewport. In either case, as this sliding takes place, time moves forward or back through the viewport; images from different periods of time appear and disappear.

The viewport never changes its position in screen space—it always remains at the same location and stays the same size. But the amount of virtual space it presents can be changed—zoomed in or out against the virtual space to show a longer or shorter period of history in its window.

In AthenaMuse the virtual space, like any other space, is defined with dimensions. A span of time can be defined to be any length at all. The connection to screen space is made by linking an AthenaMuse screen to these dimensions. The process is as simple as telling the screen which dimension to link to for x and which to link to for y. Once the connections are made, the screen will behave as a viewport onto the space defined by the x and y dimensions.

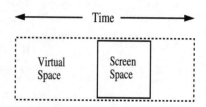

Figure 6.3 Virtual space and screen space as they relate to the timeline

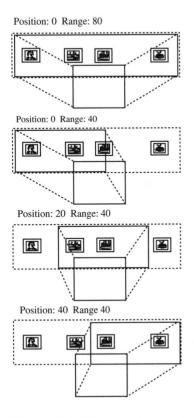

Position: 0 Range: 80

Position: 0 Range: 40

Position: 20 Range: 40

Position: 40 Range 40

Figure 6.4 The position and range of dimension *time* determine what part of the virtual space is projected onto the screen space.

How does the screen know which part of the virtual space to display? It simply follows the *current position* and *range* of the dimensions to which it is linked. The current positions on *x* and *y* determine the origin (upper left corner). The ranges on *x* and *y* determine the width and height of the region displayed (Figure 6.4). The viewport can be moved around the virtual space with the same *set_position* and *set_range* actions used in any other application (see Chapter 21).

The last detail is the placement of the images in the virtual space. In AthenaMuse all display materials are assigned some position in the space of the *package* to which they belong. It is precisely this mechanism that is used to place the images in the virtual space. When the package space is being used as a *virtual* space (when a screen has been connected to it), then the placement of the images in the package space is used to determine where they appear in the screen space. In effect, then, the only explicit change needed to implement a virtual space is to tell the screen which dimensions to connect to. This instruction triggers a small avalanche of computation internally, but that need not concern the author. The only extra consideration is the care that must be taken in placing the images into the package space.

First Snapshot

Figure 6.5 shows the first implementation of the *Chrono-Scope's* timeline. It consists of two "packages" in AthenaMuse. The first is the timeline itself, which lays out a blank area on the screen where the "ArtLines" will appear. It has five dates across the top and a scrollbar to pull time forward and back. The second package defines an "ArtLine," where the images of an artist's work will actually appear. When it is activated, the ArtLine package is placed on the timeline, registered with the dates at the top. In the final version, the ArtLine is used as a template; it is copied each time a new artist is added to the timeline.

Fabricating Images   When an artist is selected from the catalog, the timeline must go to a database and retrieve the list of images to display. The database for this project was made with a simple utility

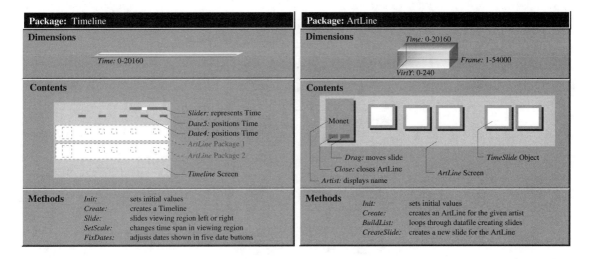

Figure 6.5   The Timeline and ArtLine packages

called *mdb* (the AthenaMuse data base). This utility works with ASCII text files, treating each line as a record. Within each line, fields are separated by a special character (|). The first line in the file contains the names of the fields or other information that helps manipulate the data. Figure 6.6 shows what the mdb file looks like for Cézanne's paintings.

Figure 6.7 shows the methods involved in loading the slides onto the timeline. The process begins when the *Cézanne* button is pressed and the object *ArtLine* gets a *Create* request. After creating the necessary screens, the process calls its *BuildList* method to open the mdb file and

```
MDBINFO | Title | Short | Artist | circa | Date | Date2 | Med | Len | Wdth | Cat | Frame | Details
Village Road, Auvers | AuverRoad | Cez | x | 1872 | 1873 | cvs | 55 | 66 | Rf 1973-12 | 1051 | 3
Dalhias | Dalhias | Cez | c | 1873 | 0 | cvs | 73 | 54 | Rf 1971 | 931 | 1
Self Portrait | Self1 | Cez | c | 1873 | 1876 | cvs | 64 | 53 | Rf 1947-29 | 977 | 1
Three Bathers | 3Bathers | Cez | c | 1875 | 1877 | cvs | 22 | 19 | Rf 1982-40 | 1062 | 5
Poplar Trees | Poplars | Cez | c | 1879 | 1882 | cvs | 65 | 81 | Rf 2324 | 947 | 3
Apples and Oranges | ApplOrange | Cez | c | 1895 | 1900 | cvs | 74 | 93 | Rf 1972 | 934 | 6
```

Figure 6.6   Mdb records for Cézanne's paintings. Each line records one painting. The lines are divided into fields for title, abbreviated title, artist, date (three parts), size, catalog number, frame number on the videodisc, and number of details.

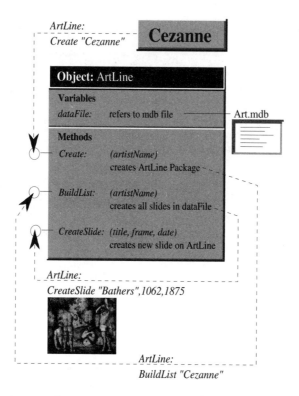

Figure 6.7   A click on the *Cézanne* button triggers a flow
of messages that load the slides onto the timeline.

read through the records one by one. Each time the artist's name is found, *BuildList* sends the frame number and date to the *CreateSlide* method, another of object *ArtLine's* resources.

CreateSlide generates a new display element and adds the frame number to it. It uses the date to determine where to place the slide in the virtual space. It gives the new element a "script" to follow (called *TimeSlide*), which is described below. Finally, it activates the new element, which appears on the screen at the appropriate location. Figure 6.8 shows the appearance of the screen at this point.

As it happens, Cézanne painted more than one picture per year. The practical consequence for our purposes is that more than one image may be assigned to the same position. The *CreateSlide* method avoids putting images directly on top of one another by spreading them out vertically as shown in Figure 6.8. The images still overlap, however—it seemed better to stack them than take the space needed

Figure 6.8   Slides appearing on the timeline

to show each one. Therefore some basic window management functions were required to shuffle through the stack.

Basic Image Behavior Each image placed on the timeline was given the same script to follow, which is contained in the *TimeSlide* object. Figure 6.9 shows this object and its methods; at this point in the development there are only two—*SetPkgInfo* and *Button-Released*. *SetPkgInfo* is a record-keeping function that stores some basic housekeeping information: what the slide represents, what other resources it can access, and so on. The other method is for responding to *ButtonReleased* events. Because the images were getting stacked up on the timeline, there was no way to see those near the bottom of the pile. The *Button-Released* method watches for mouse clicks. If the mouse button is clicked on the image, the image is raised or lowered depending on which of the three buttons is used.

This was the first implementation of the timeline context. Although incomplete, it had enough functionality to move to the next context, the NoteCards used to inspect individual paintings.

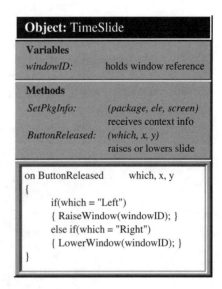

Figure 6.9 *TimeSlide* **object in Event-Script. The code for the** *ButtonReleased* **method is shown.**

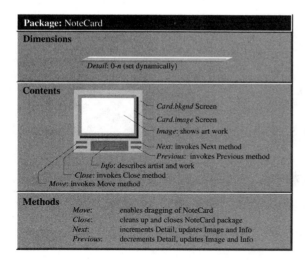

Figure 6.10   NoteCard package and display

NoteCards

If you want to see a piece of art displayed on the timeline, a click of the mouse should bring up a copy, larger than the one on the timeline and with all the basic information contained in the database file—title, artist, dates, and so on. The first step in adding this function to the application was to make a template showing what this "notecard" would look like. This is the package *NoteCard*, shown in Figure 6.10. The NoteCard context consists of a 640 × 480 pixel copy of the image, along with several labels and control buttons.

The next step is to clone this whole package each time an image is selected from the timeline. A method called *ShowCard* is added to the *TimeSlide* object, which gives this cloning ability to each of the slides on the timeline. *ShowCard* makes a copy of the template, then modifies it by putting the correct data into the various display elements so that the proper images, titles, and so on are presented.

The Second Iteration

Creating a series of images on the timeline, with the ability to open a NoteCard for any one of them, is the core of the application function.

The second pass of development generates enhancements—critical to the application, but not necessary for "getting off the ground."

Modified Zooming

Normally, zooming in on a virtual space makes everything get larger. In the case of the timeline, zooming in from an eighty-year view to a five-year view would make all the images grow by a factor of sixteen. If they overlapped at the eighty-year level, they would overlap the same amount at the five-year level; they would simply be much larger. The goal for the *ChronoScope* was to spread the images more as the zooming occurred, but not make them grow to enormous size.

Accordingly, with each step "closer," the images needed to *shrink*— then they would appear to spread out rather than grow, as the zooming took place. To do this, each image had to have a method for scaling itself. The behavior of each image is defined in the *TimeSlide* object; to handle scaling, a *Resize* method was added, as shown in Figure 6.11. The user pushes a button to change the scale. A set of fixed intervals was chosen for simplicity; the user can view eighty-, forty-, twenty-, ten-, or five-year intervals on the timeline. A click on one of the scale buttons sends a message—*Timeline: SetScale 40*, for example. *Timeline* is responsible for changing the dates at the top of the timeline. Then it must notify all of the *ArtLine* objects that have been opened—one for each artist.

In addition, the *TimeSlide: Resize* message is sent. Every image is a clone of *TimeSlide.* To get all of the images to resize, the message is sent

```
on Resize
{
    if(NOT IsClone(theObj()))
    {
        SendToChildren(theObj(),theCurrentMessage);
        exit Resize;
    }
    if(Scale <> MyScale)
    {
        put GetMapPosIn(MyMap,1) into x;
        SetMapPosOut(MyMap,1,(x + VW));
        put GetMapPosIn(MyMap,2) into y;
        SetMapPosOut(MyMap,2,(y + VH));
        put Scale into MyScale;
    }
}
```

Figure 6.11   The *Resize* method

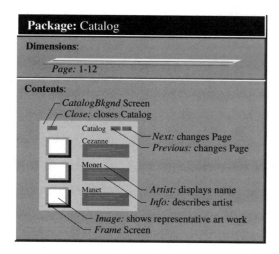

Figure 6.12   The catalog package

to the original *TimeSlide* object, which then uses the *SendToChildren* function to pass the message on to all of its "children."

Initial Catalog, Title, and Book

In the second iteration, the catalog is elevated to a simple menu with artists' names and a representative image of one piece of their artwork. This is implemented as a single package in AthenaMuse, illustrated in Figure 6.12.

Unlike the timeline and notecard contexts, which depend heavily on procedural methods defined in EventScript, the catalog is a straightforward construction of buttons and images. Each button uses a "send_message" command to communicate with the timeline—using the same message that was used in the first round of development.

Two more contexts were added at this point. One was the title context—a simple combination of labels, buttons, and images, overlaid on the timeline itself. The title is similar in form to the catalog. The other new context was a book to let users select images from the timeline and keep them in a personal "photograph album." The book was added as a complete document; it was modified from a similar document developed for a different project, described in detail in Chapter 11. It took nearly two hours to add the book to the *ChronoScope*.

FUTURE DEVELOPMENT

At this point, the prototype exhibits the basic functionality for which it was designed. To reach this point took approximately five days of effort for one person. Obviously, further development is needed to move beyond a prototype version of the application, and many possible extensions and variations could be added.

The general technique suggests many other applications. Some of these would follow the idea of a timeline but present different content; many aspects of history and of science would be possible. There are business applications where this form of presentation is useful as well—refer to Chapter 12 for one example.

Beyond the notion of time, the images can be arranged according to any attribute that can be mapped against a discrete dimension. The idea of the virtual space, as presented here, has to do with mapping an imaginary space against the x and y axes of a physical screen display. In AthenaMuse, the space can have many more dimensions, and each element of content can be placed in this space according to its attributes. Remember that the screen can be attached to any dimension. With a simple request to the screen to change its virtual x or y to another dimension, all of the contents automatically reposition themselves on the screen according to their positions along this new dimension.

This enters the domain of *visualization,* where relationships among the various attributes of complex data can be explored visually—in this case by positioning them in a complex space and then inspecting this space two dimensions at a time by simply remapping the virtual x and y bindings of the display screen.

We have here a powerful tool for discovering relationships along different dimensions. Even this simple prototype of the artwork from the Musée d'Orsay makes it clear that this "visualization" of one or more artists' work spread out in chronological order affords new ways of seeing that will be of great value to anyone interested in the history of the period. The timeline gives a visual structure to time, which begins to act as a conceptual framework. One quickly develops a sense of the position of any work within this frame—*where* it is equals *when.*

This presentation model has broad application; it can be used not only with time-ordered data, as its name suggests, but in any case where a set of data have some interval or rational data attribute (such as age, weight, or size).

7. *Navigation:* Design for a Visual Learning Environment

At the Outward Bound School on Hurricane Island in Maine, young people learn to navigate by going out in an open boat with a compass and chart and finding their way home. In the Power Squadron courses on navigation, things are handled differently: the students learn theory in the classroom, and only then go out on the water for practice. The *Navigation Visual Learning Environment* is an experiment in educational computing that was designed to integrate the two aspects of knowledge, theory and experience, by presenting the theoretical components of navigation in the context of a simulated experience. The student is therefore able to get a better grasp of the relationship between the two. Coastal navigation is a perfect subject for such research, but the idea has much broader applications in education and training. The objective in this case was to develop tools and techniques that would be transferable to other uses. What follows is an example of application-driven design: we chose an interesting target and let that guide the design of tools.

In *Navigation*, the simulation is a model environment and boat that students can use to practice navigation—in other words, this provides the basis for the experience. For the theory, the system is designed in such a way that tutorial and reference materials can be drawn directly into the context of the simulation. The following section gives an example of what it is like to use the application.

The *Navigation* videodisc was developed in 1983 by Digital Equipment Corporation.

Figure 7.1   The screen display for the sailing simulation in _Navigation_

EXPLORING HURRICANE SOUND

The student begins on the water somewhere in the Hurricane Sound area of Penobscot Bay along the coast of Maine. The problem is to plot a course and sail to the town of Vinalhaven, near the southern end of the sound. The surroundings appear in a 90-degree viewport window, as shown in Figure 7.1. Below are the controls for the boat and other resources needed for navigation. The principal controls allow the student to steer, set a speed, and change the direction of view. The field can be changed to show any 90-degree section out of a full 360-degree panorama. The viewing angle is independent of the boat's heading—it is possible to look in any direction, regardless of which way the boat is moving.

The speed control sets the boat in motion. As it moves through the environment, the field of view is updated periodically with new image sets (Figure 7.2). These image sets are drawn from a database of about a thousand views, and are chosen according to the boat's current location. Features of the boat, such as the prow and the stern, are overlaid on the image near the bottom, so one gets a sense of how the boat is oriented. In effect, students can move anywhere through an area of roughly two square miles, changing direction and speed at any time. This environment encompasses nineteen islands, and a variety of hazards to the novice pilot. To increase the challenge, a thick blanket of fog can be switched on, reducing visibility to about fifty feet. There are plenty of rocks, shoals, and shorelines on which to run aground, and plenty of ways to get lost.

Successful navigation in this area requires a compass and a nautical chart. Measurements with the compass can be made directly within the field of view because all of the images are keyed to true north. The compass simulates a hand-bearing compass; clicking the mouse anywhere on the main viewing window gets a bearing in that direction (the compass bearing is visible in Figure 7.1 at the top edge of the

This feature uses a virtual coordinate space. Refer to Chapter 6 for more detail.

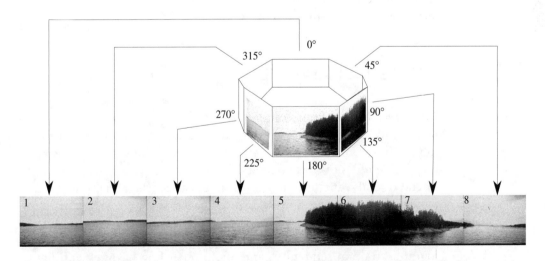

Figure 7.2. An image set contains eight views, each of which records 45 degrees. Spliced together, they give a full panorama.

water level view). The nautical chart is accessed through the Reference Materials, below the water-level view. The nautical chart covering Hurricane Sound opens up in a separate window with its own set of controls.

The chart is implemented as a composite video image. Zooming in is not done by pixel replication, but by resampling the original video data, where more detail is available.

It is important to be able to see the whole chart, then zoom in to see the details of any region. A click-and-drag action of the mouse selects a region to zoom in on. A customized graphics editor is used to create lines of position and to plot a course.

Some of the chart symbols will be unfamiliar to a novice. He or she can point to any of the symbols on the chart and ask for explanation. The chart symbols are cross-referenced to a guidebook (NOAA Chart 1), which will automatically be opened to the appropriate page. If the symbol represents something visible on the water, the system can find a view of the object from the water surface or from an aerial photograph of that sector.

Eldridge Tide and Pilot Book, Robert Eldridge White, Commercial Wharf, Boston MA, 1984.

In addition to the compass and charts, a variety of other tools and materials is available. Simple binoculars will enlarge any region of the viewing window. Other books are useful, especially the *Eldridge Tide and Pilot Book*, which gives important information on the tides. There is also a simulated depth finder and a loran electronic navigation system. Together these make up the navigator's kit. They are implemented as a set of interconnected multimedia documents.

The sections that follow describe the design and implementation of the simulation in more detail, including a general discussion of surrogate travel environments. The use of the *Navigation* system as a visual learning environment is discussed in Chapter 3.

THE VISUAL DATABASE

Navigation is based on a videodisc that holds all the raw imagery needed to simulate coastal navigation. This imagery includes panoramic photos taken from the top of a boat in Penobscot Bay over the two square miles of coastal waters.

The disc also includes images of nautical charts, aerial photos, tide tables, current charts, light lists, a reference manual of chart symbols, and other relevant materials (Figure 7.3). In all there are twenty separate bodies of information on the disc including tables, graphs, photographs, motion sequences, and audio recording of buoys and lights. Other kinds of nonvisual information, such as Loran-C radio data,

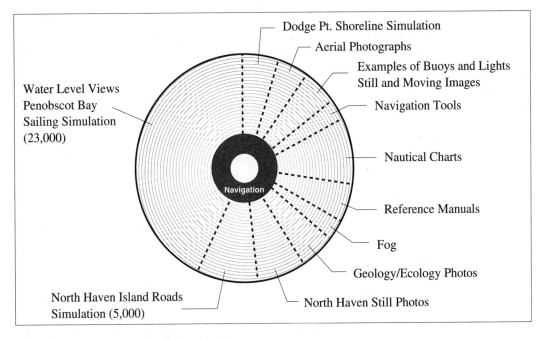

Figure 7.3   Contents of the *Navigation* disc

depth soundings, currents, and so forth, are stored directly on the computer. These materials constitute a database that can be drawn upon in different ways by the separate information accessors. Some of these are described in the following sections.

SURROGATE TRAVEL

Surrogate travel refers to a form of simulation whereby a physical space is represented with photographic or video data showing a real place. Users have some freedom of movement within the space. Such a system can be quite effective for presenting an actual location, or as an interface to a database that can be organized geographically.

There are three surrogate travel environments on the *Navigation* disc. Two are "fixed-route" environments—one on North Haven Island and one on Dodge Point on Vinalhaven Island. The North Haven materials document about twenty miles of roads through the village and around the island. The Dodge Point photos constitute a close-up world

There are other forms of spatial interfaces as well. "Cyberspaces" or "virtual realities" are similar to surrogate travel systems in that they use spatial models as an interface device but they typically are based on computer-generated images rather than photographic data. →

→
These more complex
systems fall outside the
scope of this book.
Our aim is to discuss
how spatial models in
general can be treated
as documents in a
larger information
context.

of footpaths, on which you can explore the rocks and plants along the water's edge. They supplement the navigation materials to support lessons on geology and coastal ecology. The third environment is the navigation environment in Hurricane Sound, which models a boat on the water.

The difference between traveling on roads and traveling on the water is that on a road, you turn only at fixed intersections; on the water, you turn whenever you want to, and you move in any direction. This makes a fundamental difference in how a surrogate travel environment works in an open terrain such as the water compared to a fixed-route terrain such as a system of roads.

The fixed-route terrain is best modeled as a network of nodes and arcs. Examples are described in Chapters 8 and 10.

The open-terrain approach used in the Hurricane Sound environment is quite different because there are infinite pathways though the data; you can take a different direction at any time. Here the environment is best modeled as a spatial framework with data points scattered throughout (Figure 7.4).

Think how you would build such an environment: the problem is to generate a space big enough for students to navigate in, but with fine enough resolution to mark the position of small objects such as rocks.

Around Hurricane Sound, two square miles is sufficient space to learn the basics of navigation: the Outward Bound School on Hurricane Island uses this area as the heart of its training ground. However, if you make a rock-sized grid of two square miles, you end up with a large number of nodes—a one-yard grid has 8 million points. With eight images per node, this calls for 64 million images and hence a great deal of storage (roughly 32 million megabytes)—more than most multimedia workstations are designed to handle.

a. The fixed-route model uses a network of nodes and arcs.

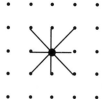

b. The open terrain model allows movement from node to node in a spatial framework.

Figure 7.4 The two models of travel environments in *Navigation*

Here is one of the principal issues in the design of any surrogate travel system; namely, the balance between *depth*, or *density*, of the data and the *breadth*, or *distribution*, of information. Given the limits on how much data can be stored, processed, and displayed, do you pour more data into fewer individual points, or do you make more points with less substance in each one? There is no right answer—it depends always on the application.

For a project such as *Navigation*, a starting point is to determine how much space is needed to satisfy the purpose of the application. For the East Coast of the United States, Hurricane Sound has a very rich diversity of navigational features in a small area. Even so, two square miles is the smallest possible space that could be used for the application.

A second step is to decide what information is needed. For the *Navigation* disc, we needed full panoramas at each point. In the other surrogate travel environments on the disc we used only forward- and backward-looking views taken with a wide-angle lens. In both cases we needed photographic data rather than synthetic images generated by the computer. Therefore the storage requirement was larger.

In the *Navigation* project we developed a two-tiered model to keep this manageable. We needed a grid of moderate density to record the fine-grained features such as rocks. The base level we chose was a grid of 700×1000 units. In terms of physical space, the smallest increment of movement is about 4 yards.

But it was impossible to store images for all 700,000 nodes (5.6 million). So the images themselves were taken farther apart—from 50 to 200 yards instead of 4 yards. As a result, there are a little more than a thousand panoramic views. These image sets make up the second tier; they are scattered unevenly over the grid. The boat moves from point to point on the 4-yard grid, but the view you see is only guaranteed to be the closest set of images available to the node the boat is currently on. The presentation is not continuous motion but an irregular animation of 50-yard to 200-yard jumps; nevertheless, it gives a sense of motion through the environment. This was our trade-off between image density (*depth*) and free movement through a large area (*breadth*).

Simulation as a Form of Document

Floating on this database of images is a simulated boat that can move through a two-dimensional space and give users the means to steer, change speed, look around, and make simple measurements. This "boat" is not one of the million-dollar models found in a full-scale training simulator. Our goal was to have a moderately complex simulation as one part of a multimedia document.

The process of writing the simulation and coupling it tightly with other documents was the primary focus. What tools would be needed to make the writing easy? Could this type of simulation be brought out of the realm of software engineering and into the domain of personal communication? Could we create a simulation of this sort and cross-reference it with reference and tutorial materials?

The AthenaMuse authoring language was designed in part to answer these questions; certain features of the language allow a very efficient description of the simulation and its interconnections with other documents. The remainder of this section describes how the simulation was

A common mistake in the design of surrogate travel systems is to underestimate the need for continuity from one point to the next and not provide enough context at each point: the result is that users lose their orientation.

implemented in AthenaMuse, and how it was joined to the other documents that make up the application.

Structure of the Application

With *Navigation* there are three main choices: one is either "sailing" on Hurricane Sound, "driving" on North Haven Island, or "walking" on Dodge Point on Vinalhaven Island. The system is always in one of these states, and it is possible to move directly from one to another at appropriate points. These are the *second-level contexts:* the highest-level context of *Navigation* is a background screen with a title and the general-application controls such as "Exit." The second-level contexts are embedded within this frame (Figure 7.5).

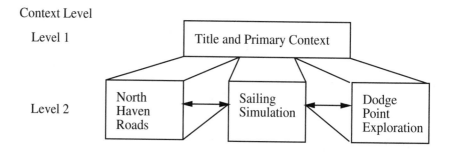

Figure 7.5   **Map of the first- and second-level contexts in** *Navigation*

Within the sailing simulation itself, the application is further broken down into more localized contexts, as shown in Figure 7.6. The boat view, the helm, the reference materials and the tools menu are permanent components of the simulation. From here, through the reference materials and the tools menu, the other resources can be accessed—charts, guidebooks, tutorial materials, binoculars, depth finder, and so on. These pop up on the screen as needed.

The Simulation Packages

Navigation is implemented in AthenaMuse, so the major components are defined as *packages*. These can be thought of as separate docu-

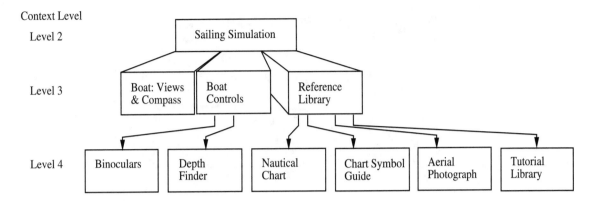

Figure 7.6   The context map of the sailing simulation

ments that are linked together to make the application. Each of the contexts is composed of one or more packages. Some of these are described in the paragraphs that follow.

The Boat   The central package for the sailing simulation is called the Boat. Figure 7.7 outlines the structure of this package. The seven dimensions correspond to the main attributes of the boat and set out the limits of its movement.

The *X*, *Y*, *Speed*, and *Heading* are used to update the boat's position. A timer is set to go off every 100 milliseconds; each time, it sends a message to move the boat. The *Move* method reads the four dimension positions and sends them to two external routines that do the computation. These routines are written in the *C* programming language. They are linked to AthenaMuse and communicate through the EventScript component of the system. One of the procedures is responsible for moving the boat, given position, heading, and speed.

The other routine manages the database. Whenever the boat moves, this module checks the attributes of the new node to make sure the boat hasn't run aground and to see that local wind and current effects are taken into account. Most important, it decides which of the thousand picture sets should be displayed. If it decides that the pictures need to be updated, it returns a new picture set identifier. Whenever a new picture reference is returned, a message is sent to the eight still images listed in the content list. These adjust their frame numbers and refresh the display to show the new images.

Not all of the eight images are visible on the screen at the same time. They are handled with the virtual coordinate facility provided in

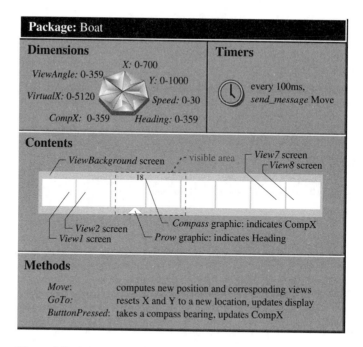

Figure 7.7   Specification of the Boat package

AthenaMuse. The dimension listed as VirtualX defines a length of 5,120 units (the total width of eight images). Each image is assigned a position along this dimension, arranged edge to edge with its neighbors.

The viewing window *ViewBackground* is then coordinated with this dimension in such a way that it will display any 1,280 units (pixels). Once this relationship is defined, any movement along the dimension will cause the viewing window to scroll through the panorama as a viewport, clipping out pieces of two or three of its subwindows (View 1, View 2, etc.) for its display. The dimension itself is defined as a closed loop, so the images at the two ends are automatically pasted together.

The CompX and Heading dimensions are used to position graphic elements for the compass and prow, which are both defined as dynamic graphics constrained to follow these dimensions. The compass is a number; whenever the mouse is clicked on one of the eight views, the Compass *ButtonPressed* method picks up the mouse event, computes a new position and value for the compass, and resets the CompX dimension. As soon as the dimension changes, the new value is propagated out to the graphic element, which redisplays the new value just above the point where the mouse button was pressed.

The prow icon behaves similarly, automatically repositioning itself according to the Heading dimension. In this case the input comes from the Helm, described in the next section.

Boat Control   Below the water-level view is the Helm, which provides the basic control of heading, speed, and viewing angle for the Boat. The contents of the Helm are listed in Figure 7.8.

The dimensions are used to control the positions of the graphic elements for the *BoatIcon* and *ViewRange*. The boat icon is a set of thirty images of a boat pointing in different directions. They act as an animation that is controlled through the dimension *IconPos*. When the left button of the mouse is pressed in the icon window, the *LeftDownMotion* method computes an angle from the center of the window to the mouse position and resets the *IconPos* dimension. The new position is automatically propagated to the *BoatIcon* element. The icon tracks the mouse as it moves. When the button is released, the new angle is sent to the Boat package as its new Heading.

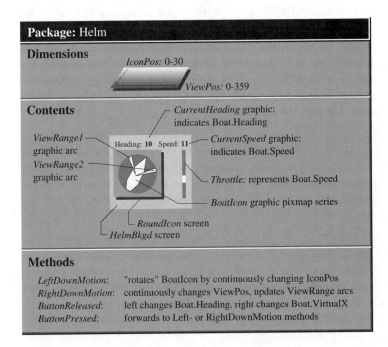

Figure 7.8   Specification of the Helm package

The *ViewRange* indicators work in the same way. Two narrow arcs mark out the 90-degree field currently being displayed in the water-level view above (*ViewRange* 1 and 2). The right mouse button is used to reset the *ViewPos* dimension, which sends its current setting to the two dynamic graphic elements. When the button is released, the new viewing angle is sent to the Boat package as its new VirtualX position, which causes the water-level view to adjust accordingly.

The throttle is implemented as a slidebar tied to the *Speed* dimension of the Boat package. The current setting is picked up and displayed by the *CurrentSpeed* indicator. *CurrentHeading* reads and displays the value of the Boat's *Heading*. Both are updated whenever their respective target dimensions change.

The Nautical Chart   The Boat and Helm make up the core of the simulation. A look at the nautical chart package shows how other kinds of documents can be cross-referenced to the simulation. In this example, the nautical chart can be used to move the boat through its environment to display some of the features indicated on the chart. The contents of the package are outlined in Figure 7.9.

The chart is a composite video image, defined as a 10 × 10 array of frames. When it is displayed, the software digitizes, scales, and positions one hundred frames of video.

Here the *X* and *Y* dimensions use the same scale as the corresponding dimensions in the Boat package. These define a virtual coordinate space over which the image of the chart is mapped. The viewing screen for the chart is linked to the dimension as in the Boat package. Changing position and range on *X* and *Y* cause the screen to select a subregion of the image. The same technique is used with the aerial photographs—a composite image mapped to the same coordinate space. Thus there are three representations of the environment.

The *PutBoat* method gets a screen position from the mouse when it is clicked on the chart. It converts the actual coordinates into virtual coordinates and sends a *GoTo x y* message to the Boat. When it receives the message, the Boat simply resets its *X* and *Y* dimensions and the change is complete: the display updates automatically when the dimensions change.

This example shows how easy it is to make a cross-reference into the simulation. Knowing the dimensions of the package is enough. The boat can be placed in any position, facing in any direction, moving at any speed, and controlled over time from any document with the same degree of control the user has. Through the construct of dimensions, AthenaMuse provides a consistent, simple way to address any document, whether text, video, or simulation.

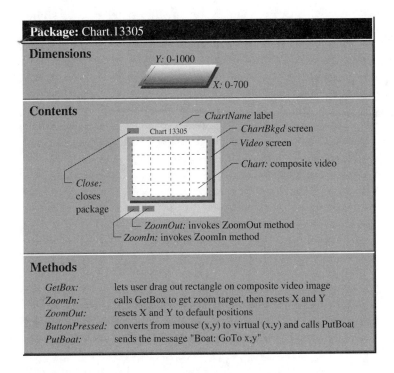

Figure 7.9 Specification of the Chart 13305 package

SUMMARY

Bringing the simulation to the level of personal communication is a challenging prospect. Simulation certainly qualifies as a form of expression, but not many people are skilled in using it in this way. Part of the reason is the difficulty of building such a simulation and then of fitting it into a normal communication context; the tools have not been available to write a simulation and send it as a mail message.

The experiment with *Navigation* highlights some of the issues. AthenaMuse allows a relatively efficient implementation—the algorithms to move the boat are difficult and the database management is difficult, but most of the interactions, the manipulation of images on the screen and the control interface can be defined very efficiently.

One may still question whether this procedure is *easy*. Efficiency is different from ease; in order to be considered easy, the encoding must of course be efficient, but in addition the writer must be able to see how to achieve the objectives. Whether or not the writer can do so depends on how closely the conceptual framework embodied in the tools matches the way that person thinks about what he or she wants to make. The problem is difficult because there are no conventions—people don't normally think about how a simulation is constructed. The challenge is to design tools that are clear enough and efficient enough to become truly easy to use.

8. *Dans le Quartier St. Gervais:* An Exploratory Learning Environment

Contributed by: EVELYN SCHLUSSELBERG

The best way to learn about a language and its culture is through *cultural immersion;* that is, by making a direct visit to the country involved. At MIT, students are approximating cultural immersion with interactive multimedia learning environments developed by the Athena Language Learning Projects.

Dans le Quartier St. Gervais is the part of this material that was developed for second-year French students. It lets them explore St. Gervais, the oldest neighborhood in Paris. This area of the city brings a strong sense of history together with the people, opinions, and issues of today. Students learn about French culture and language by visiting points of interest in the neighborhood, listening to interviews, and browsing through archival photographs and texts.

The French Language Learning Project was produced by Gilberte Furstenberg. Janet Murray is director of the Athena Language Learning Projects, which were made possible with the help of the Visual Computing Group at Project Athena and with funding from the Annenberg/CPB.

There are three principal ways to access this body of information. The main purpose of this chapter is to show how these access pathways are designed and to discuss how this and other features of the application transform a *database* of information into an *exploratory learning environment.* The following scenario describes the three access pathways in the context of the application. It gives examples of how the points of interest in the neighborhood are presented and enumerates the supplementary materials and comprehension aids that are available to help students.

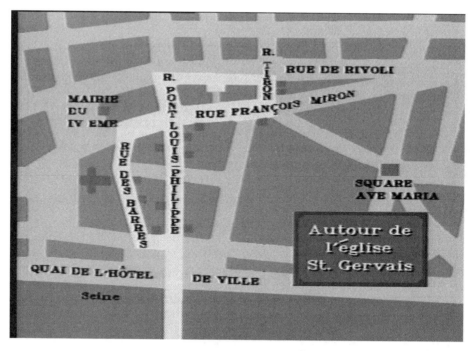

Figure 8.1   A map of the St. Gervais area. All of the highlighted streets are accessible through the application.

Note the differences in the types of information, the timing of their appearance and how the three access pathways work together.

A VISIT TO THE QUARTIER ST. GERVAIS

The visit begins with the click of a button on the title screen. This calls up a map of the St. Gervais area, which shows all of the streets that can be visited (Figure 8.1).

1   Going to a Specific Location

With the selection of one of the highlighted streets (clicking on it with the mouse), a second-level map of the street is displayed that gives more detail. For example, if one chooses the street "Rue François Miron," the screen changes to a map showing the points of interest

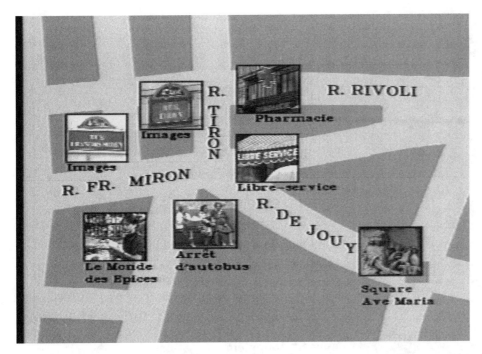

Figure 8.2 **The visual icons represent the different locations that can be visited on Rue François Miron.**

that can be visited on this street. These locations are indicated on the map by visual icons, as shown in Figure 8.2. These maps constitute the first access pathway; they let students choose a location and go directly to any of the major sites in the neighborhood.

On Rue François Miron are several points of interest including a bus stop, a neighborhood pharmacy, and an architecturally rich corner. One of the choices is a small food shop called "Le Monde des Epices" (The World of Spices). With a click of the icon, the map disappears and the student is placed on the street in front of the small shop.

At this point, one can either enter the shop or go up or down the street. If one enters, a short documentary video introduces the shop-keeper, Madame Izrael. She gives a tour of her shop and talks about the different types of food she has for sale (Figure 8.9).

This figure shows a typical video presentation. The student has a great deal of control: the motion video can be stopped at any time and can be backed up to any point with a click of the mouse on the slidebar below the image. This is a powerful tool for language students because they can hear any phrase repeated immediately.

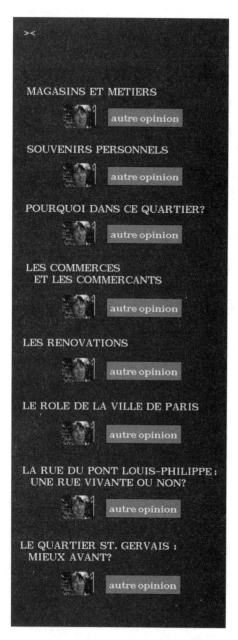

MAGASINS ET METIERS

autre opinion

SOUVENIRS PERSONNELS

autre opinion

POURQUOI DANS CE QUARTIER?

autre opinion

LES COMMERCES
ET LES COMMERCANTS

autre opinion

LES RENOVATIONS

autre opinion

LE ROLE DE LA VILLE DE PARIS

autre opinion

LA RUE DU PONT LOUIS-PHILIPPE :
UNE RUE VIVANTE OU NON?

autre opinion

LE QUARTIER ST. GERVAIS :
MIEUX AVANT?

autre opinion

Figure 8.3 This is the list of topics on which Madame Izrael speaks. By clicking her image, one can hear the segment of her interview that refers to a particular topic; by clicking on the other button, one hears the other people who have expressed an opinion on the same issue.

If they cannot understand all of what the speaker says, subtitles are available as a comprehension aid. There are two levels of subtitles (both are written in French). The first level, for advanced students, provides only key words critical to the meaning of the phrase. The second level, for beginning students, gives a full transcript. The subtitles stay synchronized with the video regardless of the direction and speed at which the video is playing.

As a further comprehension aid, students can select words from the subtitles and get their definitions from an on-line glossary. In this way they can find the meanings of unfamiliar words without spending time thumbing through the pages of a dictionary. The glossary definitions can combine text, images, and graphics (of course, the glossary is in French as well).

After the introduction one can choose to browse through the shop. A collection of close-up images shows many of the items for sale and how they are arranged. Supplementary texts describe the items (some descriptions include the prices, which serve as a starting point for discussion of money matters).

The third resource available at this location is a personal interview with Madame Izrael. She speaks about growing up in the neighborhood, what life is like in the quartier, and how things are changing.

This and the other personal interviews are really the core of the application material, for here the bulk of the spoken language is presented. There are twenty-nine interviews in the database; these were not scripted, but were structured in such a way that people speak on several topics out of a fixed set. Students can hear other people's opinions on some of the same topics that Madame Izrael addresses simply by calling up a topic list (Figure 8.3).

2   Selecting a Topic

The topic lists constitute the second access pathway through the St. Gervais material. At Le Monde des Epices one can select from Madame Izrael's eight topics to see who else from the neighborhood has addressed the same issue. The menu shows a small image of a person's face, together with a quote that summarizes that individual's opinion. By clicking on one of these choices, the student moves to a new location and sees the portion of that person's interview addressing the topic of interest. Different perspectives on an issue can thus be explored quickly. At any point, one can either return to Madame Izrael's shop or continue the exploration at the new location.

3 Walking the Streets

Choosing a topic is one way to leave Madame Izrael's shop (second access pathway). Otherwise, one can continue either by going back to the maps to choose a new location (first access pathway) or by going out the door into the street. Going out the door takes advantage of the third access pathway—surrogate travel. One can move along the street in either direction, viewing a sequence of still photographs that were taken every three feet. A sense of what it is like to move along the street is conveyed. At each intersection, one can choose to follow any of the adjoining streets in the same fashion.

Other choices come up along the way. Options appear as one passes the major points of interest, where one can stop to hear interviews or explore other resources similar to those at Le Monde des Epices. In some cases there are photographs of historic buildings with explanations or close-up images showing architectural detail. The option to return to the street maps and go directly to another location is always available.

GENERAL STRUCTURE OF THE APPLICATION

Dans le Quartier St. Gervais is built around the twenty-nine locations in the neighborhood that have been documented in detail. At each site there are interviews, short documentary videos, collections of photographs, and archival information.

The interviews are among the most important elements, since they give the students their exposure to the spoken language. People were interviewed on a variety of predetermined subjects. Overall, there are twelve topics, although no one person speaks to all twelve. Included are gentrification of the neighborhood, historical events, and personal histories. The interviews were not scripted, so they offer natural examples of spoken French in a variety of accents and manners of speech.

The short *documentary videos*, called "sons et images," show the neighborhood in motion. People were filmed on the streets, in the parks, and sitting at the cafés to show what they do and how they interact. Some of the videos present architectural details from the more important buildings or simply capture the general atmosphere of the neighborhood.

The *archival photographs and information* supplement the twenty-nine locations. They provide historical images and information regarding the sites or the events that took place there. The collections allow students to travel through time as well as space, looking back to see how the neighborhood has changed.

Beyond these basic presentation materials, *comprehension aids* were designed to help students understand what is being said. Some of them, like the subtitles and the glossary, help students with interpretation of the literal word. Others provide cultural background so that students can understand underlying meanings of phrases or gestures.

Turning Materials into an Exploratory Learning Environment

What is an exploratory learning environment? We call it a set of materials that enables students to participate, explore and discover a "world of knowledge." Students learn through the interpretation of their own observation and experience. Reference materials help them to make conceptual links between theory and their experience. They make decisions on where to go and what to see based on either their own motivation or an assignment. This type of environment needs to be rich in content, flexible in design, and attractive to the student.

Dans le Quartier St. Gervais is an exploratory learning environment. Students are in control; they decide where to go and the amount of time to spend at each location. The people they encounter are an engaging force, helping with the development of language comprehension and cultural understanding. Comprehension aids and supplementary information are available at every turn to assist students in interpreting what they see and hear. They can visit the neighborhood many times in different ways. The environment is nonthreatening, so students explore and review the material as they wish. Different activities can be planned so that students apply their understanding in a number of different ways.

The structure of the application and the design of the interface are the means for giving users freedom of action, and at the same time are a reflection of the content. To transform a database of information into an effective learning environment, the following issues need to be addressed:

- designing multiple paths of access through the material;
- cross-referencing supplementary segments and comprehension aids to the main components of the application;
- providing navigational instruments to help students explore.

Designing Multiple Paths of Access through the Material

The starting point for *Dans le Quartier St. Gervais* was to design multiple paths of access that would not only connect information in a logical way but which would facilitate discovery. The three access pathways implemented were "selecting from a map," "selecting a topic," and "walking the streets."

Although each path structures information using its own criteria, each facilitates student exploration and discovery. The criteria become evident; students know the type of options they will encounter on each pathway. However, the content within the options is revealed only when students probe for more information. Fluid movement through the material is made possible: one access pathway or a combination can be used. The students' choice of access pathway will be based on interests, objectives, and skill level. To ensure that students are able to navigate through the material using all of the pathways, the material is structured independently for each one. The first and second access pathways, "selecting from a map" and "selecting a topic," offer hierarchical branching structures (Figure 8.4 and Figure 8.5).

In "selecting from a map" the locations are organized by streets. The hierarchical structure is well known to the students, since they go from a map of the neighborhood to a street map showing specific sites and from there to a specific location.

In "selecting a topic" the material is organized by what people talk about. Students have access at once to all of the relevant topics when they hear an interview segment—they do not go up and down the hierarchy to get to the different topics.

The third access pathway, "walking the streets," is also organized by streets, but is based on a network structure (see Figure 8.6). Here, the

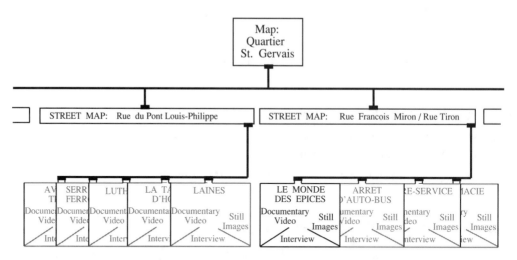

Figure 8.4 **The map of the Quartier St. Gervais gives access to the individual street maps. These in turn provide access to the separate site visits, such as Le Monde des Epices. The figure shows how the material is organized for the access pathway "selecting from a map"; the organization represents a branching scheme in which you go from a general map to a more specific map to a specific location.**

streets themselves are connected in a way that corresponds to their real structure. Sequence becomes important since options are available depending on where you are on a specific street.

A juxtaposition of the underlying structures helps to locate crossing points between access paths and to identify where communication between pathways is needed so that the correct options are available no matter which access path has been used (Figure 8.7).

A crossing point is where two or more access paths meet—here is where a student can choose to change pathways. Crossing points can exist at one or several points in the application or can be available throughout. Crossing points can also be *unidirectional* (if the user from one path can access the other) or *bidirectional* (if from the other path you can also access the path the user is on).

In our scenario most of the crossing points are bidirectional, allowing students to change access path regardless of the pathway they are using. Some of these crossing points are available throughout the application, whereas others are available only at certain points. For example, the crossing between the paths "selecting from a map" and "walking the street" is always available—students can always access a street map when walking and can always begin their walk from a street map. However, the crossing points between these two paths and the

do users get disoriented ?

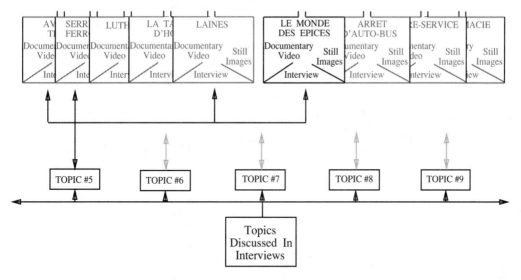

Figure 8.5   The menu of topics connects each topic to one or more of the interviews, which are contained in the site visits. This diagram shows how the material is organized using the access pathway "selecting a topic."

path "selecting a topic" are relatively few, because this third path is available only when listening to interviews.

Up to now, the discussion has focused on using multiple pathways for accessing the *same* set of material. It can become more complex. Instead of accessing the data without regard to the access path, the data will change in some cases depending on what pathway is used. In the case of Madame Izrael, if we arrive at her shop by walking, instead

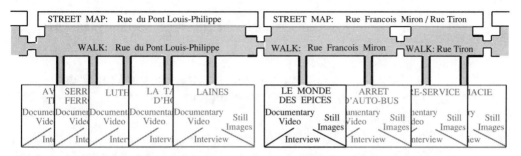

Figure 8.6   The walking segments are organized by street. They give access to the site visits, but only in the proper sequence. They are shown allied with the street maps; one can move back and forth between the two at any point. This diagram shows how the material is organized using the third access pathway—"walking the streets."

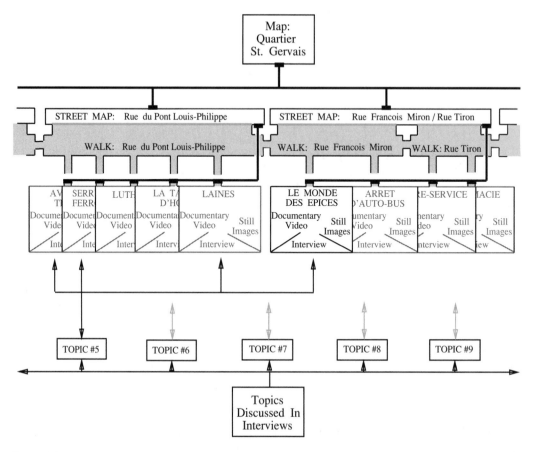

Figure 8.7 This diagram shows how the material is organized using all three access paths. Although two of the three are based on a branching scheme, when they are combined they form a web-like scheme that enables students to move through the environment in a nonstructured manner.

of by selecting it from the map, she will suggest other places to which we can walk.

Cross-Referencing Supplementary Segments and Comprehension Aids to the Main Components of the Application

In *Dans le Quartier St. Gervais* the twenty-nine principal locations are the core of the application. They provide the environment in which the student roams. Supplementary materials provide interesting additions to the environment, but they are not central. The archival photographs fall in this category; although they add a historical perspective, they are not critical for visiting the neighborhood. The comprehension aids, such as the glossary and the subtitles, are other examples of supplementary material.

The main components of an application and the supplementary segments can become overwhelming if students are bombarded with information. The amount of information they receive must be balanced with their needs and interests; the information resources have to be coordinated and their presentation controlled.

The students in this illustration have a great deal of control over the display of the supplementary information. The archival material is linked in through icons and buttons that appear and disappear as the student moves through the environment; they become additional parts of the surrogate travel network (Figure 8.8).

The interface mechanism used is essentially the same as that used for the primary material. A button or an icon appears on the screen, as when one approaches a major site. The presentation is of course different; for instance, the browser for the historic photographs does not take over the whole screen.

The subtitles are cross-referenced to the video segment via the dimensional document structure in AthenaMuse. Each video segment (Madame Izrael's interview, for example, as shown in Figure in 8.9) is implemented as an AthenaMuse package.

The subtitles and glossary are associated with the video segments. These can be turned on or off by the student (although the teachers choose not to make the subtitle option available until after the student has first listened to the segment once without them).

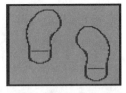

Figure 8.8 Image and graphic icons appear and disappear to indicate when supplementary information is available.

Navigation

The last part of changing a database into a learning environment is the provision of a strong set of navigational aids to the user. These convey the structure of the information available and provide the actual means of movement within the application.

Dans le Quartier St. Gervais is largely based on a geographic model, so much of the information structure is conveyed through the maps of the neighborhood. These have been modified to reflect the distribution of information in the environment, and as described above, they

Figure 8.9 An interview segment with Madame Izrael. Each interview has a dimension of time used to synchronize video and subtitles.

act as the first access pathway to move into this information. The maps are also equipped with a "you are here" feature, which indicates the student's current position within the environment. This element is especially useful when walking the streets—it helps to pop up to the map to check the current location—for the sense of space is greatly weakened in peering through a workstation window.

On the streets most of the navigation aids appear as "point-specific" indications, functioning much like street signs. Left-turn and right-turn arrows appear when there are options to turn, icons or buttons appear when additional information becomes available. Within the video segments, a slidebar shows the passage of time and indicates the relative length of and the position within the segment. The student can drag this bar to move the video forward and back.

SUMMARY

Dans le Quartier St. Gervais is a learning environment where students participate and discover a "world of knowledge." Learning is closely coupled with observation and exploration.

Multiple paths of access allow fluid movement through the information: the maps allow direct access to any of the documented locations, the surrogate travel gives a sense of the spatial arrangement, and the topic menus allow movement based on the subject material of the personal interviews. Various forms of supplementary materials help students make conceptual links between their experience and the theoretical or historical frameworks.

To keep a balance between the amount of information presented and the students' needs and interests, supplementary options and comprehension aids do not appear except when requested. The navigational instruments not only enable students to access information, they also reflect the application's material and support its underlying structure.

This application shows how a database of information is transformed into an explorational learning environment that lets students explore, observe, and learn about French language and culture. It develops skills and helps students acquire the knowledge needed to close the gap between language in a classroom and language in its native environment.

9. Man Ray

Contributed by: BEN DAVIS

"The possible, implying the becoming—the passage
from one to the other takes place in the infra-thin."

Marcel Duchamp, *Notes*,
arranged and translated
by Paul Matisse, G. K.
Hall, Boston MA, 1983.

Paris in the twenties was a mythical time saturated with literary and
artistic energy. Man Ray, an American artist living in Paris, produced a
brilliant photographic record of the faces populating that moment in
history. This chapter describes a multimedia presentation of *Man Ray's
Paris Portraits*. The document was inspired by the publication of a book
on the same subject, but the portraits actually become an entry into a
whole world of information about the artists, the work they produced,
and the electric milieu they created.

Man Ray's Paris Portraits was designed with three purposes in mind:
(a) to explore the differences between printed books and multimedia
documents; (b) to experiment with a new interface design for multimedia archives; and (c) to reflect on the nature of Man Ray's work and
its relation to *multimedia* as a presentation modality.

This chapter is intended to give a sense of the conceptual foundations of the document design and to show the evolution of these ideas.
It gives a portrait of the first stages of authorship of a multimedia document.

THE SOURCE

Timothy Baum, a poet and authority on the surrealist and Dada art movements, had made a list when he was in college of the ten most interesting people in the world he wanted to meet. One was the American photographer Man Ray. As it happened, Baum later spent many years with Man Ray and knew many of the individuals he photographed: Hemingway, Picabia, Picasso, Braque, Duchamp, Breton, Stein, Stravinsky, Léger, Miró, Satie, Gris, and others.

Baum, Timothy, *Man Ray's Paris Portraits: 1921–39,* Middendorf Gallery, Washington D.C., 1989.

In 1989 the Middendorf Gallery in Washington, D.C., published *Man Ray's Paris Portraits: 1921–39.* Baum provided many of the photographs and anecdotes for the exhibition, as well as the foreword to the book. For him, the book is an album of seventy-four old friends and inspirations; for us, it is a treasure trove of people who changed history, for these were the thinkers who were our most direct artistic ancestors.

The inspiration for a work of art or for a book such as *Man Ray's Paris Portraits* is difficult to trace. It often comes when one sees things put together in new ways. Expressing such a vision depends on understanding some presentation medium; indeed, for artists in any domain, grasp of the medium is intimately linked to the vision that is eventually realized. The multimedia computer is a new expressive medium, with the potential to support new expressive formats. The processes of inspiration in the face of this new medium are especially interesting. What follows is a narrative description of the inspiration that led to the interactive *Man Ray's Paris Portraits* described in this chapter.

Figure 9.1   Self-portrait, Man Ray

THE INSPIRATION

I was invited by George Hemphill, then Curator of Photography at the Middendorf Gallery, to visit Franklin Graphics in Providence, Rhode Island, and see the Man Ray book in production. As we paged through the proof sheets, I saw the photograph of Marcel Duchamp, one of the leaders of the "Dadaist" art movement of the twenties (in which Man Ray was completely immersed). I remembered Duchamp's idea of the infra-thin: *"The possible, implying the becoming—the passage from one to the other takes place in the infra-thin."*

Duchamp, *Notes*, p. 45.

Another favorite was Marcel Proust. Man Ray had been summoned to photograph Proust on his deathbed. The man who had written *A la Recherche du Temps Perdu (In Remembrance of Things Past)* was himself a dead photo memory—the ultimate surrealist/dada image! Sad and funny, juxtaposed with Duchamp, this image started Hemphill and myself thinking of multimedia and the infra-thin.

This experience was the catalyst for preparing *Man Ray's Paris Portraits* for their entry into the electronic age. Projecting this book into an electronic, hypermedia format would provide insight into how a visual history book based on portraiture could provide a "human-face human-interface."

The prospect was deliciously dada, in the spirit of Man Ray. It might elucidate the relation of multimedia and Duchamp's definition of the infra-thin: "The exchange between what one puts on view...and the glacial regard of the public (which sees and immediately forgets). Very often this exchange has the value of an infra-thin separation, meaning that the more a thing is admired and looked at the less there is an infinite separation." How then to create the interface? Where to begin? Man Ray's images were the answer, of course.

Duchamp, *Notes*, p. 21.

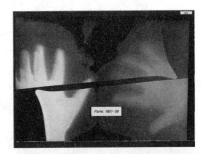

THE EXPERIMENT

The first step was to produce a small visual database of about a thousand images of various artists' work. A section of Léger's *Ballet Mécanique* and an analytic paper on the film were added, along with selections from Stravinsky's *Firebird* supplemented by some notes from Hemphill. How would one enter the electronic book? Initially some thirty postage-stamp-size copies of the portraits were created and laid out on the main screen (Figure 9.2). The familiarity of some of the images and the striking mystery of others (Lenore X, for example) made a comfortable balance.

But something was missing.

Computer artist Paul Rutkovsky looked at the interface. His first reaction was, "Can you go in there and manipulate the images, the way Man Ray would have?" After all, this was the group of artists who took pride and pleasure in putting a mustache on the Mona Lisa!

Figure 9.2 The "portal images" leading up to the main screen

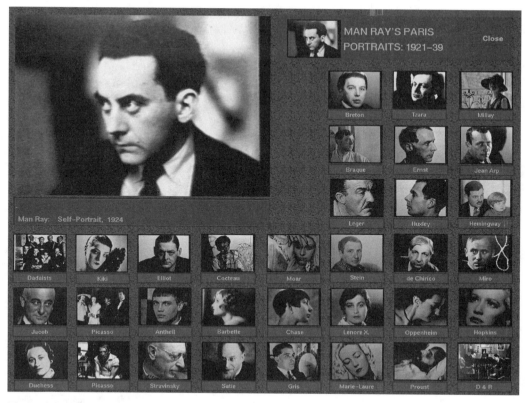

Figure 9.3   Thirty portraits make up the main screen of *Man Ray's Paris Portraits: 1921–39*.

Suddenly it was apparent that the spirit of the period was missing from the design. What we had made was merely a slide library interface, not a "Paris 1921–39" interface.

The initial screen presented to the user should *intrigue*. Certainly any of Man Ray's images would do so to some degree. His "rayograms," the stylized photograms made by laying three-dimensional objects on a sheet of photographic paper, seemed most appropriate. They were simple uses of photo technology that created complex, almost x-ray-like images.

Man Ray's rayogram of a man and a woman kissing became the "portal image." At the outset one is confronted with that sepia image full screen and a small gray rectangle that simply says "Paris 1921–39." With a click on this screen the image fractures into dozens of stretched and shrunken versions, making a collage that presents another "key" that says *Man Ray's Paris Portraits, 1921–39*. A click on this screen takes one inside the book, where the thirty portrait options are displayed.

Fernand Leger

| Search | Close |

Aspects of Fernand Leger's Ballet Mecanique

Ben Davis

Perroquet

There is a single sequence of a few frames in Leger's Ballet Mecanique that seem to sum up the both the intention of the film and its mystery. At exactly two minutes and fifteen seconds into the film a BIRD appears. It is a parrot (a cockatoo) turning to face the camera and then turning away.

It disappears in a flash of light and is not repeated.

Why in a film composed of repetitions and enlargements of everyday objects do we find this single bird? Was its lack of repetition intentional?

Leger's structure for Ballet Mecanique seems to be what Roland Barthes has called a "cycle of avatars"@Foot(The Metaphor of the Eye, essay in George Bataille's Story of the Eye, Penguin, 1979.}. Everyday objects enlarged to archetypical status passing one from the other, repeating, transforming, and interupting each other. A good deal has been written about the animated construction of the film from cleverly lit fragments of ordinary objects, faces, and the looping of sequences. The pattern of Leger's visual judge-ments are apparent. this film, the first declared "sans scenario" in its text introduction, is a collage. The swinging chrome balls, the gears of machines, the dancing bottles, the rotating disks juxtaposed with femine lips and are all awaiting the female form trudging endlessly up and down stairs with her burden. The symbols seem obvious to us in an age technology and sexual advertisement/ liberation.

But what about this single BIRD ?

Ballet Mecanique

===> | II | > | < + > | < - > | Quit

Leger's Paintings | Ballet Mecanique | Biography

Film Analysis

Return

Figure 9.4 Each artist can be studied in depth. Here Léger's film *Ballet Mécanique* appears on the left, with text analysis on the right. Points in the text are cross-referenced to points in the film.

Each portrait then becomes a visual signature representing re-positories of hypertext, images (moving and still), audio, and graphics.

By questioning Léger's portrait for instance, we can transform the screen into a visual and textual catalog (Figure 9.4). A full-motion video window (640 by 480 pixels) appears with on-screen buttons for slow, fast, step, and real time speeds. The clip from *Ballet Mécanique* is displayed along with a text. Various words and phrases are highlighted in the text and as the reader clicks on them the images referred to in the film appear in the video window. Other options in the video package allow you to review Léger's paintings from the period, as well as text descriptions.

You may return to the main screen and select other options from the portraits. You may, for instance, select Picasso and Braque, split the screen, and review the contents of their visual files simultaneously in order to compare paintings made during the same years (Figure 9.5).

Figure 9.5 Artists can be compared directly by opening separate pages side by side. Braque is shown on the left, Picasso on the right.

Text descriptions are also provided. Stravinsky's file contains a text on *Firebird* and by accessing highlighted phrases you can hear sections of the work. The main screen also holds the option for investigating Man Ray through his paintings, photographs, and written material.

MULTIMEDIA AND THE INFRA-THIN SEPARATION

The potential of this electronic "virtual museum" as an intellectual resource must be close to what Duchamp referred to as a "delay." If we liken the interface to the "infra-thin" filter between the "implying" and the "becoming," the veil of authorship between the artist and the viewer, then we have used technology much as the Dadaists employed it—as a *dynamo.*

The exploration of this subject matter, *Man Ray's Paris Portraits,* has allowed us to make a dynamic correspondence between art historical information and artistic metaphor. It has allowed us a breadth of research that pursues art as an intellectual resource, a thinking tool.

The criterion for collecting is a filter. This collection of portraits is very much like a set of baseball cards (the Dadaists would certainly have approved the comparison). Players are collected according to their fame, their professional achievements, the relative rarity of their appearance in the card medium, and anomalies in printing or other esoteric distinctions.

The same is true of the collection of artists and artistic personalities that Man Ray chose to immortalize. The difference is that Man Ray's collection uses the face as yet another filter to the enormous catalog of creative production it represents. An image of Picasso instantly conveys us to literally thousands of other images and ideas. When Picasso's face appears next to Braque's, we increase the catalog by a factor n. With seventy such faces, the collection of images and ideas is staggering. In reality the inventory would fill several museums.

The computational modeling that allows this tremendous confluence of separation and transition is the multimedia medium. The creation of prototypes such as *Man Ray* points directly to a new medium: not computing, not television, not word processing, not digital audio, but something more than the sum of its "multi" parts.

The computer phase-shifting that allows for sorting and connecting data and metaphor is something quite new. By filing ideas behind a collection of portraits, we are at once assigning authorship and implying a "community of ideas." The dynamism inherent in this construction is what Duchamp was suggesting with his idea of the infra-thin.

There is a very thin separation between individual creativity and the social creation of knowledge. The use of the computer as a filtering mechanism appears to make the metaphor concrete. We have a thin film of pixels that make a picture, but that picture can be literally transformed into text, image, or sound at the demand of the viewer. The metaphor of a "delay" is actually the nanosecond of the computer. The dada is suspiciously close to the data.

The shifts are not only from one portrait to the other, but can be from one point of view to another, one life-style to another, one philosophy to another, one medium to another. And once shifted, they can be recombined to create new ideas. Perhaps the user should be able to insert his or her portrait? Would Man Ray approve?

SUMMARY

What would electronic computing technology have meant to Man Ray? What sort of portrait would it have allowed? What sort of historical moment would it have invoked?

Man Ray was both a visual poet and a storyteller. His work provides a rich fabric that weaves iconic images into poetic narratives. His own recollection of making Henri Matisse's portrait is excellent evidence:

Man Ray, *Self Portrait*, Little, Brown and Company, Boston MA, 1988, p. 54.

When I opened my bag to set up my camera, I found to my horror that I had forgotten the lens, which was wrapped separately... Removing my glasses I taped them to the front of my camera so that one of the lenses covered the opening, but in such a manner that only a small portion of the glass showed. Then, focusing on my subject through the ground glass, I saw a quite pleasing image...All the shots turned out well...Matisse was pleased.

Those faces—Léger, Hemingway, Picasso, Satie, Stravinsky, Stein, Miró, Braque, and the rest—are the haunting visual memory of individuals who saw change and were bold enough to employ the force of the future. They have become emblems of change, of dynamic thinking. They represent the separation between object and meaning, between implication and becoming. And in their own fashion, they were friends.

The period from 1921 to 1939 was a time of tremendous technological and social change. Within those eighteen years the world would be transformed into the ever-shrinking world we live in today. The period would end in the horrors of World War II and the constant crackle of radio waves and telecommunications technologies that now force us each day to redesign our personal *infra-thin* filters of media.

We live in a similar world on the eve of the twenty-first century: tremendously accelerated global research on communications technologies, the breakdown of economic and political systems too old to keep pace, the end of the industrial era, and the search for information theories and economies. New and more new.

Multimedia computing is a new medium, but not a medium without history. What the creation of this application has pointed out is that dynamic thinking is not anything new, but it has been quite difficult to *represent*. Until the advent of computers there simply was no rendering mechanism that could accelerate the processes of inquiry and simultaneously access more information in a variety of forms.

The *Man Ray* application is like a roster of "old friends of multimedia." It is as if when we touch the portraits, they nod in the affirmative and say: "I understand what you're looking for! Here's how I expressed the same thing before you had these magic machines."

The matching of content to a new medium is vital. Prototyping is not simply a matter of finding any application and implementing a test. The careful selection of material will allow the content to inform the medium just as the medium helps to render new understanding of content. This interplay is crucial to multimedia's evolution as a unique medium, not simply a new way of seeing television or computers. The question to be asked is not what multimedia can do for a given content, but rather, what those contents *are* once they have entered the medium. If we ask Man Ray's portrait of Gertrude Stein, she will tell us that "once you get there, there's no there there!" But of course each of those "there's" is a hypertext.

10. CERN *Diorama*

CERN is the European Center for Research in Particle Physics located near Geneva, Switzerland. In July 1989 researchers at CERN turned on the world's largest particle accelerator, to study the creation of matter that occurs with the production of the Z^0 subatomic particle.

With the increasing interest in physics research, CERN found itself inundated with visitors. But it is not practical to give tours to fifty thousand people a year, as the LEP accelerator has a circumference of 27 kilometers and is buried underground. In order to cope with the influx of visitors, CERN began work on a permanent science exhibition center called *Microcosm.*

The project described in this chapter, the CERN *Diorama,* is part of this center. An interactive multimedia tour of the facilities, it presents the research through an "exploratorium" approach. Visitors are able to explore the accelerators and experiments at CERN by moving through a database of motion video images, text, and graphics.

AN EXPLORATION OF CERN

Diorama opens with an aerial view of CERN. The path of the LEP accelerator is traced on the image as a white line, as shown in Figure 10.1. A

Figure 10.1 **The main screen for *Diorama* showing the aerial view of CERN. The path of the LEP accelerator is highlighted in white.**

title is overlaid on this image in a separate window, where an introductory video runs for about a minute. This video gives a brief explanation of the research at CERN, emphasizing two main messages: that physicists there are finding increasing order at the deeper levels of nature, and that research with the LEP accelerator is studying the creation of new matter as it emerges out of the quantum ground state.

This short video leads to an invitation. First, the window for the introduction disappears, leaving the whole aerial view exposed. Then a voice-over explains how particles move from their creation in the linear accelerator to their collision in one of the four LEP detectors.

Animated particles overlaid on the aerial view illustrate these points as the explanation is given.

As the overview finishes, visitors are invited to explore any of these locations further simply by pointing on the aerial photo and clicking the button. Or they may choose a "guided tour" from a menu of choices available on the application title bar.

Suppose you wanted to visit the Aleph experiment near the village of Echenevex. You click the mouse where the site is marked on the aerial photo. A close-up aerial view is painted over the lower portion of the screen, as if laid on top of the full aerial view. Above this appears a title screen for Aleph (Figure 10.2). The title screen lets you know where you are and gives you a chance to decide whether or not to continue. It offers a few words about what a detector is and gives instructions on how to go ahead or return to the top level (by clicking on the edge of the aerial view that is still visible at the top of the screen).

If you decide to continue, the title frame is replaced with a view of the entrance to Aleph. Here you are welcomed by Jacques Le François, spokesman of the Aleph collaboration. In a short video interview he takes you through the security gates and into the elevator to the detector, which is located 150 meters below ground. While the elevator is going down, he explains a bit about how matter is created in a collision and how the detector records these new particles as they spray out through layers of iron and lead.

When the elevator doors open, you see the cavern and the detector with its four stories of electronic sensing equipment. At this point, M. Le François invites you to explore the cavern. You are now in a surrogate travel mode, where you can move through a spatial recording of the cavern. You can go forward on the main floor or up the catwalks at either side of the cavern.

As you move around the detector (using control buttons on the screen), you encounter engineers and scientists who can explain various points of interest. If you move forward toward the electronic barracks, for example, you will meet John Harvey, one of the designers of the data acquisition system for Aleph. Inside the barracks he explains how the signals from the million wires that come out of the detector are checked every 23 microseconds for signs of a collision, and how, when a collision does occur, the data are recorded, filtered, and transmitted up to the Aleph control room above ground.

As you approach the opposite end of the cavern, you can leave the Aleph cavern and enter the LEP tunnel. Here M. Le François meets you again, to bid you farewell and explain how to move down the

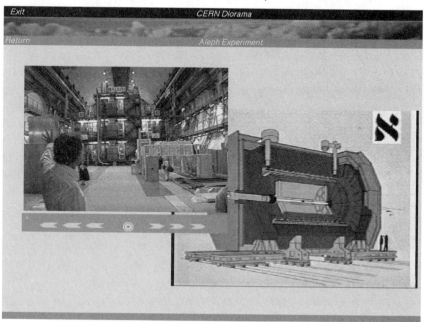

Figure 10.2 A visit to the Aleph detector begins with a helicopter view of the facility, as shown above. The lower screen shows the view of the cavern as one
leaves the elevator.

tunnel to the left to visit the OPAL experiment or to the right to visit the L3 experiment. Once you are in the tunnel, you can move from location to location directly, without going through the top-level display.

The tunnel itself is quite interesting: here you have the option of traveling at a human scale or as a subatomic particle. At the human scale, you see the outside of the vacuum tube and all the apparatus used to control the particle beam. Again, you will encounter engineers on the way who can explain the various components you see.

If you elect to travel as a particle, you see a computer-generated animation of the vacuum tube, as if you were flying along with a bunch of electrons. You pass through the center of the bending and focusing magnets and the rf accelerator cavities. You can stop at any time and change to the outside view to see the equipment you are passing through.

An exploration of this kind gives a real sense of discovery. You can follow your nose and see things you would never be able to see otherwise. At the same time, the materials are coordinated so that the important ideas come through no matter which path of exploration you choose to follow.

The *Diorama* Database

The core of *Diorama*, as is true of most of the educational materials described in this book, is a database of presentation materials. In this case, the database was designed and developed in a very systematic way. It serves as a good model of how this kind of material is produced.

The Central Messages

The starting point was to determine the central messages that we wanted to convey. One of the most important design considerations was that each visitor should come away with certain carefully selected central ideas about the research at CERN, regardless of anything else they might learn during their exploration.

To achieve this goal without making it feel like a lesson was the primary design challenge. The approach was to "deposit" these central ideas throughout the database in different forms and in different contexts. They were to be packaged and organized so that no one would miss them and no one would remember them in a negative way.

Formulating these central messages was the most critical part of the design process. Particle physics is extremely difficult to explain, and it is very hard to know how to phrase a short message to a casual visitor with no background in the subject. This part of the process alone took nearly two months of research, including review of popular books and articles on physics, interviews with physicists, and trial presentations with members of the target audience.

In the end, two central messages were chosen for the project and were approved by a number of the project organizers. Briefly, the central messages pertained to (a) unity at the microscopic levels of nature and (b) the creation of matter. These topics were clothed in a variety of expressions and presented to the visitor as short packages interspersed with other materials at strategic points throughout the database.

The Logical Network

Once the central messages of the project had been isolated, the next step was to define the contents, to identify everything that should be described for the inquisitive visitor. The starting point for this was a logical network that broke down the various components of the accelerators, the detectors, and the related theory of physics.

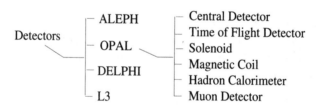

Figure 10.3 Logical network shows the topics to be included and their conceptual relationships. It does not show the pathways the user will follow to access these topics.

Figure 10.3 shows a sample of this network describing the LEP accelerator and experiments. When complete, the network contained about two hundred nodes.

This certainly does not exhaust the possible topics of interest at CERN, but given the scope of the *Diorama* project and its role as a prototype, this was an acceptable compromise. The threshold for what was finally included fluctuated as the disc space was filled—in the end, the space limitations dictated that many pieces be omitted or shortened.

The Access Pathways

The logical network defines the basic contents of the database in terms of what material is to be covered. It has nothing to say, however, about how the materials are presented. For this one needs to think about the visitors and how they will be seeing the material. The result is a separate network, which we called the *access pathway* network. The access pathways show the sequence of steps one needs to pass through in order to get to any of the documents in the database.

Structure of the Application

At the top level, *Diorama* was to run as a programmed loop, as shown in Figure 10.4. From the *Top Level* context, the *Title* is triggered first and includes the introductory video. When this video is finished, the particle animation and Invitation begin. After the invitation to interact, the system waits for the visitor to choose a location to visit or to initiate a tour (this choice is made in the context of the animation). If nothing happens, the animation times out and switches back to the title and introduction to begin again.

The top-level context for the application puts up a title bar and exit button at the top of the screen. It also paints the aerial photo that remains as the background image as long as the application is running.

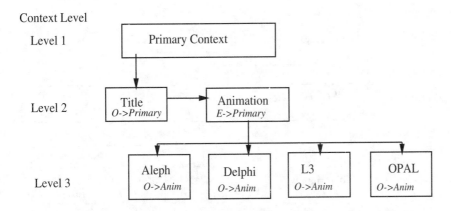

Figure 10.4 The high-level context map for *Diorama*. *O* indicates the context is overlaid; *E* indicates it is embedded in the referenced context.

The *Title* context, overlaid on the background image, presents the title, credits, and the introductory video.

When the introduction is finished, the overlay window disappears, exposing the aerial view of CERN. The *Animation* context uses this image for its primary display (it is *embedded* within the top-level context). It also overlays close-up views at certain points in the presentation. The animation is a time-based document: its display involves synchronized graphics and audio. When it reaches the end of its time span, it expires and restarts the introductory video; in this way the loop continues. The options to visit the different locations covered in the application remain available as long as the animation is active.

A Visit to Aleph

Figure 10.5 shows the architecture of one of these site visits, in this case the Aleph experiment. The *Aleph* title serves as a brief description of the site; it gives a title and several pictures of the Aleph detector. A short text explains that Aleph is one of the four principal LEP experiments and that the particle detector located here is used to analyze the collisions of positrons and electrons in the LEP accelerator. It is designed to give visitors a sense of where they are before the action begins, and a chance to retreat if this is not the place they want to be.

If the visitors decide to continue, they press a button to go on. The context shifts to the *Aleph Visit*, which begins by taking over the lower portion of the screen with a closeup view of the Aleph site.

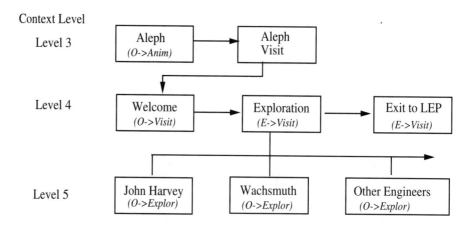

Figure 10.5   The context map for the Aleph visit in *Diorama*. *O* indicates the context is overlaid; *E* indicates it is embedded in the context referenced.

The visit itself is divided into three segments, the first of which is a welcoming video. This *Welcome* runs automatically as soon as the screen is set up, and switches over to the second portion of the visit as soon as it ends. As described earlier, this video features M. Le François, spokesman for the Aleph project. He leads visitors from the main entrance into the Aleph cavern, where the detector is located.

As he concludes his remarks, the visit switches to the second stage, the free exploration of the cavern and the detector ((*Exploration*). Visitors are free to move about the cavern and can pause, if they choose, to hear the explanations offered by physicists and engineers. They can also access a diagram of the detector that lets them look inside the machine and obtain a brief description of each part by clicking on the diagram.

From the *Exploration*, the visitor may choose to go into the LEP tunnel. This selection leads to the third part of the visit, the *Exit* to LEP, where instructions are given as well as the choice to go to the left or right.

The *Aleph-Exploration*

The exploration is constructed as a surrogate travel document, with the range of travel limited to fixed pathways through the cavern. In all, there are five pathways that run from one end of the cavern to the other, as shown in Figure 10.6. One of these runs 30 meters down the center of the floor, from the elevator doors to the "electronic barracks" in front of the detector. On each side of the cavern are two more tracks, which follow catwalks mounted about 10 and 15 meters above the cavern floor. Each pathway consists of a series of photographs taken 3 meters apart.

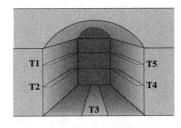

Figure 10.6 Arrangement of the five pathways in *Aleph-Exploration*

Figure 10.7 shows how this arrangement is specified in the dimensional system of AthenaMuse. In this system the document is constructed as a package. The range of travel is defined with the two dimensions *Track* and *Position*. *Track* ranges from 1 to 5 and determines which of the five pathways the viewer is on. *Position* ranges from 1 to 27 and determines how far from the detector the viewer is.

The sequences of photos are specified in the five display elements labeled *Track1* to *Track5*. Each of these identifies a sequence of frames on the video disc and defines a mapping between these images and the space defined by the two dimensions. Each sequence has a different number of images. The reason is that some of the pathways on

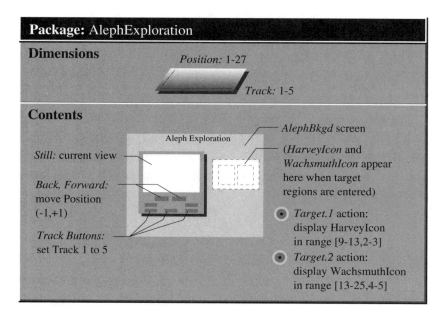

Figure 10.7   Contents of the *Aleph-Exploration* package

the sides allow the visitor to move farther up along the sides of the detector. The longest pathway has twenty-seven positions, so the overall space is set to this size. All of the sequences start from position 1 and fill the positions along their respective tracks with as many photos as they have. Accordingly, four of the tracks have empty positions at the end of the space.

Viewers have the freedom to move anywhere in the space, including these unfilled regions. To avoid having the image disappear completely if someone steps into a "black hole," the extra space on the shorter tracks is filled up with the last valid image on that track. Although the viewer may step into one of these areas, they are not permitted to remain there. In addition to these *Filler* elements, each of the short tracks has a corresponding *Eject* element mapped into its empty space as well.

These elements are called action elements in AthenaMuse—no video or other display material is associated with them. Instead, they map an automatic action into some region of the package's space. In this case, the action is to reset the viewer's position to the last valid position on the track in question. The action is triggered automatically whenever a viewer steps into the region of one of these elements. Together these elements completely define the space and its representation. A set of buttons is used to move around—left and right to change tracks, forward and back to move up and down the length of the cavern. The only other contents of the package are the mappings for the supplementary information. Buttons for the detector diagram and exit to the LEP tunnel are always available. Pressing one of these buttons calls up the corresponding package.

The references to the supplementary interviews are handled in a slightly different way. Each of the engineers is assigned a region in the package's space. If a viewer moves into this region, the picture of the engineer pops up on the screen to indicate that more information is available. Each of the pop-up icons is itself a small AthenaMuse package, containing a picture of the engineer, a short text description of what it is he or she will be talking about, and a "Start" button to let viewers call up the full document if they so choose. Figure 10.8 shows the structure of one of these packages called *HarveyIcon* .

Notice in the *AlephExploration* document shown in Figure 10.7 there is an element to display *HarveyIcon*. It defines a region of space in which the *HarveyIcon* package will be active. One package is given a mapping in the space of another package. Moving into this range automatically activates *HarveyIcon;* moving out of the range automatically deactivates it. This is a tangible way to program the whole interaction and proves to be quite efficient and easily understood.

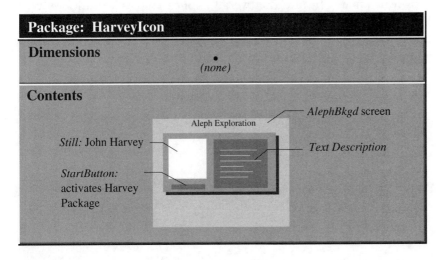

Figure 10.8   Contents of the *HarveyIcon* package

SUMMARY

Diorama is an example of a database with a "geographic" access model, where most of the access to information is based on location, either within an image or within the space of an exploratory environment. The application is also equipped with a supplementary index as an alternative access path, but this is not normally utilized by casual visitors using the system. The two access paths, the geographic and the topical index, are not tightly coupled in this case, as they are in the French language application, *Dans le Quartier St. Gervais*.

Diorama is an experiment in education, using a database model to communicate simple messages to an audience whose motivation is primarily entertainment. The most difficult aspect of the design was to keep these messages in view, yet not let them overshadow the other information or become tedious. We used physicists and engineers as the talent, partially scripting their comments. This procedure lent a freshness and sense of reality to the material. It also conveyed some of the human quality of CERN and shows the broad international collaboration that has been established there.

At the same time, this decision made it more difficult to control the presentation of the central messages. We therefore developed the project through several iterations. The people involved could then understand how the system was meant to work; they could begin to see how their own remarks fit into the overall application. As a result, we were able to achieve a good balance among all the parts and the whole, and still let a wide variety of people who actually work at CERN explain in their own words what they do.

11. Electronic Books

Contributed by: MICHAEL WEBSTER

"What is the use of a book without pictures or conversations?"
Lewis Carroll, *Alice in Wonderland*

Alice's question goes to the core of electronic books. While conventional books can contain both pictures and conversations, they are static documents; the pictures are frozen and the conversations are cast in print. Electronic books not only bring pictures and conversations to life, but also allow many different pathways through their information "landscapes." Their size and structure can be changed in ways that would fit well in Wonderland.

This chapter presents a number of applications that are based on the concept of the book. We examine these electronic books in terms of three areas where they offer distinct advantage over conventional books: (a) dynamic cross-referencing, (b) kinetic imagery, and (c) fabrication and reconfiguration.

DYNAMIC CROSS-REFERENCING

Bibliographies, concordances, indexes, and footnotes are all familiar features of books. Simply by automating their use, electronic books virtually redefine the role of cross-referencing. The *Engineering Geology Educator* and the *Neuroanatomy Learning Environment* are two applications that exemplify some of the cross-referencing capabilities of electronic books.

Engineering Geology Educator

The *Engineering Geology Educator* was developed under the direction of Professor Herbert H. Einstein at MIT.

The *Engineering Geology Educator* uses images, text, and graphics to teach the fundamentals of geology. As used in introductory civil engineering and geology courses at MIT, it has three major sections: a textbook, a quiz, and a workbook. The *textbook* is essentially an encyclopedia with 236 pages of text and over 1,000 images of geological features and processes. The *quiz* consists of multiple-choice questions based on the materials in the textbook. The *workbook* allows students to exercise their skill in identifying geological formations; they can use the mouse to draw outlines around features in an image.

Figure 11.1 illustrates the physical layout of the pages in the textbook. Each page contains up to eight still images; the user can obtain an enlarged view of any of the images by clicking on it with the mouse.

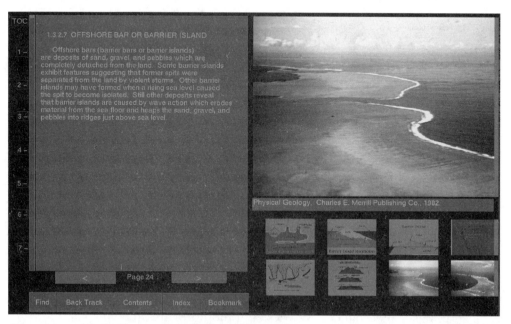

Figure 11.1 Each page in the geology textbook presents a different geological feature. Up to eight images are included with the text description.

The pages are organized in a linear fashion—in AthenaMuse, they are arranged along a single dimension, called *page*, defined with 236 positions. Browsing or cross-referencing the textbook merely involves changing the reader's current position along this *page* dimension.

The sequential organization of the pages in *Geology* can be viewed as an atavistic feature carried forward from its paper-based forebears. The contents of this book have a significant hierarchical grouping, but in essence there is no strong linear continuity from one page to the next. Instead, each page describes a different geological feature in encyclopedic style. The textbook could readily have been organized as a set of independent pages accessed from an index or table of contents. Such an organization appears in the *Neuroanatomy* project, discussed later in this chapter.

Browsing and Cross-Referencing

A number of features help students move through the *Geology* textbook:

Page Turning   Simple *Forward* and *Backward* buttons provide a way to step through the pages in the predefined sequence.

Table of Contents   Beyond its conventional role as a book outline, the table of contents contains dynamic linkages that take the reader to the chapters and sections of the textbook. In AthenaMuse terms, the table of contents enables the reader to jump to specific positions in the *page* dimension.

Scrollbar and Chapter Icons   The scrollbar and chapter icons are located to the left of the text window (Figure 11.2). The scrollbar represents the entire *page* dimension of the textbook. It is used for scanning or for jumping to a point in the text based on approximate position. Each chapter icon takes the reader to the first page of the chapter it represents; it is aligned with the point on the scrollbar where its chapter begins.

There are two interesting aspects of the scrollbar/icon relationship. First, if viewed together as a unit, they give the reader an idea of the relative length of each chapter. Second, they indicate the reader's current position in the textbook. For example, the configuration shown in Figure 11.2 indicates that the reader is halfway through chapter 3.

Index   Like the table of contents, the index in the *Geology* textbook has a dynamic quality; the reader can select an entry and move immediately to the desired page.

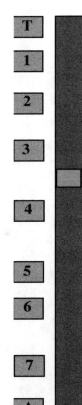

Figure 11.2   A scrollbar and chapter icons show the reader's current position along the "page" dimension. They serve as tools for moving through the material.

Keyword Searches   The same search function can be applied directly from the text body of any page. The reader can select any keyword and press a button to jump immediately to the page where that topic is discussed. This procedure works across all three parts of the *Geology* material, so if a question arises in the context of the workbook, the jump can be made directly into the textbook to find the answer.

In the case of *Geology*, uppercase letters were used to mark the key words. In other applications italics, boldface or underlining may be used to make the key words conspicuous—or they may not be marked at all.

Bookmark   The reader can create bookmarks to help return to specific points in the text. These are created dynamically—at any point the reader can press the Bookmark button. The program will ask for a name, then create an entry in the bookmark list linking the name to a position in the book. To use a bookmark, the reader chooses a name from the list of entries and the book is reset to that page.

The bookmark functions in the same way as the index or keyword look-up: an association table keeps a list of keywords and page positions. The button press triggers a keyword search. When a keyword is found in the list, the book is reset to the corresponding page. In the case of the bookmark, the association table is constructed dynamically.

Path Tracing   In somewhat the same way, as the reader moves through the text, the program itself constructs a list of the page numbers visited. It is therefore possible for the reader to backtrack and work up the path to the original point of reference. The reader can pursue multiple trails of interest without fear of losing his or her place in the document.

Neuroanatomy Learning Environment

The *Neuroanatomy Learning Environment* was developed by Dr. Steve Wertheim. Development is being continued under the name *NeuroDatabase* for Apple Macintosh computers using the Oracle database and a SuperCard interface.

Neuroanatomy is an electronic reference designed to supplement classroom instruction in medical and neuroscience courses. It contains over 1,400 descriptive text documents and an archive of still and motion images of the brain (Figure 11.3). Each page treats a single feature or brain structure, with a text description and (where available) three different views of that structure. One view is a micrographic cross-section of the tissue—the reader is placed at an appropriate point in a sequence of cross-sectional views that move all the way up the brain stem.

The second view is a three-dimensional model of the brain rendered as a computer graphic animation. It is recorded in video as one complete rotation of the model that the reader can manipulate.

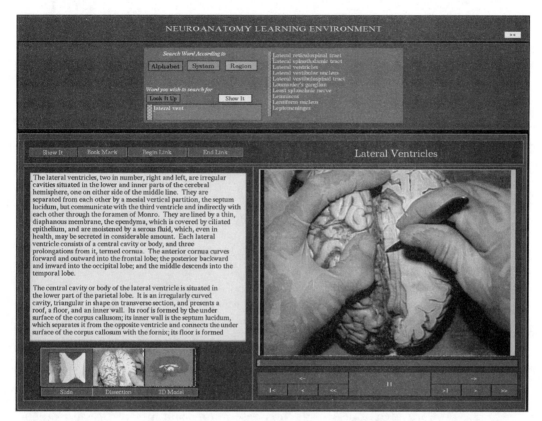

Figure 11.3 **Each page in the *Neuroanatomy Learning Environment* provides text description of one anatomical feature along with options to view micrographic cross-sections, a dissection video, or a three-dimensional graphic model.**

The third view shows the structure as it appears in a brain dissection. The dissection is recorded in video so that the student can see the process and understand the relation of the structure in question to the rest of the brain. As a page is called up, the text is displayed on the left and any imagery is indicated by small image icons on the right. A mouse click on a video icon causes the appropriate segment to be shown in the video window.

Structure and Organization Each page in *Neuroanatomy* is a separate node. There is no sequential order to the pages; the material is accessed only through a set of indexes and cross-references. This is a fundamental break from the normal structure of a book. For this reason, some of the "navigation tools" used in *Geology* are inappropriate. For example, there is no place for the table of contents, the page-turning

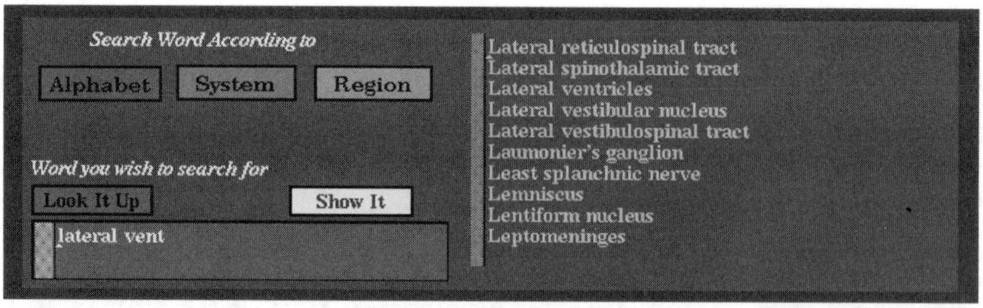

Figure 11.4   Indexes in the *Neuroanatomy Learning Environment* allow students to locate features by name, structure, or function.

buttons, or the scrollbars. Instead, the documents are accessed via three major indexes: an alphabetical listing, an index of neuroanatomical structure, and an index organized according to brain function (Figure 11.4).

Accordingly, students can locate features based on name, location (relative to other structures), or function. They can either type in the name directly to go to the correct page, or they can search through the three indexes in scrolling windows, using partial spellings to help with the search. A mouse click on an index item calls up the indicated page.

Keywords   As in *Geology*, the texts in *Neuroanatomy* contain keywords, which provide another way to move through the document. The keywords that appear in the text descriptions and indexes are all symbolic linkages, referenced through an association table.

User-Defined Links   *Neuroanatomy* also lets readers define their own cross-references. These are made with a tool called the *Reference Builder*, a prototype link editing facility written in AthenaMuse. A link builder of this sort is one of the basic features of a hypermedia system. In the case of AthenaMuse, however, the links are not stored in a global database as they would be in a more complete hypermedia system.

KINETIC IMAGERY

"A picture paints a thousand words."
                              Ancient Chinese proverb

Some concepts are hard to explain without pictures. For other concepts, even pictures are not enough—they need motion. The added di-

VISUAL OVERVIEW

Chronoscope: Musée d'Orsay

The *Chronoscope* application spreads out an artist's works on a timeline. Paintings by different artists of the same period can be studied side-by-side to explore the cross-fertilization of ideas. Based on impressionist paintings from 1848 to 1914, in the collection of the Musée d'Orsay in Paris, France. Interface: Matthew Hodges. Content: Musée d'Orsay, Paris, France.

Navigation Learning Environment

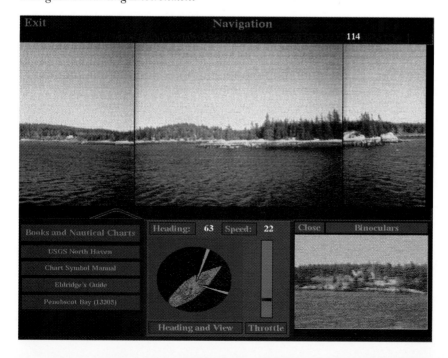

The *Navigation Learning Environment* is a complex simulation designed to teach the basics of coastal navigation with "surrogate travel" techniques. The software can render a view in any direction from the pilot's perspective, using a database of 360-degree panoramas. Maps and charts help to set a course, while a throttle control determines the rate at which the boat's position is updated. Interface and content: Matthew Hodges.

Dans le Quartier St. Gervais

This interactive documentary lets students explore the sights and sounds of an historic neighborhood in Paris. Here the student is watching an interview with a resident; a stream of French subtitles synchronized to her speech can be used to look up unfamiliar words in a companion glossary.
Interface:
Evelyn Schlusselberg.
Content:
Gilberte Furstenberg.

Real Estate

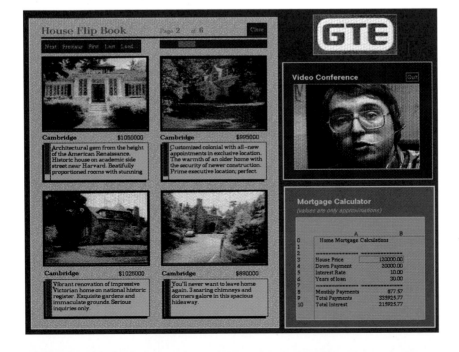

This prototype real estate application was developed with the AthenaMuse software at GTE Laboratories. House descriptions and color images are retrieved from a multimedia database and placed in a customized listing booklet. The client and Realtor can discuss candidate homes and financing options via desktop videoconferencing and a shared document facility.
Interface:
Russell Sasnett, at
GTE Laboratories.

Evelyn Schlusselberg and Ben Davis of MIT's Visual Computing Group are in the Project Athena Visitors Center. They are discussing the interface design for the surrogate travel module of *Dans le Quartier St. Gervais.*
Photo:
Courtesy of Millipore.

Faye Slayton is using the real estate prototype at GTE Laboratories. The video codec in the foreground links the multimedia workstation to a switched fiber-optic network which supports the real-time video connections used in the application.
Photo:
Dick Gaskell, courtesy of GTE Laboratories Incorporated.

Understanding Visualization

This prototype application is part of an experimental curriculum meant to give students an appreciation for the role of rendering technologies, the images they produce, and the changes in thinking that have occurred because of new kinds of images.
Interface:
Michael Webster.
Content: Ben Davis.

MuseBuilder

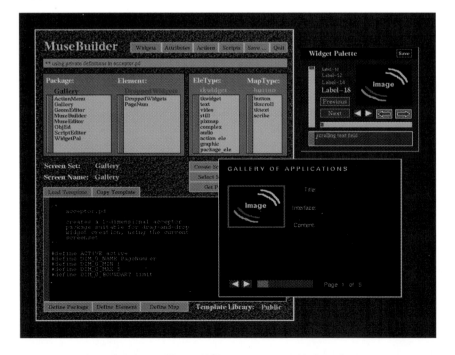

The *MuseBuilder* is the core of an interactive editing system of cooperative tools for producing multimedia applications. It is implemented as a "plastic editor" in Athena-Muse, created out of the same material it is designed to manipulate. In this illustration the *MuseBuilder* is being used to construct a "Gallery of Applications," a dynamic catalog capable of launching demonstration applications.
Interface:
Russell Sasnett, at
GTE Laboratories.

VISUAL OVERVIEW

Editor Collage

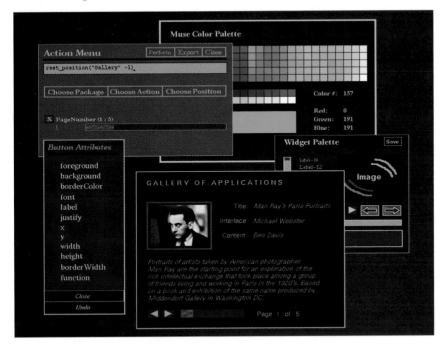

Template widgets are dragged from the user's custom *Widget Palette* into the new application. Here they are being modified with the *Attribute Editor,* which is used to manipulate the layout, color, and general appearance of application elements. The *Action Editor* (shown at upper left) is being used to attach behavior to the "forward" and "backward" buttons for changing the PageNumber dimension.
Interface:
Russell Sasnett, at
GTE Laboratories.

EventScript Editor

The *EventScript Editor* is used to extend the fundamental capabilities of the built-in AthenaMuse objects. In this case a special behavior is being written to launch an external application when the user clicks on its image in the catalog. This editor allows the author to view and modify any of the EventScript objects in the system.
Interface:
Russell Sasnett, at
GTE Laboratories.

Mechanical Bearings

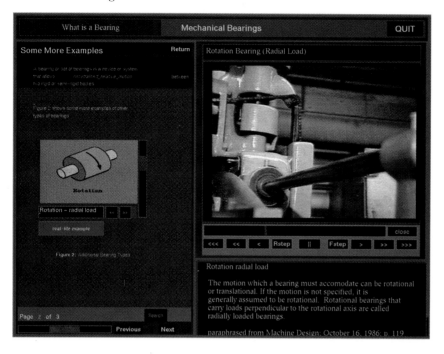

A prototype application intended to teach undergraduates about the most common types of mechanical bearings and how they are used in everyday items from skateboards to lawn mowers. Students can link from conceptual diagrams of bearings directly to real-life examples showing them in action.
Interface:
Michael Webster.
Content:
David Wilson.

Seeds of Change

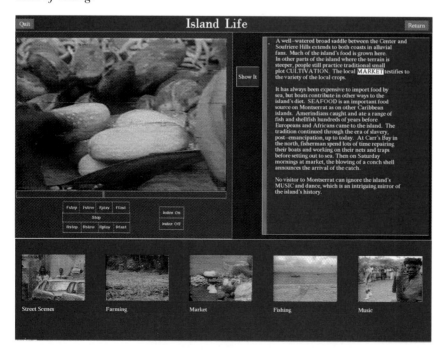

This application explores the cultural upheavals brought about by the European colonization of Caribbean islands. Each topic has a visual table of contents accompanied by a textual commentary linked to video clips and still images.
Interface:
V. Judson Harward, MIT CECI; and Conrad Goodwin, Univ. of Tennessee.
Content:
Conrad Goodwin and Lydia Pulsipher, Univ. of Tennessee.

VISUAL OVERVIEW

MITSI Collection Image System

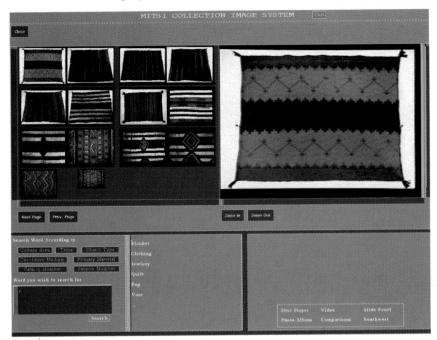

A prototype application designed to help museum curators maintain a collection of artifacts with the aid of a visual cataloging system. The interface shows two views of the same "virtual space" in the form of a light table; each view can be zoomed, panned, and scrolled independently.
Interface:
Evelyn Schlusselberg.
Content:
Janet Gomon, Smithsonian Institution, Native American Collection.

Neuroanatomy Learning Environment

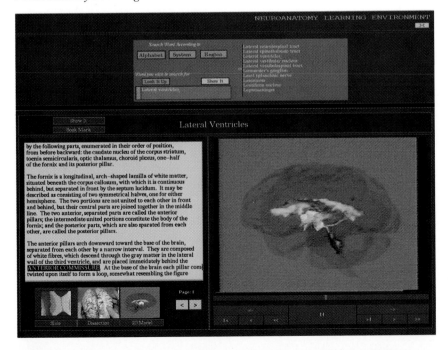

The *Neuroanatomy Learning Environment* lets students explore the anatomy of the human brain. Hypermedia cross-references link the text to video footage from a brain dissection, cross-sectional micrographs, and a three-dimensional model.
Interface:
Evelyn Schlusselberg.
Content:
Dr. Steven Wertheim.

Laboratory sessions for French, Spanish and Geology classes were held in this cluster of multimedia work-stations at MIT. Students continue to use a growing body of multimedia learning materials on a regular basis.
Photo: Ben Davis.

Students in Douglas Morgenstern's Spanish class work with *No Recuerdo,* an inter-active mystery story set in Bogotá, Colombia.
Photo: Ben Davis.

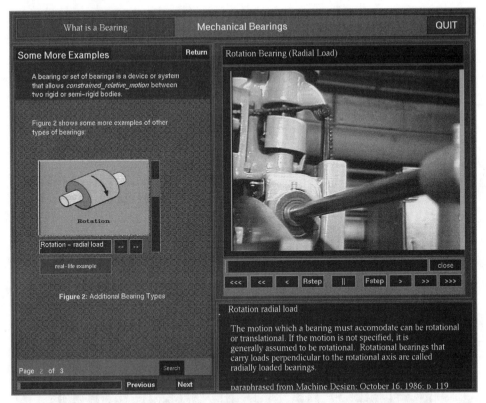

Figure 11.5   A page in the *Mechanical Bearings* Project has formatted text on the left side. Interactive AthenaMuse documents can be included as illustrations. On the right is a video illustration showing how a rotation bearing operates on the machine.

mension of time allows illustrations to show *process* and *perspective*, information that is usually lost or unavailable in a static medium.

Neuroanatomy uses a computer-generated animation to help show brain structure. Students can rotate a transparent model of the brain to better understand its internal structure. The animation is recorded in video; it is not implemented as a real-time graphic animation. But being able to rotate the image—to see it from different perspectives—gives a much clearer sense of its three-dimensional form.

Another example is the *Mechanical Bearings* Project (Figure 11.5). This material covers the design principles of mechanical bearings for engineering students. It is difficult to visualize the operation of various bearings from text descriptions or still images alone. Video illustrations help to demonstrate the underlying mechanics involved. In this electronic book, the text is formatted in pages, with the dynamic video

The *Mechanical Bearings* Project was developed under the direction of Professor David Wilson of MIT's mechanical engineering department.

illustrations inserted directly into the text with captions and control to play forward, reverse, stop, or drag the video.

Interactive Illustrations

See Chapter 17 for a technical presentation on the use of hotspots.

Beyond simple motion to show a process or different perspective, illustrations can be made interactive. A quiz module of *Mechanical Bearings* uses "hotspots" to get student input. The students are asked to identify the bearings in a device by clicking on the illustration itself. The image responds by displaying graphic overlays over correctly identified bearings. The *Geology Workbook* has a more elaborate form of interaction. The student is asked to draw a polygon on the image, to pick out a geological feature. The vertices drawn by the student are passed to an external routine, which compares them with a region defined by the professor. The routine returns an acceptable/not acceptable result and the "book" responds with appropriate feedback to the student.

Another example, perhaps the best, comes from the interactive *Dimension Tutorial*, part of the on-line documentation prepared for AthenaMuse that focuses on the use of dimensions. Figure 11.6 shows

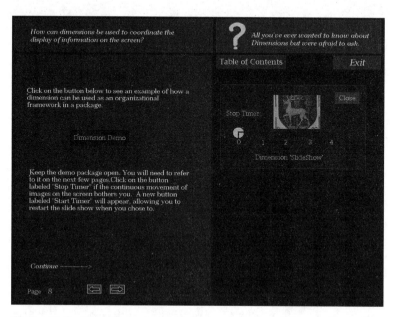

Figure 11.6 The *Dimension Tutorial* incorporates elaborate interactive figures in the text. This one allows students to watch a schematic model work alongside the application it represents.

part of a presentation on how to use an AthenaMuse dimension to control the timing of a simple "slide show." The illustration is embedded in a page of text, but it is a fully functional AthenaMuse package. The reader can activate a timer and watch the slide show in operation while the schematic portion of the illustration shows what is happening "behind the scenes." The reader can stop the timer and use the scrollbar and arrows to change the current position of the dimension and see what happens in both parts of the figure. The *Dimension Tutorial* contains a number of these fully functional applications.

AthenaMuse, as an authoring system for multimedia documents, should be an ideal vehicle for its own documentation; the result would be an interactive reference and tutorial written in AthenaMuse. Various parts of such a document have been designed and implemented.

RECONFIGURATION AND FABRICATION

There are limits on how much a reader can modify or customize a printed book. Electronic books, on the other hand, are quite malleable and can be easily restructured, annotated, augmented, or even refabricated dynamically. These properties are important in many situations, including business, education and training, and research. Electronic libraries are fluid; the information they store can easily pass from one document to another.

This section is divided into two parts. The first discusses how annotations or modifications can be made to *existing* materials; the second concerns the dynamic construction of new books by drawing material from larger collections.

Modification of Existing Documents

Annotations   Readers often customize conventional books by annotating them or by highlighting sections of text. No further modifications are really possible, short of using scissors and paste. Electronic books offer much richer possibilities. Annotations can be *layered*—segmented into different "streams"—and they can be *personalized*—more than one person can add annotations to the same text without effacing the original.

An annotation facility was added to the *AthenaMuse On-Line Documentation*. It takes the form of a personalized "annotation notebook," a private space where the reader can create pages of text and images. The pages in this annotation notebook are automatically cross-referenced to the pages in the AthenaMuse documentation where the annotations are made (each page of the notebook is associated with a single page of the documentation).

The annotation notebook functions in two ways. While moving from page to page in the AthenaMuse documentation, the annotation notebook will automatically display any personal notes associated with the specific page. Or the annotation book can be read independently; one can leaf through the pages of annotations separately, then call up the corresponding page of the manual from any annotation. So the system is useful as a "bookmarking" facility, as well.

Reconfiguration   As suggested above, the only way to reconfigure a printed book is physically to dismember it and paste it back together; then the original order is lost. Reconfiguring an electronic book can be a useful action, depending on how the material is to be used.

A modified version of the annotation notebook lets the reader overlay a customized page sequence on an existing book. The new sequence is made on a page-by-page basis. (This is certainly not an efficient approach; in practice, the interface should permit cut-and-paste operations on whole sections of text.) The reconfigured text is controlled by a separate set of page-turning buttons and sliders, assuming, of course, that the source material has a form that makes the page sequence relevant.

Now You See It, Now You Don't   There are some apparent advantages to having a format that preserves the integrity of the information. Modifications to printed documents are usually very conspicuous. There is a certain element of volatility in an electronic book; information can be easily written over or erased. Therefore, it is imperative that an electronic book be able to save multiple versions and editions of a document.

The physical nature of printed books ensures that the information is there when you need it. If you forget where you last read something, chances are that you can rediscover it by searching through the index. Likewise, each electronic book needs to come equipped with powerful search and navigational tools that will allow users to get to the information they want when they need it.

Generating New Documents

In addition to modifying existing materials by adding annotation or overlaying a different presentation structure, users can fabricate entirely new materials with relative ease. One of the classroom assignments for *Dans le Quartier St. Gervais* (see Chapter 8) was that the students create an electronic "guidebook." This assignment required a simple set of tools for creating a new "book" designed especially for students, with the interface presented in French. The result was a "notebook editor," which allows users to create new documents by cutting and pasting information from one document into another. It is a generic tool that can be incorporated into any AthenaMuse application (Figure 11.7).

In *Dans le Quartier St. Gervais* the notebook editor allows students to take snapshots of people, places, and things and annotate them with text descriptions. In this first implementation students are given a notebook with a hundred blank pages. The book is manipulated with page-turning controls and a scrollbar. Buttons are provided to add text or take snapshots from the video windows. Edit functions are available

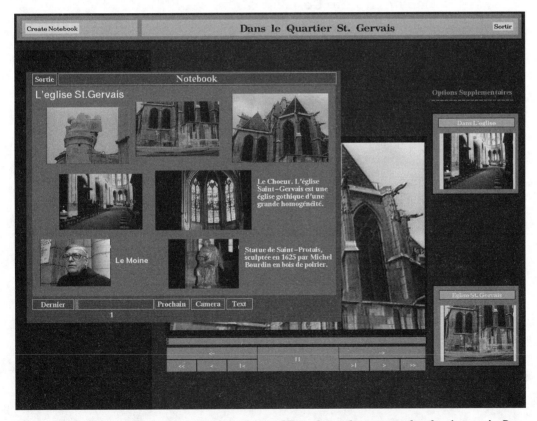

Figure 11.7 The notebook editor allows students of French to take notes and gather images in *Dans le Quartier St. Gervais*. The interface is customized to the French application.

to change the colors, fonts, and layout of the book. This simplified set of tools, written entirely in AthenaMuse, lets students create new "books" that they can share with other "visitors" to the quartier.

In this case the book is constructed by hand; it is also possible to have the computer automatically generate a book based on a specific request for information. The *Real Estate* project (Chapter 2) is an example: the raw material is a database of real estate listings, with pertinent facts and photographs of residential properties. The user initiates a query, based on whatever criteria are of interest. When the database search is complete, the results are compiled and presented to the user in the form of a book, with page-turning controls and slidebar as in the previous example. Each page contains the information on one house. The book becomes an independent document that can be saved, stored, annotated, or modified as needed.

Redefining the Concept of the Book

We have invested over five hundred years in carefully designing and honing the features of the printed book. Multimedia does not imply a radical departure from the paradigms and lessons learned from this experience. It does, however, suggest a redefinition of the concept of the book to a form where the information presentation can be interactive, kinetic, reconfigurable, and multisensory.

In this chapter the focus has been on three specific areas where the electronic book offers advantages over its paper-based counterpart. First is the change that ensues from automating the mechanics of cross-reference; even though this can be viewed as a simple labor-saving device, it promises fundamental changes in the way people interact with information. Second is the ability to include dynamic illustrations—not only allowing motion imagery and audio, but the whole range of computer interaction as well. Third is the ability to dynamically modify or refabricate books by adding annotations, filtering or reconfiguring the presentation of their contents, or fabricating entirely new materials, either by hand or automatically. For some book lovers these changes may seem nonsensical, or an inconsequential picture of an Alice-like Wonderland; the difficulty sometimes is to know which side of the looking glass one is on.

12.   Designing for Quality

In the process of developing the AthenaMuse system, coping with seasonal turnover in our academic engineering staff and unfamiliar design principles, we realized that multimedia technology could play an important role in supporting design and product development activities. This concept struck a responsive chord in a number of corporate visitors, so we began a series of experiments with "design information services." In this chapter, we describe a design support system based on the Quality Function Deployment (QFD) method.

Hauser, John R. and Clausing, Don, "The House of Quality," *Harvard Business Review,* May–June 1988, pp. 63–73.

QFD is a formal technique for recording customer requirements and building directly from these to a product specification. With this approach, quality is determined by what the customer perceives as important; the QFD method retains the "voice of the customer" through the product design phase and uses it to build a shared vision of the product requirements among the design team.

We wanted to design a set of tools to help apply the QFD process; naturally, we intended to use QFD in designing this system. The first step, therefore, was to talk to customers—users of QFD—and understand their views on the basic system requirements. We would then link those observations with the design features of the system.

We found a number of needs that were being met poorly with the conventional paper-based approach to QFD, problems that pointed to a computer-based approach.

These are reflected in the comments below, excerpted from interviews with product development managers:

"We lose the customer's input—the information is filtered too much by the time it reaches the engineers. We need a way to hold onto more of the customer's original words so that they can be called back later—the engineers don't believe the marketing people."

"Customers have some needs that they can articulate, and others that they cannot. We need a way to help access the unarticulated needs—to meld with the customer's mind—and then to capture what we learn and communicate it effectively."

"The problem is that people forget the QFD. We spend a day doing the analysis and then it goes in a drawer. That information needs to be used more through every phase of the design."

"We have people in Singapore, Vancouver, and Toronto who all need to be involved in the design. We can't even agree on a time to meet, so it's very difficult to work together to design a quality product."

"Basically, if the project is big enough for a change in staff, we can't do it. If someone leaves and we have to bring in a new person, the project usually dies. We need a way to communicate the design to new people so they can pick it up."

"Above all, we need to build quality methods into the fabric of our operation. People always view QFD as an extra. There need to be tools and processes that make it fit in better with the whole product development process."

To show how QFD works, we can associate these statements with different functional characteristics of a computer-based system. Figure 12.1 shows an example of a QFD "House of Quality" matrix, where customer needs and product features are correlated. Need statements are weighted according to their relative importance to the customer. These weights, along with correlation strengths, are used to compute a priority level for each product feature. These values help clarify how design trade-offs should be made and how resources should be allocated.

In general, the House of Quality matrix gives a snapshot of what the principal design features of the product are and how they relate to customer needs. This knowledge can be invaluable in building a shared vision among a group of designers and in communicating this vision to other groups of individuals involved in the product development process—even the customers themselves!

QFD works at different levels of detail. The example above looks at the most general system characteristics. As the design proceeds, the focus shifts toward finer levels of detail. The following section de-

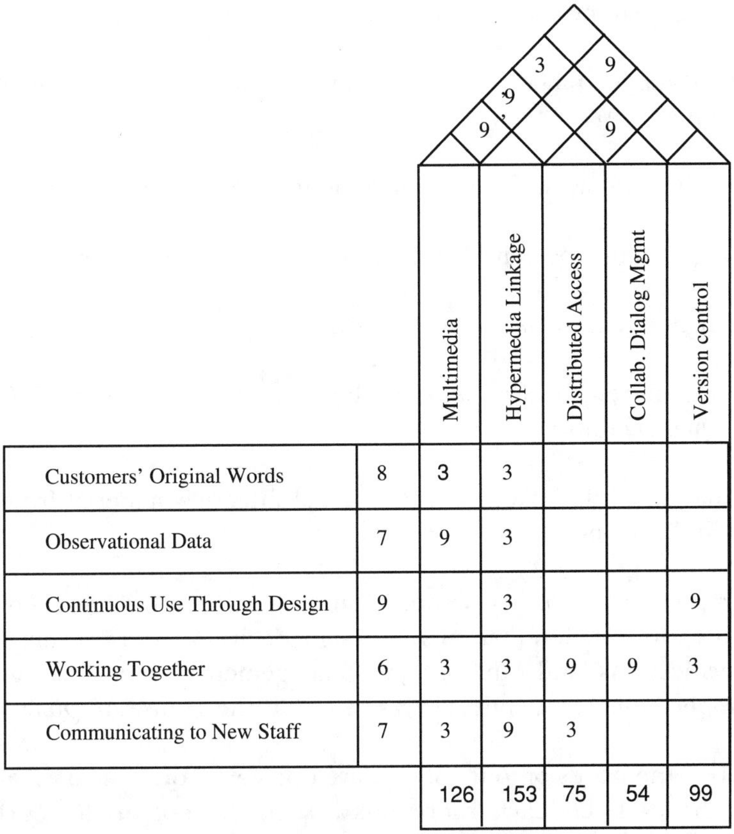

	Multimedia	Hypermedia Linkage	Distributed Access	Collab. Dialog Mgmt	Version control
Customers' Original Words	8	3	3		
Observational Data	7	9	3		
Continuous Use Through Design	9		3		9
Working Together	6	3	3	9	9	3
Communicating to New Staff	7	3	9	3	
	126	153	75	54	99

Figure 12.1 House of Quality Editor, with the need list on the left side and the feature list across the top. The relations between needs and features are indicated by the numbers in the central matrix. The "roof" of the house shows the feature-to-feature relationships.

scribes the basic processes involved in developing a QFD analysis and shows how these correspond to the major components of the prototype QFD toolkit we developed.

THE *QFD TOOLKIT*

QFD begins with customer interviews or observations, where the aim is to understand the customer's view of what is needed and what is important in a product. Processing this information involves several steps:

1   Gathering customer data in video or audio;

2   Locating and extracting "need statements" from these interviews (or from other sources);

3   Organizing and saving the need statements as "requirement lists";

4   Applying customer-perceived priority weights to the need statements;

5   Constructing feature lists for the product;

6   Putting requirement lists and product feature lists into a QFD House of Quality editor;

7   Defining cross-references back to original interview material from any point in the system.

It was clear that the process could continue beyond the House of Quality to provide a foundation for design decision histories, functional specifications, and other project management documents, but for this application our boundary was drawn at the House of Quality Editor.

To address the needs on our list we developed a set of "primary features" of the tool set. Each represents a separate tool in the *QFD Toolkit*. These are designed to work together to support the flow of information from the customer interviews through the QFD analysis.

1   Interview Analyzer, for encoding audio and video interview data;

2   Need List Editor, to transform "raw" needs into hierarchically ordered sets;

3   Feature List Editor, for creating and presenting feature sets to address needs;

4   House of Quality Editor, for the central presentation construct in QFD;

5   Project Notebook, to hold all preceding documents on a project basis.

The product features described at this level still articulate relatively broad requirements for the system. In this case each product feature represents a separate tool in the toolkit. The following sections describe several of these tools. Here the more detailed requirements are outlined—the need statements are developed through the process outlined above. The aim is to show how every major feature of the software design can be linked to the customer statement of needs and priorities.

INTERVIEW ANALYZER

The first tool in the set is one used to clip important segments of video from customer interviews or documentary videos. Given a stream of video as input, this tool produces a set of *need statements*. Figure 12.2

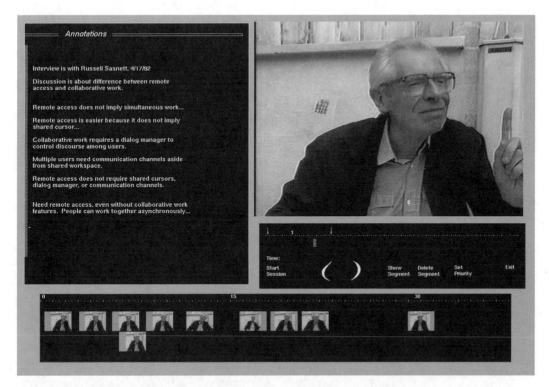

Figure 12.2   The Interview Analyzer is used to identify segments of a video sequence where the customer mentions a need or comments on some aspect of a design. The individual segments are added to the clipboard at the bottom of the screen. Text annotations can be appended in the window at upper left.

shows the interface to the Interview Analyzer. On the right is the video control panel, where the video material is viewed and useful segments are identified. Left and right bracket markers identify the beginning and end of segments. Small segment markers appear on the timeline at the upper edge of the control panel as the segments are defined.

When a closing bracket marks the end of a new segment, a video icon is placed on the clipboard at the bottom of the screen. These icons are placed according to their time of creation. A mouse click on one of the video icons calls up a special viewer to display the corresponding segment of video, along with any text annotations associated with it. The text annotations are entered via the window in the right-hand portion of the screen. All annotations are written into the same window, but they are extracted on a segment-by-segment basis and attached to the individual pieces of video. Each of these need statements is added to a list as it is created; this list is passed along to the Project Notebook, where it can then be accessed from the Need List Editor or other tools.

NEED LIST EDITOR

In a normal QFD process, the designers produce a number of interviews with customers, not just one. Each interview produces a number of need statements, which must then be sorted and categorized. The ideal method is to use a wall, adhesive notes, and a pen; the notes can be moved around the wall and grouped in clusters. But the wall has a short memory and is difficult to distribute. Our aim was to capture some of the same ease of use in a computer interface.

Figure 12.3 shows the prototype version of this interface. On the left are a set of icons showing which interviews have been opened. An interview is opened by picking it up from the Project Notebook and dropping it on the Need List Editor. The need statements from the interview are then automatically spread out on the work surface. There they can be moved around and placed in clusters, with statements from different interviews combined. At any point a category can be defined by drawing a rectangle on the work space and giving it a name. Any need statements within the rectangle become members of the category. They can be dragged in or out of the boundary to change membership. Categories can be nested inside one another and they can be opened or closed for better space management.

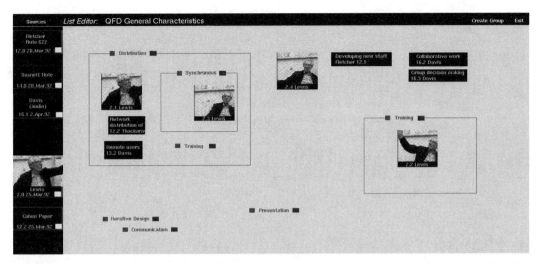

Figure 12.3   **The Need List Editor is used to organize the various need statements gathered from interviews, mail messages, or other sources. Items are placed into named clusters; the result is a hierarchical Need List that can be passed along to the House of Quality Editor.**

A similar list organizer is used to generate a product feature list. It functions in much the same way as the Need List Organizer but focuses on product features. It can be helpful to have both lists visible at the same time through the organization process. The process of clustering and organizing these lists is a free-form activity, normally undertaken together by a group of designers. The end results are more formal listings of the sort that appear on the top and left side of the House of Quality Editor. In the computer version, these lists are generated out of the cluster labels from the work space. They can be dropped into a House of Quality Editor as the next step in the QFD process.

HOUSE OF QUALITY EDITOR

The House of Quality diagram is central to the QFD method. It is essentially a correlation matrix relating needs to features in a product specification. There are significant quantitative aspects to this diagram. The needs are weighted according to customer priority. The product features are weighted according to how difficult they are to implement. The need-to-feature correlations are weighted according to the strength of their interdependencies. All of these values are used to

The House of Quality Editor was based on extensions to Athena-Muse developed at Digital Equipment Corporation.

compute the overall priority rating of each feature. The House of Quality Editor in our prototype has some of the traits of a spreadsheet calculator, where the cells in the grid are linked to one another. A change in one cell propagates changes to other cells in the matrix, as shown in Figure 12.4. The need lists are loaded into the left side; the product features are arrayed across the top.

A mouse click on any of these cells can initiate a cross-reference back to the original need statements, all the way back to the source video from the Interview Analyzer. The lists are editable—categories can be added or removed. The weights can be adjusted and the correlations can be added in the central part of the matrix. As these values are modified, the summary values are computed across the bottom.

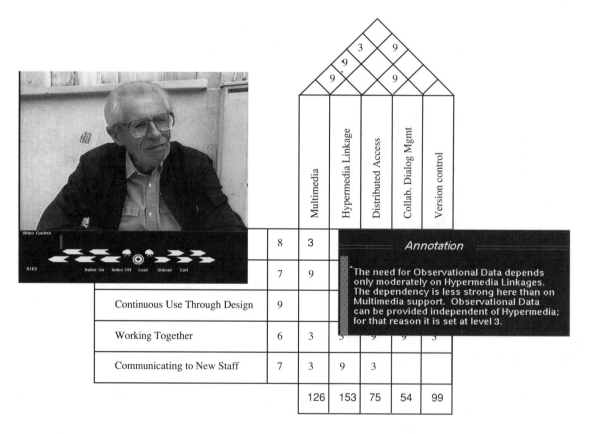

Figure 12.4 The House of Quality Editor is a dynamic matrix that computes product feature values. At the same time, it serves as an interface to all of the source material used to construct it and the annotation and commentary that explain it. In this illustration several of the cells have been probed for background information.

On the right side are the competitive analyses, the part of QFD that compares the performance of other competitors in satisfying customers' needs. Explanatory notes can be attached to any of the cells in the matrix. We use a number of these House of Quality diagrams to describe a project fully. They relate to different levels of detail or different classes of customer requirements. All of the diagrams are stored in the Project Notebook. Taken together, they represent the complete functional specification for the project. They serve as both table of contents and summary to a web of information that constitutes the complete rationale and priority for every product feature.

SUMMARY

The role of multimedia in business is communication. In this application, the aim was to explore how information can be collected and organized into a "stream" that carries through from the initial requirements definition phase to the functional specification and implementation notes of a product. Our intent was to preserve the "voice of the customer" throughout the development process, adding to it the voices of the development team. As a product emerged, it would therefore carry with it a living history of its design and development.

As noted above, this prototype was partially implemented using AthenaMuse. The level of dynamics and flexibility required go well beyond the architecture provided by AthenaMuse. However, the design approach used in AthenaMuse is a step in the right direction; for, above all, tools of this sort must be *flexible*. The QFD process is neither fixed nor universal; neither are the pathways of information flow through the design process. Constructing tools at the "document" level, as we have done in this prototype, leaves them highly adaptable. This promises a much easier growth path than the approach of tying together a set of hard-coded tools.

In many business situations people need to manage small but dynamic information resources, similar to the ones illustrated here. Tools for constructing these resources cannot remain the province of "programmers," where results are difficult to attain, expensive, and inflexible. As one advances on the "human dimension" of multimedia computing, the need for diversity and flexibility increases enormously. The *QFD Toolkit* stands as a target application for this model of software development.

In the end, tools should be manipulable at about the level of complexity of the spreadsheet calculator. It is not uncommon to see people struggling to make a spreadsheet perform a task it was not designed for. People will work to create what they need, as long as they can see how to apply the tools they have (however ill-suited they may be). When we look ahead at the use of multimedia in business settings, it is inevitable that there will be major changes in the ability of nonspecialists to design, construct, and maintain dynamic information resources as well as the tools needed to manipulate them.

Part 3

TECHNICAL ISSUES

Introduction

The following chapters present a number of technical issues in the design of multimedia applications and systems. The first three address fundamental considerations of how multimedia documents are produced, covering the plastic editors used in AthenaMuse, the use of templates as a strategy for code re-use, and the pragmatics of creating compound multimedia documents.

The next three chapters address problems of integrating different forms of information in a multimedia environment—issues of synchronization of time-based material, ideas on generating references to and from visual imagery, and some experiments with constraint-based graphic objects.

These are followed by a discussion of the Galatea video device control software developed at MIT and a review of the evolutionary trajectory of broadband networked computing environments as they relate to multimedia computing. The final two chapters present an overview of the AthenaMuse system, one discussing the PackageSpec data specification component and the other addressing the EventScript programming language.

13.　Plastic Editors

The notion of a reader is in transition, for interactive documents let the reader do more than just turn pages. A reader's interaction with a document may take many forms, but an important threshold is crossed when the author decides to give *generative* powers to the reader— powers of creation, annotation, reorganization, customization.

For any of these changes, editing tools are necessary: to produce new material, to modify the composition of a page, to change the ordering, or to add cross-references from one part of the document to another. Document preparation systems in general have *static* editors, compiled to perform a fixed set of tasks. They are designed to provide all the functions needed for a certain type of editing, and normally they are not meant to be changed.

When an author wants to give readers control, it is usually in a specialized context where a particular type of modification is supported but readers do not have license to revise the entire work. General-purpose editors are often inappropriate for these situations. Because they offer a broad set of functions, the control interfaces to these editors tend to be far too complex for casual readers. Also, it can be quite difficult to integrate the editor smoothly into the application; the interface may be inconsistent, the data may not transfer easily, and so on.

With the AthenaMuse authoring system, we began experimenting with the notion of "plastic" editors—tools that can be molded to meet the specific requirements of an application. The idea is to make the editor itself behave more like a document. In this way application developers can use customized editors in their applications without having to modify and recompile some major part of an executable image.

EDITOR AS DOCUMENT

R. Stallman, *GNU Emacs Manual,* Free Software Foundation, Cambridge MA, 1988.

One might say that a text editor such as *GNU Emacs* is a plastic editor, because the key bindings to the interface can be modified and new functions can be added dynamically to the system. These are indeed the characteristics of a plastic editor, but the feeling is somewhat different from what we intend. Changing the editor should be more like changing a document with cut-and-paste, point-and-click manipulation. In the case of *emacs*, the sense of separation between the editor and the document remains quite clear; furthermore, any substantial changes must be written as *LISP* expressions, so they quickly fall outside the province of the non-specialist.

As documents, plastic editors are more complex than most. However, compared to compiled editors they are quite simple to modify, and they retain the feeling that they are "cut of the same cloth" as any other document.

Making the editor behave as a document is our central goal. Plastic editors should be as mutable as other documents, and heighten the user's sense that the editors themselves are the same type of material as the documents being manipulated. What we need is a compromise: the notion of a document must be expanded to encompass the interactions needed in an editor, and the notion of an editor must be broken out of the usual "closed box" model.

Editors in AthenaMuse

An editor is a set of tools for creating, deleting, modifying, combining or connecting information. It consists of a set of functions operating on a known data format, where the data specify displayable information such as video, text, graphics, or audio. Editors function at three levels: data definition, composition, and document interconnection. "Data" editors are those that produce simple forms of independent display material—pieces of text, graphics, video, audio, and so on. "Composition" editors combine these basic elements into aggregates, handling the tasks of layout and media integration. "Document-interconnection" editors control higher-level organizational issues across sets of documents—cross-reference linkages, logical flow of control, query hierarchies, and the like. We have built a number of interactive editors with AthenaMuse (Figure 13.1) and explored some of the details of combining them into "workbench" combinations. The list includes editors at all three levels, although in some cases they are quite rudimentary:

1 *Attribute Editor:* for point-and-click editing of the appearance of AthenaMuse objects;

2 *Group Editor:* for creating groups of objects for manipulation by the Attribute Editor;

3 *Subtitle Editor:* for synchronizing text subtitles with motion video sequences;

4 *Pixmap Editor:* for clipping subregions of images and storing them in image sequence files;

5 *Video Editor:* for defining video sequences and storing them in a local database;

6 *Figure Editor:* for creating simple drawings and video overlays;

7 *Font Selector:* for previewing and choosing text fonts;

8 *Color Palette:* for selecting red-green-blue color combinations;

9 *Action Editor:* for constructing valid *action* parameters in the PackageSpec language and attaching them to interface objects (see Figure 14.5);

10 *EventScript Editor:* for inspecting and modifying EventScript objects, variables, and methods (see Figure 14.7);

11 *MuseBuilder:* for developing AthenaMuse documents in a "workbench" environment; includes many of the editors listed above, along with support for loading new document elements from a template library (see Figure 14.1).

All of these editing tools are implemented as AthenaMuse documents. As noted earlier, AthenaMuse is not based on the usual paper

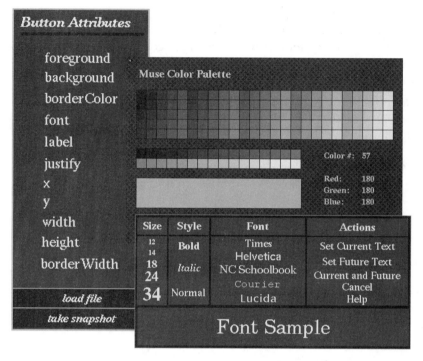

Figure 13.1 Plastic editors for modifying AthenaMuse documents. The *Attribute Editor* (left) displays the list of button parameters. Color and font values are chosen with the *Color Palette* and *Font Selector*.

metaphor common to most electronic document systems; the architecture is broad enough to encompass dynamic systems as a fundamental form of document. Aside from making the editors mutable, implementing them as documents has another important consequence: an editor can be included as a component of any other set of documents.

An illustration of this point is seen in the *Dans le Quartier St. Gervais* application. As noted earlier, the material is designed as a learning environment in which students explore a database of imagery and interviews with people who live and work in a historic neighborhood of Paris. As part of the learning experience, the students were to create their own guide books for the neighborhood. This task required a customized set of editors, designed especially to produce such a book quickly, easily, and in French (the aim, after all, is to teach French, not to turn students into multimedia producers). Having created a notebook in which students could write text and add images, we needed to

les habitants du Quartier St. Gervais

Le Moine: L'Eglise St. Gervais

Madame Izrael: Le Monde des Epices

Préférences

font

couleur du fond

couleur du texte

échelle

position

Dernier   Prochain

3

Figure 13.2   The AthenaMuse *Attribute Editor*, modified for inclusion in a French educational application

provide layout and attribute editing capabilities. Rather than building from scratch, AthenaMuse allowed us to include the entire *Attribute Editor* as a content unit within the book.

First, the *Attribute Editor* was used to rearrange its own appearance. This process included translating the English labels into French. Then some functions were removed, and a copy of the modified editor was saved under a new name. Finally the "new" editor was plugged into the master document (Figure 13.2). The above procedure illustrates the nature of the plastic editors—taking an existing editor, copying it, cutting out functions, even using the editor itself to modify its own appearance, then embedding it as part of another document.

DIMENSIONS OF PLASTICITY

Editors can vary widely in their degree of *plasticity*—their ability to be molded and shaped to a new purpose. We have explored the following dimensions which characterize an editor's plasticity:

1 Ease of appearance modification;

2 Ease of behavior modification;

3 Capacity for integration with other applications;

4 Capacity for coordination with other applications.

Mutable Appearance

Changing the appearance of an editor is the simplest form of modification. Users should be able to change the colors, fonts, labels, positions, and sizes of an editor's interface components. Any alterations to an editor's appearance must be saved so that they can be recalled at the next time of instantiation.

These appearance attributes are maintained as a set of values commonly referred to as *resources*. In some systems these are saved in a special database that programs read during initialization. The purpose of extracting attribute values in this way is to allow personalization of a piece of software without having to change its source code. For example, Apple encourages developers to store the labels for buttons and menus as text resources. As a result, many applications can be translated from one language to another simply by editing their resource files.

The X resource database is a list of name/value pairs initialized from a user's preference file.

The X Window System uses a similar scheme, drawing default values for a wide variety of attributes from an X resource database. Unfortunately, X resources can only affect an application when it first starts up; they cannot be used to make changes once it is running. Another problem is that the resources of ordinary X applications cannot be inspected or modified by external programs. This makes it difficult or impossible to create a generic attribute editor which works with any X application, and which allows users to see immediate results from changes they make. In AthenaMuse, we overcame these limitations of the X resources scheme by adding our own attribute management layer. Any document or editor can have its appearance modified by the Attribute Editor, even while it is being used. This editor can load and execute any AthenaMuse application and allow the user to change the layout, color, text, fonts, and other aspects of its interface components. Users are free to create different versions of the basic editors mentioned above. Even high-level authoring tools like the MuseBuilder can be customized for special applications.

Mutable Behavior

Changing the appearance of an editor can be quite important, in terms of making it look and feel like part of some larger system. But it is usually necessary to modify an editor's behavior as well. Behavior modification falls into two major categories: *recombination* of pre-defined functionality, and *fabrication* of new functionality.

Recombination   Often the desired modification of an editor's behavior can be achieved by simply enabling or disabling some of the functions which it already supports. This can be done in a number of ways. For example, most X applications allow a flexible mapping between an input event and the program action it triggers. Users manipulate these by setting resources in the resource database. This can be used to define short-cuts for common actions, such as a keyboard equivalent for selecting the "Save" item on a menu.

The AthenaMuse *Video Editor* was the frequent subject of functional recombination of a more elaborate form. Many AthenaMuse applications require video editing of some kind; but the degree of complexity can vary greatly. As a lowest common denominator, most of these interfaces involve a number of "playback controls" to show specific pieces of video content. This paradigm is so pervasive that we frequently ask novice users to create a video control panel as their first exercise, by recombining the basic video control capabilities provided by AthenaMuse. We have collected many of these video viewers over several years (see Figure 4.4). All of them draw from the same set of built-in actions to control the display of the video material, but these actions can be triggered in new ways from an endless variety of interface objects. We use the analogy of the "software deli," where users can make custom interfaces like sandwiches. Most of the work involves adding or deleting buttons and re-attaching library functions to them. These reconfigured control panels can usually be cut and pasted from one document to another without difficulty.

Fabrication   Fabrication is the process of building entirely new functionality into an editor. AthenaMuse provides two avenues for developing new editing capabilities. The first choice is EventScript, the AthenaMuse scripting language (described in Chapter 22); the other is the C programming language. Achieving fluency in EventScript is more difficult than learning the PackageSpec specification language. And programming in C is still more demanding. Therefore, developing new editing capabilities is not an activity for the non-programmer. The layers in the AthenaMuse system are like rungs on a ladder, with authors starting out at the top. Each step down grants greater flexibility, but requires more skill to take advantage of it. When authors find themselves standing on the ground all the time, the authoring system is of little or no use to them.

The *Boston Suburbs* project was produced by Lois Craig, Associate Dean of Architecture. The Light Table Editor was written by V. Judson Harward.

One of the more interesting tools created with AthenaMuse is the Light Table Editor, a tool for viewing and organizing images that was developed for the *Boston Suburbs* project (Figure 13.3). The user works on a virtual "light table" surface which may be filled with still image "slides," each of which represents a video segment. The slides can be moved around the table, resized, and rearranged to form conceptual

Figure 13.3   The Light Table Editor, from the *Boston Suburbs* project

groupings, or loaded into a "projector" for viewing. None of this functionality was built-in or hard-coded into the AthenaMuse software; it was written as an AthenaMuse document using PackageSpec for the display objects and control interface and EventScript objects for the slide behaviors.

The Light Table Editor is based on an EventScript object called *Table*, which is responsible for managing a group of slides. The *Table* object has a method named *NewSlide* to handle requests for creating new slides, given a frame number and caption. This method creates a new *Slide* object and assigns it a position. When activated, the *Slide* object invokes its display method and appears on the *Table* at the appropriate location. Each *Slide* object also has methods which let it respond to mouse input for moving and resizing operations.

The alternative to coding in EventScript is to write functions in the C programming language and then invoke them from the EventScript interpreter. At the C level, programmers have access to all of the internal data structures in the AthenaMuse "kernel." The power to extend the base system carries with it a great deal of responsibility, for authors must learn how to fit their ideas into the existing architecture without breaking it. Although C programming is not an option for non-specialists, it does provide an important level of flexibility to the authoring environment as a whole.

In operating systems without a dynamic linking capability, external functions must be compiled into the AthenaMuse software system.

Integration

In many cases an application can be extended very easily by embedding one or more stand-alone editors inside it. The editor itself may be used as a component that may find a place in many applications. An author should be able to uproot the editor from its original context and graft it onto an unrelated application with a minimum of effort. Figure 13.4 shows the complex relationships among some of the AthenaMuse editors mentioned earlier, with arrows indicating where one editor includes part or all of another. An editor designed for integration should have as few external dependencies as possible. Any kind of run-time resource limitation, such as requiring a specific type of video display hardware, can cause the editor to fail in an unexpected context. In AthenaMuse documents, the most common obstacles to integration are name clashes (two objects with the same name), references to missing files, and unavailable fonts. A careful author can minimize such limitations and thereby simplify the process of transplanting the editor into another document.

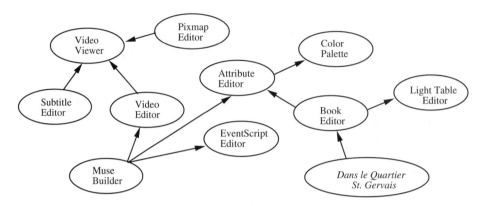

Figure 13.4   Patterns of inclusion among the AthenaMuse editors (and the French language application). Arrows indicate that an editor contains all or part of the editor to which it is pointing.

Embedding an editor in a foreign application is easiest when its functions are largely self-contained. As dependencies between the editor and the surrounding application increase, the difficulty of integration increases correspondingly.

Good programming practices can avoid some typical pitfalls, but the problems are not all technical. Whenever two pieces of software come together, the most important factor in their successful integration is likely to be the quality of their respective documentation. If future system-builders don't know which parts of an editor are reusable or how to exploit them fully, integration cannot be achieved without great risk.

Coordination

Some editors and the functions they provide are so pervasive that it doesn't make sense to embed them in individual applications or documents. A single editor can serve the needs of many applications if given the proper communications facilities.

Two of the AthenaMuse editors designed for such coordination are the *Font Selector* and the *Color Palette*. The *Font Selector* displays a list of available font families and shows how various attributes (such as bold or italic) will affect their appearance. The *Color Palette* provides a rainbow of color swatches and a large preview area for choosing foreground and background colors. These editors export the names of chosen fonts and colors using the X Window System *selection* mechanism. A user can paste these values into other applications using the "clipboard" facilities provided by the window system.

Getting editors to cooperate using communications channels leads to a much looser style of integration than with the technique of embedding whole editors as described above. Here the editors remain independent programs, using well-defined *protocols* to service requests from client applications. When an editor wants to send a message to many clients at once, it can use a *broadcast* protocol instead of performing a series of one-to-one transactions.

Conceptually, the editor places key values into named slots; any applications expressing an interest in these slots receive notification whenever their values change. X *properties*, which are arbitrary values attached to X windows, behave in this manner. We experimented with broadcasting the state of an AthenaMuse document by placing its dimension settings in an X property attached to the main window. A related context-sensitive help package was able to synchronize itself to the first document by tuning in to these signals.

More powerful editors require more elaborate communication techniques, which are normally expressed through an Application Programmer's Interface (API). An API opens up an editor to external manipulation, letting other programs access its internal functionality in an approved fashion. An API can support different language bindings, so that programmers can use either object-oriented messages or remote procedure calls to control the editor. Although application programmers have been using APIs to request system services for some time, the concept of controlling applications themselves in this way is quite new.

Graphical user interfaces add some unexpected wrinkles to the idea of interconnected editors. In many cases a developer will want to create a seamless "virtual application" out of independent editors. Difficulties arise if the functionality of these editors cannot be decoupled from their control interfaces. Users can become understandably confused when several coordinated editors offer simultaneous overlapping functions, such as multiple "Quit" or "Save" buttons. More subtle problems arise when combining the "look and feel" of different user interface toolkits, including mismatches between their interaction techniques or aesthetics. Today these matters are challenges to the specialist; our current focus with plastic editors is on the countless small modifications and extensions to editors that can be employed by the non-programmer to enhance their expressive power.

Refer to Chapter 15 for further discussion of these issues.

SUMMARY

The idea of plastic editors becomes important when authors want to give readers control. In our experience, the majority of multimedia applications and documents benefit from some such capability. This area is not well addressed in the existing approaches to document preparation nor in the design of programming environments for non-specialists. The "plasticity" of editing resources should be a primary consideration in evaluating or designing a multimedia authoring environment. It should extend through the four dimensions outlined earlier, which include the ability to modify the editor's appearance, to modify its behavior, to incorporate it within another document, and to coordinate it with other documents through a programmatic interface.

With AthenaMuse, we found that we could produce a variety of high-level editors using the same document production tools available to authors. These editors can be molded to meet the needs of custom applications much faster than traditional compiled editors, which by comparison seem cast in stone. Such flexibility is only possible when the base architecture of a document is rich enough to describe procedural interactions as well as static information.

These experiments helped us to realize the importance of plastic editors within the scope of multimedia authoring. But the techniques we explored in implementing our plastic editors seem hardly sufficient. There is still too much procedural coding involved; too much falls out of the hands of the author and into the hands of the programmer. We are continuing our research in this area with the intent of discovering new ways to turn readers into participants and to erode the distinction between document and document processor.

14.   Templates for Form and Function

An electronic spreadsheet model is a computer program; so is a Hyper-Card stack. Most mainstream software for personal computers has some kind of programming capability, usually in the form of a "macro" or "scripting" language. But the users of these systems do not perceive themselves as software developers or engineers—they are simply authors. Yet these authors are still bound by the same difficulties that have plagued software engineers for decades.

One of the most persistent problems in software engineering is the inability to reuse existing components reliably and predictably. Most software systems are built entirely from scratch, even if they bear a striking resemblance to their ancestors.

In other large-scale engineering efforts, such as automotive design or building construction, most of the components come in standard sizes and conform to rigid specifications. The same is true in computer hardware design, where semiconductor microchip components from several manufacturers all provide equivalent functionality and interfaces. Why is software different?

As others have pointed out, plasticity, complexity, and interdependence are part of the essence, the very nature, of software systems (see Brooks or Cox). At least in theory, a computer program can be written to simulate any real or imaginable process or phenomenon, including other computers and programs.

F. P. Brooks, *The Mythical Man-Month: Essays on Software Engineering*, Addison-Wesley Publishing Company, Reading MA, 1975.

177

F. P. Brooks, "No Silver Bullet: Essence and Accidents of Software Engineering," in *Computer*, Vol. 20, No. 4, April 1987, pp. 10–19.

B. J. Cox, *Object-Oriented Programming: An Evolutionary Approach*, Addison-Wesley Publishing Company, Reading MA, 1986.

Software can address any problem, but it may not provide an appropriate solution. While the software domain expands, machine capacity in terms of speed and storage continues to increase at a phenomenal rate, with ten-fold improvements every three to five years. Ultimately, there are no upper bounds on software complexity, other than the human capacity for understanding.

This statement gets to the heart of the difficulty with reusable software components: understanding complexity. Essentially, the problem involves being able to recognize patterns or models in a software architecture which can be applied to a number of different domains.

Typically this recognition comes as a result of studying existing software systems and then trying to adapt them to new problems. The approach is inductive; the software designer tries to generalize backward to first principles given a working model.

A. Goldberg, *Smalltalk-80: The Interactive Programming Environment*, Addison-Wesley Publishing Company, Reading MA, 1984.

Smalltalk was the first software development environment to tackle this problem from the opposite direction, by providing a hierarchy of generic software elements that can be specialized to meet the situation at hand. This deductive approach to software leads to a more coherent body of reusable components, because every system spawned from the environment shares a common architecture.

The fundamental structure in Smalltalk is the object, which binds together a set of data resources and a messaging protocol for manipulating them. Everything in the system is an object, giving the user a common framework for investigating any application. Smalltalk was also the first system to provide reusable architectures, with the Model-View-Controller application paradigm. Users can make a copy of this design, then customize it to the task at hand.

Software libraries, in contrast, provide a grab bag of related functions. The order and context in which the functions are applied is critical to obtaining proper behavior, but usually no assistance is provided other than written documentation.

Similarly, the splitting of functionality into tiny modules makes it difficult to comprehend the overall pattern the software designer is trying to create. With complicated libraries and protocol sequences, such as the X Window System library, reuse is hampered by too much detail—you can't see the forest for the trees.

The X11R4 library contains almost five hundred unique functions.

One principle worth remembering is that designs are more reusable than implementations. If an architect's client wants a house just like one that Frank Lloyd Wright built, there is no call for the architect to travel to Chicago and rip pieces out of a historic home. Besides being illegal, the scheme probably would miscarry because Wright did not design the house to be taken apart and reassembled. Instead, the architect gets a copy of the plans that were used to build the original house, and creates a new house based on that design.

Many informal efforts at software reuse, in which modules are scavenged from existing systems and transplanted directly into a new framework, fail for exactly the same reason. The modules were probably not designed for reuse, so they may carry unseen dependencies from their original context. Furthermore, a haphazard integration of widely varying programming styles can only lead to obfuscation of the overall plan. How can we create reusable software components and designs, that come with instructions, maps of the territory they inhabit, and a sense of their own history? How can we build systems that communicate their design as effectively as their implementation? In essence, how can we help future developers see the forest through the trees?

THE TEMPLATE LIBRARY

One promising technique is that of providing *template libraries* as an integral part of any software development environment. A template is a parameterized software component that can be customized by specifying different values for certain key attributes. A component is instantiated by applying a set of these parameters to the relevant template, thereby generating a new version suitable for binding into a working system. Ideally, users should be able to store many different versions of these parameter sets, designed to create custom-mixed "flavors" of each component. The concept is similar to style sheets in word-processing software, where a "style" is simply a collection of formatting instructions applied to a body of text—bold, centered, justified, and so forth. The difference is that a software template applies to both form and content—what to do and how to do it.

Suppose that we had a template for a word-processing document. Both the formatting options and the actual text could be controlled by parameterization. For example, an author could create pattern-matching rules to substitute keywords in the text for given parameters. Imagine that the following template, called NonPayment, is part of a business-oriented word-processing package:

```
[.JUSTIFY=Filled, .SIZE=12]
Dear $CUSTOMER,

Your bill is past due. We still show an outstanding bal-
ance of $DEBT on your account number $ACCOUNT_NUMBER.

If we do not receive payment from you by ($DATE+2weeks),
we shall have no option but to take legal recourse.

Regretfully,
$ACCOUNT_MANAGER
```

One could automatically create hundreds of form letters to non-paying customers by supplying a small number of key parameters, perhaps pulled from a database of delinquent accounts. The parameter list to create a particular instance of NonPayment might look like this (where .A denotes a formatting option, and $A describes the optional content):

```
.JUSTIFY=RaggedRight;
$CUSTOMER=John Doe, $DEBT=214.76,
$ACCOUNT_NUMBER=410-17-6432,
$DATE=$TODAY,
$ACCOUNT_MANAGER=Janet Smith.
```

As the number of templates grows, it becomes necessary to create a formal organizational framework, or library, to contain both the templates and their many possible sets of parameters. Obviously, users will need tools to help them locate suitable items stored in the archive. This task is easier when the various pieces contain embedded documentation, which they carry with them even after being bound into a working system. It becomes possible to "see the forest" in a large body of software—to discover how the pieces of the puzzle fit together and to trace components back to their roots.

```
Dear John Doe,

Your bill is past due. We still show an outstanding bal-
ance of 214.76 on your account number 410-17-6432.

If we do not receive payment from you by September 15,
we shall have no option but to take legal recourse.

Regretfully,
Janet Smith
```

Experiences with a Template Library System

We view the AthenaMuse authoring system as a kind of novice programming environment, with special multimedia capabilities. We have explored the use of template libraries in the *MuseBuilder* application, which lets users create and modify AthenaMuse applications with a minimum of special-purpose programming knowledge (Figure 14.1).

In *MuseBuilder* a template is not a working piece of "live" software, but rather a specification of what a component should contain, how it should behave, and how it should relate to other components. The user and *MuseBuilder* collaborate to provide all of the contextual parameters for a given template. Then the component is instantiated, plugged into the growing application.

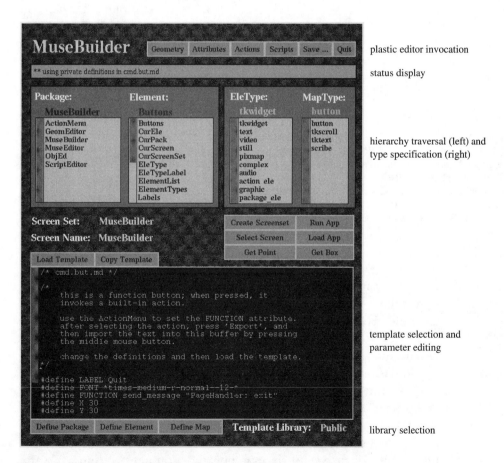

Figure 14.1 Anatomy of the *MuseBuilder* application

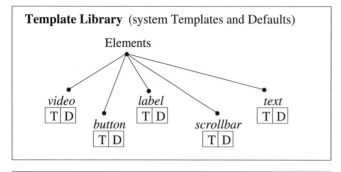

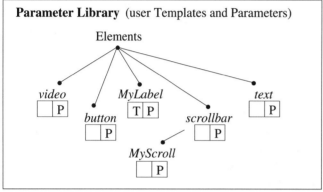

Figure 14.2   The template library is a system-level resource containing template definitions (T) and default parameters (D). Each user has a private parameter library, which stores a copy of the parameters (P) last used with each template. This user has created both a private template (MyLabel) and a private parameter list (MyScroll). MyScroll uses the same template as "scrollbar," but with different parameters.

D. Goodman, *The Complete HyperCard 2.0 Handbook*, Bantam Books, New York NY, 1990.

The *MuseBuilder* provides the system-level parameters for a template (where it will go in the object hierarchy, for example). These attributes are determined at runtime by inspecting the current state of the user's fledgling application. The *MuseBuilder* also enforces some type-checking rules, such as ensuring that the user does not specify video data for a text element.

The user is responsible for providing all of the other parameters, such as fonts, colors, labels, and options. The *MuseBuilder* makes this job easier by storing default settings for each attribute in the *template library,* and letting users save many different versions of parameter lists in their own private *parameter library* (Figure 14.2). Each parameter set includes documentation of the attribute values it will accept, and information on how they affect the created component.

This template library approach overcomes one of the problems with many WYSIWYG (What You See Is What You Get) authoring systems. Usually authors can only create a "vanilla" object. They must then spend time manually customizing its flavor—changing the font, size, line style, and the like. For example, HyperCard's "New Button" command creates a rounded-corner button with the label "New Button," the font set to "Chicago," and no functionality.

Still, HyperCard does come bundled with many sample applications, loaded with "clip art" and working button examples. Authors can cut and paste these objects, including their behavior, into their own stacks. The HyperCard stack libraries are an excellent catalog of design examples, demonstrating potential applications. But these facilities are not merged into a powerful development environment to automate the production of complex systems. Instead, HyperCard development is largely the result of manual labor—cutting and pasting, tweaking and modifying. One final point is that the AthenaMuse template library approach can be applied at any level of resolution. Most templates are variations on low-level objects, such as buttons and sliders. But a template can also describe composite objects, or even an entire application.

For example, a VideoButton template, which uses a scaled video image, a rounded border, and a text label creates something that looks like a miniature television set. (Figure 14.3). Another template contains an entire video viewer, complete with video output, simulated VCR-style control panel, digital readout, and slidebar cursor. With the touch of a button, anyone can include the entire viewer in an application or, using the parameter library mechanism, create customized versions of it.

Figure 14.3   A VideoButton

Implementation of AthenaMuse Templates

As mentioned earlier, the MuseBuilder is itself merely an AthenaMuse application. It contains a number of plastic editors (which are also AthenaMuse documents) to select fonts and colors, choose video segments, edit widget attributes, and so on. The templates are designed to generate the same input language that describes all AthenaMuse documents; thus the AthenaMuse parser already built into the system can be used to load new objects.

The templates are ordinary text files, usually just AthenaMuse specifications that have been modified to accept template arguments at key locations. The parameter files contain documentation of the available options along with any definitions. The following is an example of the parameter file for a basic text label (Figure 14.4):

```
/*
  TEMPLATE: label.but.md
  This simple label is a button without any
  attached function. It carries no dependencies
  on the dimension space in which it is placed.
  Note: The FONT and LABEL attributes do not
  need quotes around their values.
  You can use the color palette tool (musepal)
  and font selector tool (xfontsel) to choose
  appropriate values.
*/
```

Hello, World

Figure 14.4 The text label defined by the parameters in the example

```
#define LABEL Hello, World
#define FONT *book*bold-r-normal—18*
#define FOREGROUND 159
#define BACKGROUND 42
#define BORDER 60
#define BORDERWIDTH 2
#define X 30
#define Y 30
#define WIDTH 2
#define HEIGHT 2
#define RESIZE 0
```

To create this label, the user locates "label" in the template library browser and clicks the mouse on an AthenaMuse screen. After the "Load Template" button is pushed, a brief wait for processing is followed by the appearance on the screen of the new label.

If any parameters are changed before loading, they are stored persistently in the user's library. At any point the user, by pressing the "Copy Template" button, can declare the current parameter list to be a new style. The current template becomes an independent copy with its own name and persistent parameter list. By this means the user's library grows beyond the system-provided templates.

As mentioned earlier, parameters can be loaded from either system-level defaults or private user customizations. The user selects which type of object to load and its location in the application hierarchy. The *MuseBuilder* then locates the appropriate parameter file and puts it into an editable text buffer. The user modifies these parameters, possibly using some of the editors to obtain suitable values. Just before the new object is loaded, the parameters are automatically archived to the user's private library.

Next comes the code generation phase. The *MuseBuilder* writes out a temporary file containing the current application context, such as the name of the selected screen and the parent object where the template will be loaded. It also fetches the user's version of the template parameters from the text buffer.

A filter multiplexer called *mpp* (the AthenaMuse pre-processor) is run on these parameter files. It looks for special characters in the input stream, switching between filters and merging their outputs. Text substitution is done with a variety of filters, including *cpp* and *awk,* while *bc* is used for simple math.

The resulting AthenaMuse specification is put into another temporary file, which is read by the built-in parser in order to load the new object.

All of this processing is handled by a special MuseParser object, which also monitors the loading process and updates the object lists displayed to the user. Any application can add dynamic loading capabilities by including the MuseParser specification files, and then sending a message to MuseParser to "load *filename*." Our experiments with the *MuseBuilder* have shown that it is not very difficult to create a working template library system for language-based programming environments, even with the limited tools provided to AthenaMuse developers. The *MuseBuilder* is just another AthenaMuse application—no different from the applications it creates. The advantages of giving novice developers a means to snap together applications from a library of customized plug-and-play components are obvious.

TEMPLATES FOR FUNCTIONALITY

So far we have made no mention of templates for functionality. The examples have all dealt with parameterizing structural and appearance attributes, such as object attachments, fonts, and colors. Is it possible to provide similar customization capabilities for procedural behavior?

Programming languages need sophisticated parsers to verify their conformance to a syntax specification. They also require rigorous semantic analysis to guard against type mismatching, questionable use of language constructs, and the like. This very formality is what makes them simultaneously valuable and efficient to experts and frustrating to novices.

With PackageSpec, the AthenaMuse specification language, we experimented with some simple techniques for nonprocedural encodings of behavior. We felt this was important for the following reasons:

• we wanted to reduce the time and the level of skill required to create AthenaMuse applications;

• we wanted to reduce programming errors by limiting the domain of possible inputs;

• we wanted to reduce or eliminate run-time error.

The PackageSpec language supports approximately sixteen built-in actions, sufficient to create a large number of simple yet highly reli-

applications. In contrast, the EventScript object-oriented programming language (for more advanced users) can access over 160 compiled functions, many of which can easily be misused at runtime to create disastrous conditions.

The built-in actions are presented to the novice user as attributes attached to various objects, not as functions acting upon them. These actions are valid in any context, at any time. Hence there is no calling sequence or protocol to learn.

The actions all operate on packages and the dimension space inside them; all take a single parameter, a Package Position (or PackPos). This parameter contains the name of the package to affect and a tuple of integers (or coordinates), one for each dimension in the target package. For example, a button with the associated action *rset_position("self" 0 –1 0)*, would change the current position of the second dimension by one unit in the negative direction.

Every displayable object in AthenaMuse is assigned a position or region in the space described by the dimensions of its containing package. When the coordinates of the package enter an element's region, that element becomes active and displays itself. Whenever the package position leaves this region, the element disappears.

Other dependencies may be specified between dimension positions and element attributes. For example, a text label may display the current position of some dimension. Likewise, a line graphic or bitmap may move in sync with one or more dimension positions.

The dimensional notation is intended to shift the notion of program *states* to one of *locations in space.* In AthenaMuse, information is organized according to its position in a space of the author's design. The built-in actions serve to move the user through this space in various ways. When behavior is specified through data rather than procedures, it becomes possible for a limited functional domain to be mapped onto point-and-click specification techniques. An example is the Action Editor in the *Muse-Builder,* which lets authors create complete PackPos speci-

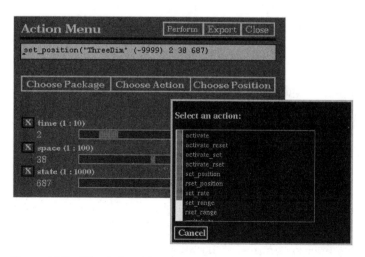

Figure 14.5   The *Action Editor*

fications with a graphical user interface (Figure 14.5). Not even the co-ordinates need to be typed; they are input with sliders to avoid out-of-range problems. As a result, it is impossible to construct or perform an invalid action using this tool.

Biological Metaphors for Software Behavior

We have described how a limited set of functionality can be presented to novices as familiar attribute/value pairs. What about a more complex programming situation: can procedures be expressed as parameterized templates?

In a sense, this capability is what the object-oriented programming paradigm provides. Traditional object systems contain a class hierarchy, analogous to those used in biological taxonomy. Each object in the system belongs to a given class, which fully describes the type and number of its attributes and the behavior it exhibits in response to a messaging protocol. To create a new object of a given type, the programmer sends an appropriate message to the relevant class object. The result is a new object of that type, which usually must be customized after instantiation. To create a copy of an object, the programmer sends it a message to copy itself. The class of the object must have built-in support for replication.

D. Ungar, R. B. Smith, C. Chambers, and U. Holzle, "Object, Message, and Performance—How They Coexist in Self," in *Computer*, Vol. 25, No. 10, 1992, pp. 53–64.

In contrast, so-called classless systems such as Self (see Ungar) and the EventScript language in AthenaMuse, do not contain any formal hierarchy of object types (Figures 14.6 and 14.7). These systems remove the subtle distinction between a class object (the mold) and instances of that class (the finished components). Instead, any object can serve as a template for any other via a cloning operation. The newly created clone is an exact duplicate of the original, down to the last "cell." After cloning, the two objects are completely independent entities, free to continue evolving along separate paths.

In class systems, every instance of a given class must conform precisely to the patterns established by the class template. An object cannot suddenly mutate to exhibit new behavior or acquire new attributes. This is not to say that one model is "good"

```
object A
{
var temp;

    on Wakeup { put 'foo' into temp; }
    on NewClone { Beep(); }
    on hi { printf('hi!\n'); }
}
object B
    uses A
{
    on wakeup
    {
        put 'bar' into temp;
        CloneObj('A','C');
    }
}
```

Figure 14.6 An example of object definition in EventScript. Any object can borrow the attributes and methods of another object.

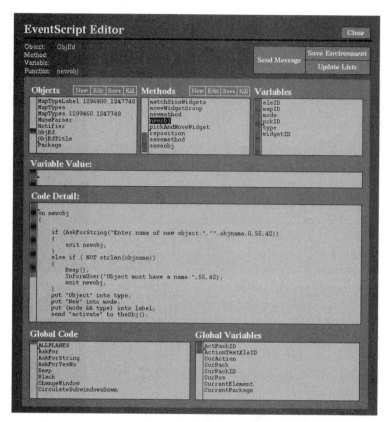

Figure 14.7 The *EventScript Editor*. All of the objects in the system are enumerated in the upper-left scrolling list. Selecting an object brings up the relevant list of its attributes (variables) and behaviors (methods). Selecting a variable displays its current value; selecting a method causes the body of the procedure to be displayed.

and the other "bad"—they are merely expressions of different philosophies, each useful for certain purposes.

In practice, the cloning metaphor is convenient for implementing the type of template libraries described earlier. A candidate object is chosen to be a template, whereupon it is molded and shaped to meet a set of requirements. This process can include changing attribute values, or even the type and number of the attributes themselves. Most important, the essential behavior of the candidate object can be modified to make it uniquely suited to its circumstances.

After the mold has been forged, this prototype object can be cloned to create any number of duplicates. Naturally, every clone will need to be specialized in some way—connected to other related objects and bound into the application environment. But the cloning metaphor lets authors create templates that are very close to finished works, needing only the smallest spark to bring them to life (see Lieberman).

H. Lieberman, "Using Prototypical Objects to Implement Shared Behavior in Object-Oriented Systems," in *Proc. of 1986 Conf. on Object-Oriented Programming Systems, Languages, and Applications (OOPSLA)*, ACM Press, New York NY, pp. 214–223.

Limitations

Unfortunately, a system that can actually synthesize behavior "on the fly" based on input parameters is somewhere between artificial intelligence and science fiction, depending on the task in question. Certainly such techniques will require an interpreted language so that object methods can be rewritten at will.

On a simpler level, many people use systems that have a limited form of this capability. The common spreadsheet calculator is able to update all of the referent cells whenever formulas or macros are moved about, cut, copied, and pasted. This capability exists because the system can make reasonable assumptions about the way input and output cells are placed on a geometric grid. As in AthenaMuse, the information is organized according to its position in a multidimensional space.

In the more general case, it will continue to be difficult to parameterize behavior without using programming languages. Most of our tools for pattern recognition and substitution are text-based, and lie outside the execution environment of typical systems. Hence behavioral templates will probably remain out of reach of novices in the immediate future.

SUMMARY

Templates for both form and function are important tools for software development environments at all levels, but particularly for novices. They provide an organizational framework for attacking a problem and encourage the design of reusable components. Users can customize templates, define new versions to meet new requirements, and quickly create several copies without manual intervention.

In addition to speeding up the development process, these techniques hold promise for building more coherent systems. Template-based construction has the potential to create software that is better equipped to communicate its design and genealogy to future authors.

15. Compound Documents

Just as a chemical compound binds different kinds of atomic elements, a *compound document* binds a variety of information types to create a single seamless presentation. The tools used to create compound documents have traditionally been closed monolithic applications. But when users need greater flexibility to create a custom "information workbench," compound document systems can be assembled from plug-and-play *plastic editors*, as described in Chapter 13. The software development community currently is engaged in something like electronic alchemy, searching for ways to create new information compounds from existing documents and applications. To a large extent this effort is stimulated by the unprecedented growth of institutional networks that interconnect large user populations in business, government, and educational settings. All of these users share a requirement for interpersonal communications systems that can handle multimedia information from a diverse set of applications.

FROM ISOLATION TO COOPERATION

Among the great hopes for multimedia computing is that it can improve organizational productivity by enhancing work group communications. Personal productivity is concerned with one person and one task; it requires high-performance software tools designed to fit the job at hand. Specialists in every domain are constantly searching for new and better software tools to help them in their work.

Unfortunately, organizational productivity requires an easy exchange of information between coworkers, frequently across functional boundaries. The overall flow of communication is hampered when large numbers of people cannot read a document because they lack the proper software.

Consequently many users are faced with a difficult choice: they must either abandon specialized tools and skills or face isolation from their electronic community. Some organizations try to avoid this problem by administrative decree, forcing everyone to use a particular application for word processing or spreadsheet manipulation. This approach is bound to alienate users at the high and low ends of the skill range, who are either pulled down to a lowest common denominator or bewildered by an overabundance of functionality.

One technical strategy is to acquire or develop software that converts every kind of document to a common interchange format (Figure 15.1). To this end, several international standardization efforts are under way to define generic document formats that applications can use to exchange multimedia information, including text, audio, still images, and motion pictures. The trouble with interchange standards is that even in the best case they limit the richness of document

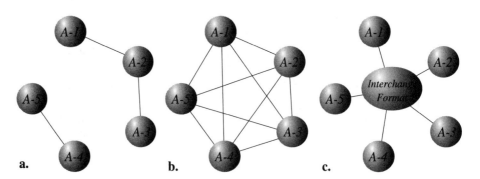

Figure 15.1   The document conversion problem. Each node represents a different vendor's offering of a common productivity application, such as a word processor or electronic spreadsheet, each with its own unique document storage format. In (a), programs require a specific converter between their native format and those of their peers; sometimes a conversion is not possible. Maximum flexibility would require the situation depicted in (b), with every format convertible to every other (a most unlikely situation). In (c), the same goal is met by having each program provide conversion between its native format and a common *interchange format* shared by its peers. This solution reduces the complexity to a manageable level, but requires cross-vendor cooperation to achieve.

representations to whatever the current state-of-the-art happens to be. Many subtleties of data description either do not fit the model or are not fully supported by vendors claiming adherence to the standard.

Neither policies nor interchange standards address the root causes of poor application interoperability. There are fundamental shortcomings in the ways in which such software is created. These include:

- The lack of a *systems perspective* on application development;

- The lack of coherent *application architectures;*

- The lack of universal *interapplication control mechanisms.*

Put simply, applications are not designed to work with one another. Each product is a point solution to a specific problem, with little opportunity for customization and no way to integrate the solution with existing systems.

New compound document technology promises to provide an integration framework to which any type of information can be attached. The challenge is how to transform the legions of independent-minded applications into well-behaved components of a larger communications system. A transition path must be found with the least expenditure of effort from both users and software developers.

Key Features

"Language was not powerful enough
to describe the infant phenomenon."
Charles Dickens

There is a fable about seven blind men who grope around an elephant, each trying to characterize the huge animal by describing one small part: the trunk, a tusk, an ear, a foot, the tail, and so on. Each investigator extrapolates a vision of the total animal from his local observations, leading to seven wildly incorrect theories. We suffer the same syndrome in trying to sketch out the key features of a multimedia compound document system based on our own limited experience. Our task is made more difficult because several software vendors have already begun spreading their own theories about this elephant.

Relevant multimedia document interchange standards activities include ODA, HyTime (based on SGML), and MHEG (see Newcomb, Dengel, and Kretz).

S. R. Newcomb, N. A. Kipp, and V. T. Newcomb, "The Hytime Hypermedia Time-based Document Structuring Language," in *Communications of the ACM*, Vol. 34, No. 11, 1991, pp. 67–83.

A. Dengel, R. Bleisinger, R. Hoch, F. Fein, and F. Hones, "From Paper to Office Document Standard Representation," in *Computer*, Vol. 25, No. 7, July 1992, pp. 63–67.

F. Kretz and F. Colaitis, "Standardizing Hypermedia Information Objects," in *IEEE Communications Magazine*, Vol. 30, No. 5, May 1992, pp. 60–70.

We see the need for a general architecture to build compound document systems that support the following features:

- Extensible data types and representations;

- Revisable component documents;

- Network distribution;

- Multiuser document sharing;

- Adaptability to available resources;

- Easy customization by end users.

Extensibility   A compound document should be able to contain information it did not create, allowing users to place radically different data types and representations into any host document. In such cases the host application should not need any built-in support for the foreign data types it uses. Thus, applications must either load new software modules to expand their functionality, or else use the facilities of other applications to render and manipulate the foreign data.

Revisability   The elements that make up a compound document should be stored in a *revisable form*. A typical PostScript document offers a counter example of nonrevisable *final form* storage: the text, the graphics, and the images are all mixed together, cast into a static presentation that is very difficult to modify. It may be convenient for users to break a compound into a hierarchy of documents (Figure 15.2). Users may want to edit the independent subdocuments in the context of the containing compound, or with a stand-alone editor application. Even if the subdocuments are stored in different files or manipulated by unrelated programs, the compound should maintain its visual integrity, reflecting the most recent changes to its constituent parts.

Network Distribution   A compound document system should take advantage of network services to enhance and simplify the process of group communication. At the most basic level, compound documents need to be packaged for travel through electronic mail systems and reconstituted on the receiving end. In addition, a compound document system should be able to find resources dynamically and make use of them regardless of their physical location.

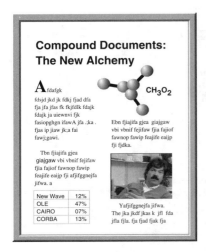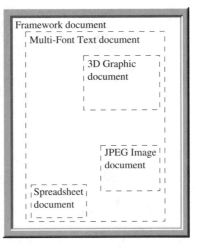

Figure 15.2 Hierarchical documents. The seamless compound document on the left is actually a composite of five different subdocuments. Different "live" application contexts can be embedded inside each other, with each subdocument managed by a corresponding object or service. The framework document provides the glue to coordinate the entire display.

For example, when a user mails a document containing a five-minute video clip to her colleagues, their mailboxes should not be flooded with individual copies of a multimegabyte message. Instead, each recipient might receive a *reference* to a single copy of the document, with the video being displayed by a special network service. Complex and expensive document services, such as 3D renderings, can become network resources available to everyone.

Document Sharing Users need to collaborate on the production of documents. Instead of the usual practice of mailing different versions back and forth, a distributed compound document system should allow several users simultaneously to edit a shared view of a single document (Figure 15.3). Participants should be able to join or leave the shared session at any time from desktops all over the network.

The system also requires conferencing facilities independent of any particular document or application. These may include arbitration to avoid concurrent updates by multiple authors, security features to protect private information, and real-time mixing and distribution of audio feeds from conference participants.

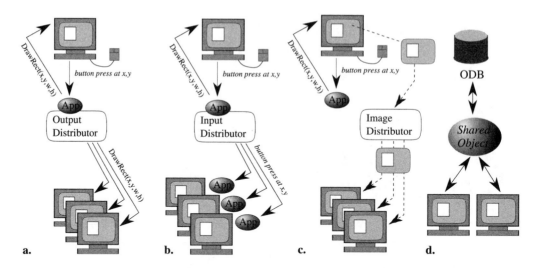

Figure 15.3 Document sharing techniques. In *protocol replication* (a), the instruction sequence used by an application to draw a window is captured and dispersed from a single master program to many slaves. With *event replication* (b), each user runs a local copy of the program and only the input event sequence (mouse clicks, key presses) needs to be distributed from the master to the slaves. With *image replication* (c), an image of the master user's screen is repeatedly "grabbed" and broadcast to the slaves, much like a video signal. With *shared objects* (d), a document is just a complex object in a distributed object database. Each user viewing or editing a shared document sees the others' changes as the database is updated.

Adaptability   Compound document systems need to adapt themselves to the set of resources available on particular computer and network configurations. Sometimes this involves taking advantage of special-purpose processors or software components; at other times it means having to make up for their absence. Another form of adaptability concerns user preferences rather than system resources: the system needs to adapt its actions according to user profiles specifying each person's primary language, favorite word processor, and so on.

An excellent example of adaptable software is Apple Computer's QuickTime system for displaying temporal information such as audio and video. When recording a movie, the QuickTime system is able to detect the presence or absence of video compression hardware and act accordingly. Video playback is similarly adept at switching between a number of different hardware or software decompression engines.

Customization   Every person or organization is sure to have unique requirements for a compound document system; customization makes it possible to service these unforeseen or unmet needs. At the corporate level, system administrators may have to create adapters or gateways that link mission-critical information systems into the compound document framework. At the personal level, users may need to create templates or style sheets that capture particular idioms.

The compound document system must accommodate differences in individual level of skill, differences in task complexity, and differences in language and culture. As noted earlier in Chapter 13, it is frequently inappropriate to expose the user to a full arsenal of editing facilities. Customization suggests the ability to select and package document handling functions at a level suitable to the application and its users.

Internationalization is another complex topic. Issues of language and culture generally permeate every aspect of a multimedia document. Comprehensive solutions to these issues imply changes at every level of system architecture, from the operating system to the user interface.

IMPLEMENTATION STRATEGIES

There appear to be three fundamental strategies for implementing a compound document system: as an all-in-one *integrated* system, as a plug-and-play *component* system, or as a *hybrid* system combining the two approaches.

Integrated Systems

One design for a compound document system is modeled after the Swiss army knife: "all the tools you'll ever need in a single package." CMU's Andrew (see Borenstein) and BBN's Slate (see Lison) are prominent examples of this approach, with integrated subsystems for word processing, spreadsheet manipulation, 2D graphics and image editing, electronic mail correspondence, and more.

In an integrated document system, the data viewers and editors are really just different modules within the same program. The Andrew system is based on *insets*, which are a pair of cooperating objects: a *data* object and a *view* object. The data object manages the actual information, while the view object knows how to create an on-screen representation of it. Andrew's insets can be placed inside one another to create layered compound documents. A multi-font text inset can be used to generate a proposal that happens to include a spreadsheet inset illus-

N. Borenstein, *Mutlimedia Applications Development with the Andrew Toolkit*, Prentice-Hall, Englewood Cliffs NJ, 1989.

H. Lison and T. Crowley, "Multimedia Systems: Sight and Sound," in *UNIX Review*, Vol. 7, No. 10, October 1989, pp. 76–86.

This architecture derives from the Smalltalk object-oriented programming environment, which first introduced the Model-View-Controller (MVC) paradigm: a data model, a view to display it, and controllers to manipulate it.

trating its financial ramifications. A footnote to the proposal can contain a voice inset to present informally an aside from the author. All of these insets are dynamic and fully manipulable within the context of the containing document.

The chief benefit of an integrated design is that the individual tools can be very tightly coupled for smooth operation. Users won't have any problems exchanging data between the built-in editors, or with trying to sort out an array of confusing or conflicting user interfaces. If the integrated toolset satisfies the majority of a workgroup's needs, it can be a highly productive "information workbench" for ordinary office communications.

Problems   The main problem with integrated systems is that they must do many things well instead of just one. Each of the included editors must provide a significant portion of the functionality of similar stand-alone tools, or else no one will use the system to do "real work." This is particularly problematic in large corporate settings, where job responsibilities are often extremely specialized and divided into functional hierarchies. For example, if the text tool does not support multiple columns and text-fitting around illustrations, it will not be used to generate the company newsletter. Specialists need special tools; all-in-one tools generally do not meet the needs of high-end users.

An integrated compound document system is most effective in a homogeneous group, when an entire project or department agrees to use it. Efforts to standardize any one tool across functional or organizational boundaries will meet with strong resistance from specialists whose needs go beyond the common denominator. The result tends to be two sets of tools: one for doing work, and one for communicating about it. As a partial solution to these problems, integrated compound document systems can add data interchange facilities that provide gateways to external applications. In many cases, *filter* programs can be written to perform automatic conversions among data formats. If the system is particularly well designed and documented, programmers can even modify or extend the set of base objects and editors. With these techniques it is possible to customize an integrated system to match a specific communications domain.

Component Systems

In a component document system, loosely coupled programs associated with independent document types are coordinated to present the illusion of a single "virtual" document. Authors express ideas using a set of *services* provided by external software packages, rather than relying on a single monolithic program to provide all of the requisite functionality.

Perhaps the most sophisticated example of this approach is Hewlett-Packard's New Wave user environment for IBM-compatible personal computers (see Heller). In the UNIX world, the Maestro system provides a good example, using a network protocol to coordinate a set of independent multimedia components (see Drapeau).

New Wave combines a document and its application software into a single abstract object. New Wave objects can be embedded inside one another. A simple mouse click on any of these objects, such as a picture inside a text document, will activate that component's editing functionality—in this case, raster image operations. Any document-oriented application that follows the New Wave guidelines can become a participant in a compound document, managing its own display, editing, storage, and printing in the context of the containing document. In addition, if several users on a network open the same compound document object, any changes to the shared document are automatically propagated to everyone's shared views of it.

Today most documents live in their own private universe, with each application completely responsible for everything that happens in it. The component document strategy is an opportunity to delegate some of this authority to external software modules. Developers will be able to concentrate on building up a set of unique competitive advantages, reusing the work of others and avoiding a duplication of effort. Users will benefit from the ability to mix and match components to fine-tune a system's behavior to their individual needs.

A simple analogy is an audiophile assembling a component stereo system, with an amplifier, CD player, and speakers from three different specialty manufacturers. The audiophile can rest assured that the stereo components will work together because all of the vendors have agreed to use standard electrical interfaces and connectors: 120 volts AC for power, 8 ohms for speaker connections, and RCA plugs for line-level audio.

Problems There are a number of difficulties with the component system strategy as it has been implemented thus far. The first challenge is to get the would-be components attached to one another via a shared interoperability framework. The software community has been slow to reach consensus on a wide range of application interoperability issues. Applications are generally seen as single-purpose tools, stand-

M. Heller, "Future Documents," in *Byte*, Vol. 16, No. 5, 1991, p. 126.

G. Drapeau and H. Greenfield, "Maestro—A Distributed Multimedia Authoring Environment," in *Proc. of the Summer 1991 USENIX Conf.*, USENIX Association, Berkeley CA, 1991.

alone document processors. A few years ago the guiding vision for the UNIX operating system was to provide a suite of small interoperable tools, in which streams of information could be piped together to create arbitrarily complex data processing systems. With the advent of modern graphical user interfaces, UNIX applications have become scattered islands separated by very deep oceans.

However, forces at work in the marketplace offer reason for hope. Recent advances in personal computer system software are setting high expectations for application interoperability and ease of use. For example, Microsoft's Object Linking and Embedding (OLE) technology and Apple's Publish and Subscribe features let documents contain dynamically updated information provided by other applications.

The second challenge is to convert stand-alone applications into well-behaved component documents. There is more to the problem than simply lashing together a set of independent editing systems. The components must submit their controls in a way that allows for coherent and flexible interface design across components. This will require a significant amount of cooperation among software vendors, who will have to agree on a common vendor-neutral architecture and protocol.

There are also issues of economics and logistics that come with the component system approach. Licensing is one example. Many of the popular editing systems have been distributed under single-user licenses. If these systems are to be incorporated into broader communication fabrics, it can only take place on the basis of a different pattern of licensing than we commonly find today. If every member of a group who wishes to communicate needs an individual license for every component of such a system, the cost quickly becomes prohibitive.

AthenaMuse as a Hybrid Model

The idea in a hybrid approach is to create a system kernel which provides integrated editing capabilities for fundamental document types but otherwise serves as a coordination framework for a component system. The architecture of AthenaMuse allowed us to undertake some experiments along this path.

AthenaMuse defines a document architecture with specific constructs for handling the coordination of subcomponents of a compound document. The display elements integrated into the system—images, text, graphics, and so on—are designed to tie into these constructs. This makes it possible for non-specialists to create a reasonably wide range of interactive documents. AthenaMuse differs from other integrated document systems in that the editing facilities for manipulating these integrated resources are accessed through the AthenaMuse documents themselves rather than through built-in editing interfaces. This extends the range of possibilities enormously, and gives rise to the flexibility and high degree of customization that has been described in Chapter 13.

But what of the problem of linking in other applications? As a first step, we explored some strategies for getting several different programs to *cooperate* in managing the display of a compound document. We used the existing AthenaMuse system to construct top-level "container" documents that coordinate with external processes to render various kinds of subdocuments. Our overall goal was to create a hierarchical compound document that appears to users as a single seamless document, rather than a collection of independent programs that get "launched" outside the central framework.

Researchers in the Distributed Multimedia Applications project at GTE Laboratories experimented with three different techniques for creating compound documents in AthenaMuse: *window transplants; application wrappers;* and *view servers.*

Window transplants   In the X Window System, client applications draw on the screen by sending requests to the X server to perform graphics operations in a particular window. Windows are rectangular regions of pixels, each with a unique identification number, that can be overlapped and shuffled like pieces of paper on a desktop. X is a fully *recursive* window system, meaning that any number of subwindows, or children, can be created inside a parent window. The X protocol supports requests to dynamically alter the parent-child relationships among windows. A window and all its children can be "re-parented" to a completely unrelated window, even one created by another application. Put together, these basic facilities allowed us to *transplant* windows from their original applications directly into AthenaMuse documents without any modifications whatsoever.

Many other window systems, such as the Apple Macintosh, maintain only a list of windows, not a hierarchical tree.

We created a set of EventScript objects to let authors "drag and drop" windows from any X application into an AthenaMuse compound document shell. These "foreign" windows are stored as part of a document's specification. Instead of taking static window snapshots, the software quietly reparents a "live" window from a hidden copy of the original application. The user sees only the AthenaMuse document with the transplanted windows; the rest of the external application remains invisible.

We created a prototype real estate service at GTE Laboratories, linking two users' desktops with a shared compound document containing a live video feed, a real estate listings book, and a mortgage calculator (described in Chapter 2). Participants can perform a simple financial analysis with the interactive spreadsheet, which is actually a window transplanted from a public-domain spreadsheet calculator called *sc.*

The advantage of this technique is that it requires no changes to existing applications, which remain completely independent. However, independence is not always a virtue. Since there is no communication protocol connecting AthenaMuse and the external programs, no information can pass between them except through generic cut-and-paste mechanisms. Furthermore, transplanted buttons retain the "look and feel" of the original application, which can lead to visual confusion if they clash with other controls in the document. Activities that require real coordination, such as getting a compound document to print all of its components correctly, are out of the question. Window transplants are not a general technique, but an interesting "hack" inspired by the recursive nature of the X window system.

Application Wrappers   Instead of pruning bits and pieces from another application's window tree, we decided to turn existing applications into more cooperative objects by giving them an API (Application Programmer's Interface), as discussed in Chapter 13. We were looking for a way to "wrap up" an application in an object-oriented abstraction, so that an AthenaMuse document could manipulate it by means of a messaging protocol.

José Diaz-Gonzalez at GTE Laboratories discovered how to use the shared library facilities in UNIX System V (SVR4) to "get inside" foreign programs. We could then load the EventScript interpreter into any X Toolkit application and define a set of object scripts to form an API. We created a library of routines called *Pmsg* to implement a message-passing protocol between any two X windows. EventScript objects in the AthenaMuse document and the application wrapper are able to communicate with each other using this protocol.

We took the *sc* spreadsheet program and a figure-drawing program called *xfig*, and built object wrappers around them. We implemented standard messages requesting each program to reparent its drawing window into the AthenaMuse document. Furthermore, we made it possible to activate functions in the external programs, such as retrieving cell values or formulas from the spreadsheet. Any direct-manipulation interactions, such as moving or resizing graphic elements on the *xfig* canvas, remain available as well. At this point we were able to create seamless compound documents containing live spreadsheets and complex graphic illustrations, all from within the AthenaMuse framework. Users had no idea that several programs were cooperating behind the scenes to display and manipulate the combined document.

View Servers   The real problem with application wrappers is that they are too hard to create. Today a developer would have to expend a tremendous amount of energy to divine the inner workings of another vendor's application without access to its source code. Eventually market pressures will force vendors to provide their own API to applications.

This thinking led us to explore a third alternative to creating compound documents, using what we call *view servers*. A view server need not contain all of the complex functionality inherent in a full-blown application. It merely knows how to render a given data type in a client's windows, as opposed to the reparenting techniques explored earlier. A view server can then manage a large number of views displayed in different documents. In contrast, an application wrapper usually has a single "canvas" per instance.

We built a prototype view server using an EventScript-based drawing package originally written for the AthenaMuse *Figure Editor*. A client document sends a message to a "directory" service requesting a view server for a particular data type. If an appropriate server exists, the client sends it a message describing the data to be viewed and the window in which it should be displayed. The server retrieves and interprets the requested data, then draws a view of it in the client document's window. Any button presses or window exposure events in the document window are passed on to the view server for processing. The display is updated as necessary.

The view server is based on a notion of document components which is different from the idea of binding together stand-alone applications. It decouples the control interface from the data management and display aspects of the software.

TECHNICAL EVOLUTION

Today there seems to be confusion about what is or is not a compound document, or even a multimedia document. Some would say that any document containing a variety of multimedia information is a compound document. This kind of static compound is easy to create using ordinary cut-and-paste facilities. Photographs, paragraphs, diagrams, and spreadsheet tables can all be placed into the same document by means of almost any page-layout program. Unfortunately, the individual bits and pieces of data have lost their dynamics; the power to control and change them was left behind in the original application.

Cut-and-paste involves a one-time transfer of data between two programs. The recipient is left with nothing more than a snapshot, a moment in the history of another document. In addition, the receiver becomes entirely responsible for managing the storage and display of the newly transferred data. The programming overhead needed to support an ever increasing variety of data types can quickly get out of hand when trying to create a generic multimedia editor for compound documents. As a result, importing and exporting these data types on a per-application basis simply does not scale well.

An alternative to cut-and-paste is the ability to create *links* between documents, by making a reference to information instead of copying it. This type of long-term relationship between documents is more appropriate for the large quantities of data consumed by multimedia information such as images, sounds, and movies. Even so, a symbolic link is only a data conduit or pathway connecting two documents; it retains the traditional distinction between a document and an application.

The next step up the evolutionary ladder will be to move to an object-oriented document model. A "document" is encapsulated inside a data object that deals with media-specific storage and transmission requirements, and responds to requests that manipulate its internal state. An associated view object knows how to create a visual representation of the document on various output devices, such as screens and laser printers. An integrated compound document system could bring together a number of these document objects inside a single object-oriented application.

Finally, we will reach a plateau where the document objects are spread across a computer network or many different networks. At this point, a component compound document system might be implemented as an object-oriented network service, with all of the data objects stored in a distributed object database. Such a system could become the basis for a wide range of custom applications that require compound document facilities.

SUMMARY

It is clear that at this stage in the evolution of compound documents there is no available solution which meets the needs of all users. The optimal strategy is to understand the spectrum of needs and how these can be placed in flexible compromise.

The component model offers advantages in supporting specialized needs of high-end users. It offers a clearer path toward an extensible architecture, and a clearer model of network distribution. Its disadvantages are that it increases complexity, both in terms of interface and internal machinery. This implies a higher degree of fragility and therefore a threat to document longevity. In addition, the component model is not so amenable to "micro-coordination" among document elements, nor to customization.

The integrated approach has somewhat opposite characteristics; improved customization and coordination capability, but at a substantial cost in functionality.

In our experience, the hybrid approach made an interesting compromise. It allowed us to explore issues of interface design with a highly flexible set of integrated resources, but at the same time to extend the capabilities of the system by adding external components for display and editing.

The subtleties of expressing ideas through multimedia documents are not yet well understood. It is important to gain experience with the details of coordinating document elements, for it is likely in the interaction of these elements that much of the interesting expression will emerge. These issues are more easily explored in an integrated framework. But it is important to be able to link high-powered editors into such a framework, for this direction seems to hold the greater promise for longer-term solutions.

16. Synchronization

Synchronization is coordination in time. Multimedia computing requires a great deal of such coordination when diverse streams of information are being integrated into a coherent presentation. This chapter presents three principal issues in synchronization:

1 Representation, how information streams and their relationships are specified;

2 Processing, how timing requests are serviced;

3 Error handling, how missed events are handled.

The focus is on how these issues were addressed in AthenaMuse. This system was an early implementation of synchronization services for multimedia, and certainly not very sophisticated. Nonetheless, all three issues were addressed in a complete system that was used for a wide variety of applications, and therefore it is a useful example.

Representation

The first problem in synchronizing a display is to specify what is to be synchronized and how the components of the presentation relate to one another. The author must identify pieces of text, video, graphics, or audio information and provide precise detail on how their display is to be coordinated over time. From this an internal representation must be produced that can be handled by the event processing machinery that will actually coordinate the display of all these materials.

The timeline is the normal method by which a user specifies timing relationships. Display information is mapped onto the timeline, and the sequence of onset and offset times defined in this way is used as the reference for controlling the display.

In AthenaMuse we used an abstract timeline as the groundwork for synchronization. As a fundamental aspect of its document architecture, AthenaMuse allows the author to define an arbitrary number of *dimensions*. Every document shares this structure, and it is quite simple to allocate a dimension within a document and let it represent time. Mapping the display data onto one or more of these dimensions is also a standard part of the AthenaMuse document architecture; in effect, everything needed to construct a representation of a time span and to position display information against it is built into the system at a basic level.

This has proved to be one of the most powerful features of Athena-Muse. Time, particularly real time, is a special case of a broad set of co-ordination issues. In many instances, coordination has more complexities than a one-dimensional timeline can capture. More than one dimension is needed to reflect the relationships among the display materials. In some cases, more than one flow of time can be used concurrently, each moving at a different rate. In other cases, time does not flow at all, but is stepped along by the user. It is important not to take a limited view of time, thinking only of a presentation that moves along one dimension at a fixed rate from beginning to end.

Video Subtitles

One of the first AthenaMuse applications involved synchronization of text subtitles with motion video. This was the French language material developed by MIT's Athena Language Learning Project, part of which is described in Chapter 8. The problem was to map a variety of materials, including multiple streams of text subtitles, a scrollbar "cursor," and "cultural flags" onto motion video sequences of native French speakers (Figure 16.1). The subtitles are divided at phrase boundaries in the discourse, so they are updated approximately one or two times per sentence (about every three to five seconds).

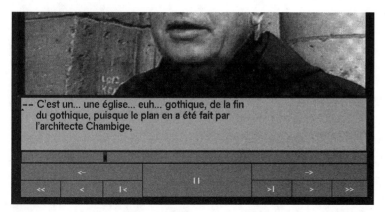

Figure 16.1   The screen layout for a typical video sequence in *Dans le Quartier St. Gervais*. The scrollbar below the video represents the passage of time and offers a way to jump backward or forward. Subtitles appear in the window above the scrollbar.

The subtitles come in several varieties. For beginning students there is a full transcription of the dialogue; more advanced students get a reduced transcription with only a few key words. It is possible to display more than one set at a time or switch streams with the click of a button for multilingual presentations.

The subtitles are stored in separate files, one for each set. These files are scrolled through the subtitle window, one subtitle at a time. The synchronization therefore depends on a mapping between character offsets in the text files and frames in the video sequence.

The following example shows the internal structure of the subtitle package shown in Figure 16.1.

```
package "Subtitles"
{
    screen_name "subtitles"
    active
    dimension "time"
    {
        min 0 max 890
        timer_fn pace
        parameter "subtitles" 1
        rate 0
    }
    element "video"
    {
```

```
    type video
    screen_name "video"
    active
    map video
    {
        pos_in 0
        pos_out 430
        in 5000
        out 5430
        label "StGervais:Side1"
        key_dimension 0
    }
    map video
    {
        pos_in 431
        pos_out 890
        in 6500
        out 6960
        label "StGervais:Side1"
        key_dimension 0
    }
}
element "titles"
{
    type text
    active
    screen_name "subtitle_box"
    filename "moine.text"
    map tktext
    {
        pos_in 0
        pos_out 890
        (20 29 646 95 67 57 67 1)
        font "-adobe-helvetica-medium-r-normal—18-180-75-75-p-98-iso8859-1"
        text_options 0
        file  "moine.text"
    }
    map textmap  { pos_in 0   pos_out 65   in 0   }
    map textmap  { pos_in 66  pos_out 123  in 70  }
    map textmap  { pos_in 124 pos_out 340  in 114 }
    map textmap  { pos_in 341 pos_out 467  in 230 }
    map textmap  { pos_in 468 pos_out 512  in 313 }
    map textmap  { pos_in 513 pos_out 890  in 462 }
}
}
```

In AthenaMuse this document is implemented as a single *package*. Within the package, the dimension *time* serves as the organizing framework. The video elements identify the source materials and their position with respect to time. In this example two video segments are defined to show how separate video sequences can be spliced together in a single document.

In AthenaMuse the video display method assumes that the individual video frames referred to in these definitions are to be distributed evenly over the time onto which they are mapped—there is no need to map each separate frame to a specific point in time.

The process for displaying the text subtitles is quite different. It is not enough to say "Here is a text file; spread the characters evenly over time." Instead, specific character offsets in the file are mapped explicitly to ranges of time. As the cursor in the document moves into one of these ranges, the text file is repositioned to the appropriate location. The text elements in the illustration each contain a list of these mappings. The offsets are generated with a "subtitle editor" that provides a direct manipulation interface for defining these mappings.

This example shows the basic characteristics of the representational scheme used in AthenaMuse. An arbitrary number of dimensions can be created, any of which can be used to model time. The display elements are mapped onto these dimensions by means of *position-in* and *position-out* attributes. As the package's current position changes along its dimensions, the display elements are updated accordingly.

This scheme turned out to be quite effective and taught us some important lessons concerning synchronization. First, the representation scheme for synchronization should not tie one stream of data directly to another; using an abstract framework to mediate between data sources gives more flexibility. This way, any of the data streams can be modified without changing all the rest. Second, there should be support for more than one dimension of time. With AthenaMuse a number of timing dimensions can operate simultaneously in the same document. This allows orthogonal timing operations within a presentation to occur independently, again providing a greater degree of flexibility. Finally, the representational scheme for synchronization should be implemented as a fundamental aspect of all documents rather than as a special-purpose appendage to an otherwise nontemporal document architecture. Inclusion of dimensions as a fundamental component of all documents in AthenaMuse has made the system much more consistent for its users.

EVENT PROCESSING

Precision is the main concern in the processing aspect of synchronization. Timing precision can be greatly affected by the speed of the CPU, the real-time capabilities of the operating system, and data access and throughput speeds of the I/O subsystems.

The issue of precision should always be discussed with respect to the needs of an application. Different applications require different levels of precision; the precision needed to display text subtitles over video is much lower than the precision needed to support seamless cuts between video segments, for example.

As a rough metric, consider three orders of magnitude, in milliseconds:

300 ms (.3 sec)	Text over video, acceptable text subtitles
30 ms	Audio over video, video cuts
3 ms	Audio mixing

Here each level of precision is sufficient to support certain classes of applications. When displaying text along with video, as with the subtitles, a slip of a third of a second does not affect the user greatly.

Where more dynamic video editing is required, the synchronization needs to be much more accurate—to within one, possibly two, video frames. An audio soundtrack that slips by more than about two frames becomes noticeable to the viewer. The normal frame rate for motion pictures varies from 24 to 30 frames per second, depending on the format standard. This translates to 33 to 50 milliseconds, roughly an order of magnitude more precise than needed for subtitles. Dynamic audio mixing would require yet another order of magnitude of precision, because phase shifts of even a few milliseconds between audio tracks can create echo effects and other distortions.

Currently, multimedia is struggling to shift from analog to digital video. Digital video requires synchronization at the 30-millisecond time scale, since digital audio and video are not packaged together as they normally are in the analog domain; therefore basic audio and video synchronization must be handled by the display engines.

The AthenaMuse Architecture

AthenaMuse has a built-in set of timing services. In distributed computing terms, the time management is on the *client side*. If the timing were available from a separate network server, it would be possible to synchronize actions *across* AthenaMuse applications. As it is, each AthenaMuse process maintains its own internal notion of time, which poses a serious constraint in developing distributed applications.

The services in AthenaMuse provide a fixed number of individual timers that can be set to go off periodically or on a one-time basis. Most applications require that the event stream remain open while waiting for a timer; otherwise, all user input is shut off until the timer expires.

AthenaMuse packages are the clients of these services. They can *start* a timer, *stop* a timer, or *set the rate* of a timer to a specified number of milliseconds. The *start* request must identify the action to be called whenever the timer expires. Normally these actions affect the position of the package along its dimensions.

In Figure 16.2, for example, notice that the timer is declared as an object with *pace* as the action. *Pace* is an AthenaMuse function that tries to keep up with real time. The argument tells it which dimension to affect and how big a step to take. The *rate* tells it how often to take such a step. *Pace* watches the system clock, and if it begins to fall behind it will take bigger steps to catch up.

Typical buttons for *Play* and *Stop* use the *set_rate* action to control the display of the package. *Play* sets the rate to 33 milliseconds, corresponding to the normal frame rate for NTSC video. A negative value here will reverse the direction of the movement, in effect reversing time and playing the video and subtitles backward. The *Stop* button simply sets the rate to zero.

Strategies

The internal handling of events in AthenaMuse is quite simple: each time the current position on a dimension changes, all package contents are checked to see if they need updating.

The various strategies to improve the efficiency of this process fall into two basic categories:

1 Precomputing event lists to reduce the need for checking;

2 Anticipating events so that resources can be organized in advance.

Precomputing an event list means going through all the display contents looking for significant events such as the *in* and *out* points of video segments, subtitles, and so on. These are put in a list and used to set the timers, so that an event is generated only when such a change is scheduled to take place, not every few milliseconds. A variation of this approach is to let each data stream maintain its own timer and event list, so that the events come directly to the object level.

The advantage of either approach is that the burden of searching for significant change is radically reduced—events are generated only when something needs to be done. The disadvantage is that the event list must be recomputed each time an element is inserted or modified.

Anticipating events means making an assumption about what is going to happen and preparing resources in advance. Queuing a video playback device in anticipation of a transition is a good example. If you have more than one video source and want to make a seamless cut from one to the other, you can anticipate the transition and queue the second device before the cut point arrives. Otherwise, you may be waiting for the search after the transition should have taken place.

The advantage here is that a little anticipation can smooth over a number of resource management difficulties ranging from device access delays to network latencies. The disadvantage is that assumptions must be made about what will happen, generally at the expense of flexibility. If you have queued some display requests, for example, and suddenly the user pushes the stop button, you may have to scramble to locate and abort those requests (if in fact they can be aborted, which is not presently the case with the X Window system).

Also, the computation of how much to anticipate a given event is quite subtle, since the display times and latencies are not at all fixed. The function to perform this computation would use probabilities based on type and quantity of material to be presented, the normal display rates for the rendering processor, an estimated resource access time for the storage device, and an estimate for the network latency given the transport pathway and buffering capabilities. To make this work across platforms and for a reasonable number of display types appears to be a substantial challenge.

ERROR HANDLING

Whatever precautions are taken, the application must still be prepared to deal with timing errors, which is the third aspect of synchronization.

A timing error means that some part of the display cannot be serviced when it is supposed to be. There are two fundamental sources of error in a non-real-time environment such as UNIX. The first involves the time needed to access and display the information (getting video data out of a file, or painting a screenful of graphics). The second stems from the operating system itself serving other processes. The result in both cases is that the process managing synchronization may not receive a scheduled signal on time.

The essential question in error handling is what to do with these missed events. Basically, there are three options: throw them away, process them "late," or slow time.

Throwing events away means jumping ahead in the event stream in order to catch up with other components of the display. This is exactly what is done with the subtitles described earlier. In our system the video is moving along under control of the videodisc player, which blindly follows its own clock. The subtitles, on the other hand, depend directly on the AthenaMuse timing services, following UNIX's view of the system clock.

As the system gets loaded, the subtitles tend to fall behind the video. It makes no sense to display subtitles after the speaker has gone on to the next remark, so in this circumstance the events are simply dropped. The effect is minimal in practice; given the normal duration of the subtitles, they never disappear entirely. The *pace* function, described above, compares the package timer with the system clock and jumps the package timer ahead if necessary, bypassing any events in the middle.

There are situations where this behavior is not acceptable, where events cannot, or need not, be discarded. For example, if a trigger point responsible for starting up some other part of the application happens to "fall through the cracks" and be discarded, the entire behavior of the application could be affected. Or, if the video was the tardy element, as might be expected with digital video (or audio) delivered over a network, it would make no sense to skip over video to keep up with subtitles.

In such cases either the events can be processed late with respect to the other data streams, or the entire presentation can be slowed down—or even stopped—to accommodate the limiting data stream. In

AthenaMuse the *set_position* calls can be used instead of *pace*. They will visit every point in time without dropping any events, but they tend to lag significantly behind a video presentation following real time (where the video playback unit cannot be slowed with enough precision to synchronize them). Here the events controlled by the system timer simply come in late. AthenaMuse has no provision for limiting this delay. A more sophisticated approach would allow the user to set a limit on the acceptable lateness, after which one of the other tactics could be employed.

In one instance we decided to stop time. We found that when a document appeared on the screen and the video material started playing, the time needed to draw any remaining parts of the display made all the other timed events fall behind. We modified the display routines to stop the timer until all display events had been processed, in effect holding back time to accommodate the extra burst of graphics activity when the display first appeared on the screen.

SUMMARY

There are three aspects to synchronization and a coherent treatment of the problem must address all three. First, there should be an efficient scheme of representation that lets the author specify what is to be synchronized and how the timing is to be arranged. This scheme should translate easily to a system-level representation that can be processed by the timing services at run time. In our experience, a document format based on abstract dimensions has been an effective start toward such a system.

The second component is the timing—or synchronization—service, which manages the event streams and calls the display servers to update the presentation of the content material. Here the principal questions have to do with the cost-versus-precision trade-off: What is the application? How much precision does it require? How much effort is needed to achieve this level of precision? What are the costs of optimizing performance through precomputation or event anticipation? These questions admit a variety of solutions, and they will continue to play a central role in the design of synchronization systems until there is a "solution" for distributed real-time performance with high-volume data throughput and negligible network latency.

The third component of the system, important in light of present technical limitations, is the error handling strategy—what to do when the timing services cannot keep up. Here the options are relatively straightforward, but the question of how to apply them is more subtle. Whether you throw away events, display them late, or slow down the other components of a display to keep pace depends to some extent on the content material. It may or may not be possible to design general policies regarding how to handle errors; we do not yet have enough experience to know.

17. Hotspots

Contributed by: BRIAN MICHON

Displaying video on a workstation screen is only part of the challenge of multimedia computing. Immediately one wishes for greater power—how can this video be connected to other information in the environment? The present chapter treats the integration of video with other forms of data in a multimedia environment.

Part of the problem is temporal. Whereas Chapter 15 discusses the integration of video by making data bindings with specific points in *time,* here we look at the issues involved in binding data to points within the two-dimensional *space* of a raster image through the use of "hotspots." Included is the description of a utility called *HotSpots* which was developed as part of the AthenaMuse environment.

Hotspots can be thought of as special buttons designed to let the user interact directly with an image and its content. They differ from conventional buttons in three respects. First, they need not be rectangular but can take the shape of any arbitrary polygon. Second, they typically have minimal or even no visual representation, and no associated labels or icons to indicate their function. Third, they automatically stay registered to part of the image to which they are linked, even if the image is scaled or sized.

The general objective is to make the user feel as if he or she is interacting with the image. Because the hotspots are transparent, users interact with the content of an image and not with some intermediate in-

B. Michon, "Highly
Iconic Interfaces," in
*Multimedia Interface
Design*, ed. by M. M.
Blattner and R. B.
Dannenberg, ACM
Press, New York NY,
1992, pp. 357–372.

terface. Interacting with a picture can be considered a more "iconic" interface than either text or graphic icons; we refer to such an interface as a highly iconic deictic interface (see Michon).

The following sections outline the principal issues in the use of hotspots by both author and reader, and describe the main points of the *HotSpots* implementation as well.

CREATING HOTSPOTS

There are two steps in creating hotspots: the first is to define the shape of the hotspot over the base image; the second is to define its behavior.

Defining a Shape

Defining a hotspot's shape involves tracing the outline of an object or region on an image. This task can be done interactively by the author with a tool that draws polygonal lines with the mouse pointer. For example, in the *Mechanical Bearings* project, the students need to click on engine parts in a video image for more information. The image is brought up as a window on the workstation screen and the author then uses a tracing tool to mark lines around each area of interest. As each line is drawn, a hotspot is created using this shape and recording the dimension of the window in which it was defined (see Figure 17.1). Today, hotspot boundaries must be entered by hand, a time-consuming process even for still images. For the mapping of objects through a sequence of motion images—following a bouncing ball, for example—the process quickly becomes impractical.

Figure 17.1   Hotspot definition

M. Piech, "Object
Tracking in Video and
Its Application to
Multimedia," BSEE
thesis, MIT, 1990.

Edge detection and image analysis techniques can automate this process, at least in part. Working with the Visual Computing Group at MIT, an undergraduate research project explored the use of edge detection to track objects automatically through a sequence of motion videos and construct hotspots to follow them (see Piech).

To start the process, the author provides an outline of the object in a "key frame," using a drawing tool as described above. The next step is to choose the beginning and end of the video segment containing this object. The system then analyzes this sequence frame by frame, trying to track the object and calculate a new location and a new shape (Figure 17.2).

Similar techniques are used in film colorization systems, where the work is done through a combination of linear interpolation between key frames, edge detection, and color map or pixel value analysis.

Defining Behavior

After the shape of the hotspot has been defined, behavior must be attached to it. This is comparable to defining the behavior of a conventional button, in that one must indicate which functions or methods to invoke for various events that may occur. In a general hotspot utility, the author should have at least as much capability to define behaviors as with a conventional button. Therefore separate functions can be assigned not only to button press and release events, but also to double clicks and *enter* and *leave* events as well. *HotSpots* also offers the option of defining a function to be called if the mouse is not in *any* hotspot in an image.

Use by Readers   Hotspots typically are transparent and unlabeled so they do not obscure the image on which they are superimposed. These properties raise two important user interface issues: (a) How does a user know where or if there are hotspots on an image; and (b) How does the user know what will happen when a hotspot is pressed?

Showing Hotspots

Given that the idea behind hotspots is to allow the user to click directly on the image without a visible button, how

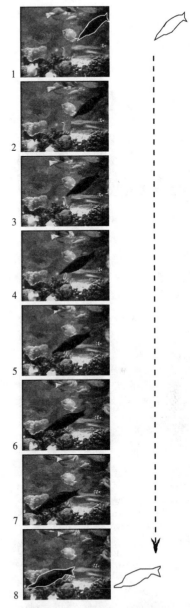

Figure 17.2   Hotspot tracking in a motion video sequence. A beginning outline is traced and then used to constrain the edge detection algorithm in the following frames.

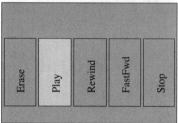

Figure 17.3 Hotspots for interactive images. A series of video frames depicts the control panel of an answering machine in each of its six possible states. A list of named hotspot areas overlays the on-screen image, one over each button. When the user moves the pointing device into a hotspot area and clicks on it, the software immediately displays the relevant image showing the underlying button in its depressed state, and invokes the associated function (in this case, playing back an audio message). When the function is finished, the software returns the display to the default image.

does the user know which objects are *hot* and which are not? There is no simple answer—different contexts call for different solutions. With regard to whether hotspots need to be shown, there are cases where they *always* need to be shown, other cases where they *sometimes* need to be shown, and still others where they *never* need to be shown.

The CERN *Diorama* uses explicitly visible hotspots to indicate active regions on an aerial photograph; these must always be available. The *Geology* and *Mechanical Bearings* projects both use images as a quiz in which students are asked to identify features of the images; the hotspots are hidden until feedback is given to the student. In *A la Rencontre de Philippe*, part of the French language learning material, images of a telephone and a telephone answering machine are used as interface devices, where hotspots are overlaid on the buttons as they appear in the image; there is no need to make the hotspots explicitly visible (Figure 17.3).

Regarding how the hotspots should be made visible, there are again several alternatives. As before, choice depends on the application. The least conspicuous approach is to have the mouse cursor change when it enters or leaves a hotspot; the user can probe the image with the mouse to locate the active regions.

A more explicit method is to highlight the hotspot in some way, either by drawing in the edge or by applying a mask to the whole region. Another approach is to add a text label or icon to the hotspot, to indicate its presence but not its boundaries.

In *HotSpots* such changes in the visual appearance are made by telling the hotspot to draw itself. A group of hotspots can also highlight themselves if the parent hotspot list is told to draw itself.

How a hotspot best highlights itself on an image depends on the image. Sometimes a simple outline is sufficient; other times it is best to fill in the object with a color or a translucent fill pattern. It may even be necessary to define a method that decides how to highlight at run time. These choices are context dependent; the system should provide enough flexibility so that the author can choose and apply an appropriate strategy.

Indicating the Behavior

There is a similar need for flexibility in defining the behavior of a hotspot. In some cases, as with the telephone interface, the function of the hotspot is self-evident, implied by the content of the image. This approach can be reinforced or supplemented through the use of labels or icons, as with the CERN *Diorama* project mentioned above.

Many times the behavior of a hotspot is a conventional action, communicated through separate instructions or left to the user's "intuition." This is typically the case where the action is to call up some other body of information, in effect traversing a cross-reference linkage. The action is the same from one hotspot to the next, although the result—the destination—may certainly be different. In instances when complex behavior is associated with a hotspot, a pop-up set of instructions can be called up on entry or button press events in the hotspot. Arbitrary complexity is thereby accommodated without burdening the user.

IMPLEMENTATION

In the *HotSpots* implementation, each hotspot has a name and method pointers for different classes of events. The methods describe actions to take when the mouse enters, exits, or stays within a hotspot, or when the user presses or releases a mouse button. Aside from its name and methods, each hotspot keeps track of its own shape, location, size, graphic attributes, and highlighting procedures. Hotspot objects are maintained in a structure called a *hotspot list*. Each list keeps track of the number of hotspots, the window and display information needed to show them, and status information on whether the pointer is in one of the hotspots on the list. It is the hotspot list that maintains the function to be called if the pointer is not in any hotspot.

The X Window System has a mechanism for defining arbitrarily shaped areas. These are called *regions*. Regions are defined by a polygon (a list of points); X provides functions for creating regions from points and other functions for determining if the pointing device is in one or more regions.

HotSpots provides a C-callable library of functions for programs to interface with the hotspots it manages. These functions allow one to create, shape, resize, highlight, and destroy hotspots. Implementation is generally straightforward; resizing is the one exception, because of the way the X Window System scales arbitrarily shaped regions.

Scaling

Once defined, hotspots will register correctly with a video image even if the image is resized, moved, or stretched. The hotspots must be scaled whenever the underlying video image is resized.

Keeping the hotspot exactly registered with the object, even when the image is scaled, is crucial. If the hotspot strays by even a few pixels, users could well get information on the wrong object (imagine a budding neurosurgeon learning to identify brain structures...).

The X Window System provides a function called XShrinkRegion for scaling regions. This routine uses a *sampling* procedure to determine the shape of the newly scaled region. But sampling intervals are not precise enough for registering hotspots, so the new regions are shaped only somewhat like the original. This imprecision is unacceptable in applications such as the *Neuroanatomy* reference browser, where the hotspots conform to the complex shapes of brain structures.

The hotspot resizing method is more precise than XShrinkRegion. This routine scales the original set of points that defined the hotspot to generate a new region. Each hotspot object consists of two arrays of points: one defines its original shape; the other defines its current shape. Two sets of points are kept because each scaling transformation may introduce roundoff errors. By transformation of the original coordinates, these errors are not propagated each time the hotspot is resized.

Event Processing

Hotspots are currently an experimental extension to the core AthenaMuse software system.

The strategy for integrating hotspots into AthenaMuse is as follows:

1 On the creation of any still image object, check for the name of an associated hotspot list.

2 If such a list is present, read in the hotspots from storage.

3 Register the window as having active hotspots.

4 On receipt of any hotspot event, dispatch a message to a recipient EventScript object.

The two points of interest in this process are the window registration and the message dispatch to EventScript. The Hotspot event handler is responsible for checking events, for determining which hotspots may be affected, and for dispatching notification messages. This added complexity is not needed unless hotspots are being used. Registering the windows where hotspots are used speeds up the event processing by calling the hotspot routine only when necessary.

The user-level event processing is routed through EventScript. Thus an EventScript object must be ready to receive notification from the Hotspots event handler. This object receives notice of any X event in which the author indicates interest; it can then be processed with any of the resources of EventScript.

In AthenaMuse even still image objects may contain a sequence of frames ("still" refers to the display mechanism, not to any fundamental difference between a singular image and a sequence of images).

Thus, a still image may reference a sequence of hotspot lists, one for each frame. A sequence of frames, each with a different arrangement of hotspots, may sound suspiciously like "motion" video. Indeed, structurally there is no difference. The important detail, though, is the *speed* at which the frames are displayed.

The difficulty is that when a new image in a sequence is displayed, the old hotspots must be removed and new ones activated. At present, accurate synchronization is difficult to accomplish at the normal video rate of 30 frames per second.

The best that can be done is to refresh the hotspots whenever the video stops playing. In AthenaMuse this restriction applies equally to motion video and to still images; if the images are keyed to a timer, the hotspots can be active only while the timer is stopped.

SUMMARY

Images in a multimedia system sometimes are treated as units, with the whole image being the lowest-level data unit. Hotspots are an important tool for developing a deeper level of integration in a multimedia computing environment, for they allow cross-referencing between the specific *contents* of an image and any other data in the environment.

In a general utility, hotspots should have a number of characteristics. They should scale accurately with the host image, they should have quick response for event processing and rendering, and they should be flexible in terms of appearance and behavior. The *HotSpots* implementation described in this chapter is reasonably successful in all these areas.

One of the serious limitations of hotspots is that they are *geography based*—defined in terms of a fixed location on a specific image. If the image changes (aside from being scaled), the hotspot is invalidated. Photographic images do not usually encounter this problem; however, if the user can edit the image, the hotspots will be affected.

Another limitation at present is the difficulty of using hotspots with motion video sequences. Part of the problem is the creation of hotspots over a sequence of frames, which in general must still be done by hand. Even after the sequence of hotspots is made, there remains the question of whether the processor can synchronize them with the display at 30 frames per second.

There are a number of other methods to integrate images with their neighboring information in a multimedia environment. The simplest, and the precursor to hotspots, is the rectangular button overlay, where the button is defined to be transparent. This widely used technique saves the time involved in defining a polygonal hotspot and takes advantage of the existing event processing (as opposed to writing a custom event handler in EventScript, for example).

Another approach is to map the video image to a three-dimensional model. The mapping can be done in such a way that a click on a particular point of a known image can be projected into the model to identify the object.

The *Navigation* project (Chapter 7) uses this technique in a limited way: the panoramic views taken on the water surface of the Penobscot Bay are registered to true north; consequently, the location of a button click on any of these images can be translated into a compass bearing. The spatial organization of the database allows a directional search from a known point. Objects in the indicated direction can thus be retrieved, although there is some ambiguity in the search process.

Yokoyama, S., Maejima T., Kawamura, N., Williams, J., Conner, J. *CAPS (Computer Aided Presentation System)*, 1990, Intelligent Engineering Systems Laboratory, MIT.

In another project the designers constructed a geometric model of a room containing furniture and other objects (see Yokoyama). Placing a "camera" in the center of this room, they created an animation of a 360-degree rotation, which was recorded on video. The mouse clicks on any frame of this video sequence could then be accurately mapped back to the original model to identify and retrieve the object. This approach demonstrates the principle of data mapping; however, for something that was created as a vector-based geometric model, the use of video makes sense only if real-time graphic animation is not involved. With real-time graphic animation, there is no point in recording the passage in video; it can be manipulated directly as a graphic model. Another technique, but one with limited application, is to work with color or gray-scale values of an image, using these as the point of reference. In some cases, the color can be used to identify an object; so, on a mouse click, one can read the color under the pointer and use it to look up a reference.

Finally, the futurist may look to techniques of fully automatic feature extraction and object recognition. Their analysis of the contents of an image could be used as the basis of cross-referencing, thereby eliminating the need for hand tracing of images. As with speech recognition, these techniques are emerging slowly and applications today are available only in specialized domains.

18. Dynamic Graphics
   and Controllers

Dynamic graphics are circles, lines, polygons, or boxes that respond to changes in their environment. Their attributes—including size, color, and position—are tied to other values in the system in a *constraint* relationship. Normally the attributes of such graphic objects are fixed; the attribute specifies a size, location, or color. In dynamic graphics these attributes can be attached to the values of other variables in the environment. The result is that as one of the key values changes, the graphic or controller automatically responds. Any change at one end of the constraint is propagated automatically to the other.

Constraints have sometimes been used to manage the geometric layout of an image: graphic objects can be made to line up or change position automatically to adjust to changes in their neighboring objects. In this chapter the focus is on a broader use of constraint relations, whereby links are made to other *content* in the information environment. The links are used either for representing the state of other objects (visualization) or for animations that can be linked to other parts of a document. This is an issue of *integration;* one of the fundamental problems in multimedia computing is to find ways for different types of representations to work together—not simply be packed together "in the same box."

CONSTRAINTS

A. Borning, "The Programming Language Aspects of ThingLab," in *ACM Transactions on Programming Languages and Systems*, ACM Press, New York NY, October 1981, pp. 353–367.

Constraints are the basis of dynamic graphics and controllers. A constraint is a functional relation between two or more variables; when one of the variables changes, new values for the others are automatically computed (see Borning). Constraints are important in multimedia for another reason: they allow authors to define processes of change without writing procedures. The best example is the spreadsheet calculator; the spreadsheet uses a simple form of constraint where a cell may use a "formula" that looks to other cells when it computes its value. The spreadsheet has expanded the definition of the electronic document. At the same time, it has rendered the computer usable to a large population who would never write procedures for the programs they routinely write on a spreadsheet.

M. Stefik, D. Bobrow, and K. Kahn, "Integrating Access-Oriented Programming into a Multiparadigm Environment," in *IEEE Software*, Vol. 3, No. 1, January 1986.

Many varieties of constraints are possible. For example, they can be set up to *push* or *pull* their values. The spreadsheet cell normally *pulls* the values from other cells when it recomputes. In the so-called *active value* model, the variable *pushes* its new value to dependents as soon as it changes (see Stefik). In other words, it actively notifies its dependents that it has changed and causes them to recompute their values.

Constraints can be set up as one-way, two-way, or multiway relations. A one-way constraint works in one direction—*from* one variable *to* another—but not in reverse. Two-way constraints work both ways; a change in either variable will affect the value of the other. Multiway constraints involve more than two variables. A simple example is an addition constraint to maintain an $a + b = c$ relation. If any two of the values are set, the third will be computed to satisfy the constraint. Multiway constraints offer rich possibilities, but they introduce more complex issues in implementation and use: relations can be overdefined or underdefined (when too many or too few of the components are set), they can involve cyclic dependencies, and so on.

The constraint-based examples described here are relatively simple, intended to demonstrate how constraints can be included in a document model. The following paragraphs illustrate the use of dynamic graphics in different applications described in this book and present some of the issues involved in their implementation and use.

Scrollbar

The scrollbars used in AthenaMuse are implemented in such a way that they can be constrained to the AthenaMuse package dimensions.

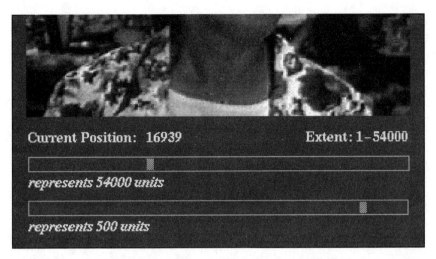

Figure 18.1   Three representations of the current position attribute of a dimension. This package has a single dimension, *Frame*, that extends from 1–54000. The current position (16939) is displayed numerically by a dynamic graphic label. The first scrollbar represents the entire extent, although not every position can be reached directly. Since this scrollbar is 480 pixels wide, each pixel must represent over 112 frames. To address this problem, every AthenaMuse scrollbar responds to a built-in action that increments or decrements the associated dimension by one unit, even if the scrollbar's thumb doesn't move at all. A more flexible solution for offering fine-grain control is illustrated by the second scrollbar above. It represents only the current 500-frame subsection of the dimension's total extent. When the dimension's position reaches 17000, the second scrollbar will "wrap around" to the left.

As an example of a two-way relationship, a change on the scrollbar (from user input) can affect a dimension, and a change in the dimension (from a timer, for example) will affect the appearance of the scrollbar. Dimensions have three principal attributes: current position, range (breadth of the active region around the current position), and rate. The scrollbars can be connected to any of these values in a two-way constraint relationship.

Most video documents use a scrollbar of this kind to serve as a "cursor," as in Figure 18.1. The scrollbar slider moves forward and backward to show the current position within the video sequence. The scrollbar acts as an input mechanism as well: dragging the scrollbar slider causes the video to scroll forward and back through the sequence. It need not be linked directly to the video—it is mediated through the dimension.

The video document in Figure 18.1 has two scrollbars. One represents the entire length of the document, in this case 54,000 frames.

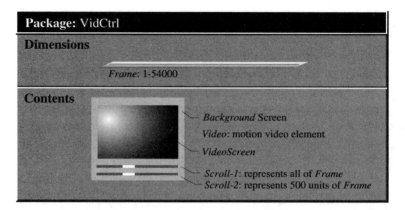

Figure 18.2   Package structure for document in 18.1

The second is defined to represent 500 frames at a time; it is used for frame-accurate searching once the general area has been located. As time advances the second scrollbar "wraps" around to the beginning after each 500 frames.

Figure 18.2 shows the structure of the document as it is implemented in AthenaMuse. The dimension *Frame* defines the overall range of 54,000 units. The *Video* element specifies the mapping between the 54,000 frames in the videodisc "file" and the 54,000 units of the *Frame* dimension. It also directs the video display to the screen named *VideoScreen*.

The two scrollbars are defined in the *Scroll* elements. Along with their general appearance attributes, some mapping information is included which indicates that they are to appear on screen *Background* as long as the dimension position is between 1 and 54000 (all the time, in other words).

The scrollbar definition has one other item, which declares the relationship between the scrollbar and the dimension *Frame*. This is the *represents* statement; its arguments declare which dimension in which package to connect to, which attribute to pay attention to, and how many units to represent with the width of the scrollbar. The first shows 54000 frames and the second 500.

The AthenaMuse parser produces objects from these definitions. Each time the *represents* directive is encountered, two things happen. First, a special "constraint" object is created, which contains the mapping information. Second, a pointer to this constraint is added to the scrollbar and to a list of constraint pointers maintained by the dimension.

In this application the *Frame* dimension ends up with a list of two constraints, one for each scrollbar. Each time the user drags one of the sliders, the first part of the constraint—*scroll_control_package*()—is invoked. This function checks the scrollbar position and uses it to reset the dimension. As soon as the dimension is changed, all of the elements in the package are updated—first the video, then the controls. As this updating takes place, the second part of the constraint is invoked—*update_dimension_representations()*. The dimension goes down its list of constraints and uses its current setting to reposition each of the scrollbars.

One could imagine an infinite loop at this point, where the repositioning of the scrollbars would cause a slight change in the dimension and thereby start the whole process again. But looping of this kind is suppressed; each item can be repositioned only once per cycle.

This example of a basic two-way constraint in operation is driven by a pair of functions that propagate values between the two connected objects. These functions are predefined. The only detail left to the user is which dimension attribute to connect to. It is possible to create new constraints with the EventScript portion of AthenaMuse. (The controller for the *Navigation* project described below is an example of a two-way constraint implemented in EventScript.) Two-way constraints each require two methods, one for each direction of the constraint.

For the most part, the dynamic graphics described in the following sections are based on one-way constraints; the dimensions affect the graphics, but the graphics do not affect the dimensions.

Page Counters

The first example of such an object is the "page counter," a graphic text object that can change the text it displays. Normally a text object is specified in terms of its screen position, font, color, and so on, and *a specific set of characters* that it draws on the screen.

In the AthenaMuse graphic text object, the quoted string can be replaced by a *constraint reference*. For a page counter, the constraint would be *set_label_equal*. This constraint is given an attribute of a dimension as its target—either its rate, current position, or range. It establishes a relationship between the graphic object and the dimension attribute. Each time the graphic is updated (each time the position on the dimension changes), this function is called to generate a new character string. It works by checking the new value of the dimension attribute and converting it into a character string.

```
element "Time"
{
    type graphic
    screen_name "Vid.bg"
    active
    map label
    {
        pos_in 1
        pos_out 54000
        label set_label_equal("Video.time.position")
        x1 12
        y1 12
        foreground 152
        erase 1
    }
}
```

From the developer's perspective, he or she has created a text object in the usual way, except that a function call is put in place of the text.

An Animated Particle

The same technique can be applied to the *position* of a graphic object. Figure 18.3 shows part of the internal structure of a graphic object, as AthenaMuse sees it — in this case a rectangle. The position and size of a rectangle are defined by four parameters: *x1, y1, x2,* and *y2*. The same is true of other graphic objects, including the line and arc. The illustration shows how each of these attributes can be set with a fixed value or computed dynamically using a function pointer/parameter pair (Figure 18.3).

When the object is displayed, the function pointer slots are checked for each of the four control points. If a function pointer is found, the function is called to compute a new value, which is stored in the corresponding value slot. This value is retained so that the previous display of the object can be erased before the new one is drawn. If the function pointer slot is found empty, the content of the value slot is used instead. The result is that each of the four controlling values can be attached to a dimension—this means the *x, y,* width, and height of the rectangle can be controlled separately.

Different functions can be used to bind these attributes to the dimensions. The most common is a simple linear function that computes the new attribute value based on one of the dimension's attributes, multiplying by a scalar and adding an offset. Figure 18.4 shows an animated yo-yo, where the graphics are attached to a dimen-

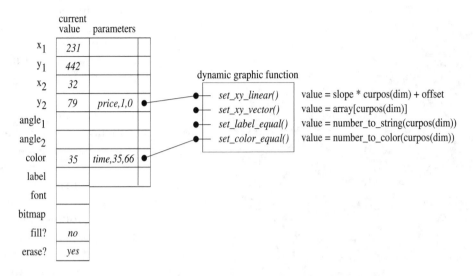

Figure 18.3   Dynamic Graphic implementation. In this example, the height of a rectangle is computed dynamically as a linear function of the *price* dimension. Its color varies over a range of values determined by the *time* dimension. The other values remain the same.

sion. A scrollbar is attached to the dimension in a *represents* relation, as described above. As the slider is dragged, the yo-yo automatically readjusts its position: the scrollbar moves the dimension, which causes the elements to update, and the graphic recomputes its position based on the new setting of the dimension. Different features of the graphic can be handled separately. Thus, the yo-yo can be made to expand as it drops and retract as it rises. Its size can be linked to a separate dimension, controlled by a separate timer or scrollbar controller to make size independent of position. In this way a single graphic object can be used to represent many independent dimensions of information.

Aside from the linear function used to control the yo-yo, a different function allows the graphic to move along a set of points in a vertex list. The graphic can follow an arbitrary path around the screen, using the dimension position as an index to a list of user-defined vertices. The CERN *Diorama* project described in Chapter 8 uses this technique to display animated particles moving around the path of the particle accelerators used for physics research at CERN (Figure 18.5).

The first step in creating such an animation is to define a path on the screen and store it in a file as a vertex list. In the case of the CERN material, this was done by displaying the video background—one of several aerial photographs of CERN with the position of the acceler-

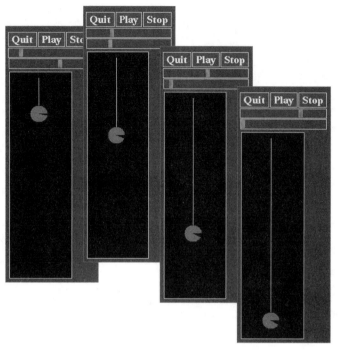

Figure 18.4   Yo-yo in action

ator highlighted. The points were defined using a simple Athena-Muse "points editor"; the author must mark each point with a click of the mouse. The points are stored in a file, which can then be used to feed a dynamic graphic. The display function uses the current position of a dimension called "Time" to index this set of points and determine the appropriate position for the graphic. At one level, a graphic object that follows a user-defined vertex list is rather ordinary. The important point is that the graphics are integrated into a much broader document architecture with a general interface. All of the cross-referencing machinery is available; the animation can be controlled by any other document in the environment.

An Animated Compass

Another of the objects defined as a graphic in AthenaMuse is a "pixmap," a raster image that can be drawn on the screen. In AthenaMuse the pixmap object can contain a sequence of images, rather than a single image only. The display routine for the object needs the name of the file containing the images, identification of the image in the sequence to display, and its location on the screen. As a dynamic graphic object, the screen position and the image number can be bound to dimensions.

Binding the image number to a dimension means that the dimension can be used to make the object step through its list of images in sequence, as an animation. The position can be bound to one or more dimensions as well, so the image can be moved around the screen.

One use of such an object was a customized controller for the *Navigation* project (described in Chapter 7). It sometimes happens in building an application that a special control interface mechanism or policy is needed. With the normal "toolkit" approach used with X

Windows and Motif, one must dive into the source code and build a new widget—something not done on a whim!

For the *Navigation* interface, we wanted the controller shown in Figure 18.6. This controller has two functions. First, it controls the heading of the simulated boat in the application. Second, it indicates the current field of view from the boat. The application shows a 90 degree photographic view of the boat's surroundings, based on its current position and "view angle." The controller is meant to determine which 90 degrees out of the full 360 are being displayed.

The controller acts on two corresponding dimensions, *IconPos* and *ViewPos*. The display of the controller is implemented by means of graphic objects. In the middle of the controller is a pixmap object showing a bird's-eye view of a boat. This pixmap has thirty images that

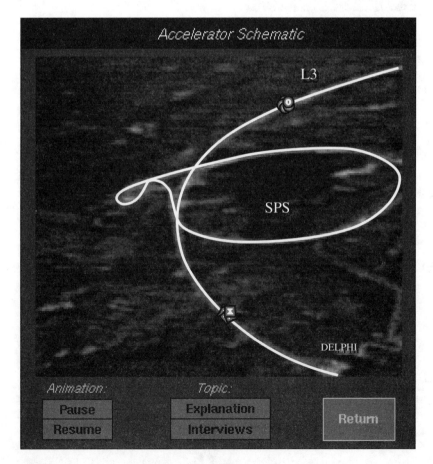

Figure 18.5   Dynamic graphics used for animation

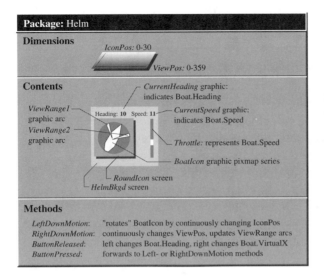
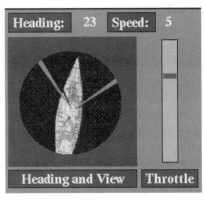

Figure 18.6   Dynamic Graphics in the *Navigation* project

show the boat turning in twelve-degree increments. The image number is bound to the *IconPos* dimension, so whenever *IconPos* changes the boat turns. The field of view is implemented as a pair of graphic arcs that respond to the *ViewPos* dimension. Both the boat and the arcs are displayed in a round window, which has an EventScript method for handling button presses and mouse movement. These methods reset the *IconPos* dimension whenever the user clicks or drags the left button, and they reset the *ViewPos* when the right button is used.

SUMMARY

In AthenaMuse we implemented limited versions of dynamic graphics and controllers. Our aim was to find better ways to integrate these graphics into the multimedia environment. Dynamic graphics, with their attributes connected to the dimensions, provide an interesting mechanism for handling both visualization and animation. The significant point is that these objects exist within the context of a broader document architecture—they can be manipulated through standard methods as normal parts of a compound document.

Other systems have implemented much more sophisticated approaches to defining and servicing constraints. The purpose here is to show how the concept can be applied in the context of a general communication environment. Constraints will be a notable aspect of such systems; they can be used to represent or visualize other data values, and they can be used to control animations. Both functions are important in terms of integrating the graphic information with other resources in a multimedia application or document. Constraints allow users to specify processes of change without writing procedures; in this respect they offer a powerful tool in reducing the burden of authorship.

To look ahead, the dynamic graphics described here can be projected into more sophisticated examples of visualization and animation; the data mapping will be more complex and the animations will move into three dimensions. What suffers under the limitations of today's CPU speeds shows acceptable performance on the next generation machines. Part of the power of the faster machines will undoubtedly be used to support this type of material.

19. Video Device Control

Contributed by: DANIEL I. APPLEBAUM

As programs were developed at MIT to provide access to visual information stored on videodiscs, it became evident that some system of remote access was needed. At first, a videodisc player was put next to each workstation. It was controlled by each application and its output was connected directly to the workstation (Figure 19.1).

Asking users to carry videodiscs to the workstation was not an acceptable solution, however. And permanent mounting of video resources locally was impractical. The only viable option appeared to be building a centralized video repository and distributing the analog video signals to the local workstations over the MIT campus cable television (CATV) system.

This chapter describes the "video server" that was implemented to perform these functions. A *video server* is a computer program that mediates access to scarce video resources among a number of competing applications called *video clients*. The server responds to client requests for performance of operations on video devices, such as playing or recording video segments. The request protocol is abstract enough to prevent client dependency on a particular piece of video equipment (Figure 19.2).

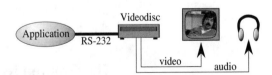

Figure 19.1 Direct device control. An application sends instructions directly to one or more video devices, making it dependent on their interface protocols. Although simple to implement, this method doesn't allow different applications to share access to the same video resources.

241

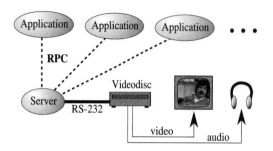

Figure 19.2   Client/Server Device Control. The limitations of direct control are overcome by having a single *server* program arbitrate access to devices using a generic RPC (remote procedure call) interface. This protocol insulates applications from idiosyncratic device-level interfaces. In addition, the *client* applications can be local (on the same machine as the server) or remote (anywhere on the network).

One may ask, "What about digital video? Isn't network access to compressed video just around the corner? Why should we be interested in anything using analog video at this point in time?" There are two reasons why an analog system is worth considering. First, many of the access and control issues are relevant whether the distribution is in the analog or digital format. Second, while digital video technology is advancing rapidly, hybrid systems employing existing analog storage and distribution mechanisms will still be widely used for some time.

DISTRIBUTED VIDEO

The *Image Delivery System*, the target application for the video server project, was intended to give network access to the collection of several hundred thousand images at MIT's Rotch Visual Library. Various parts of this collection were recorded on videodisc, with the idea of placing a video server at the library to provide access to these resources from anywhere on campus. A computer at the library would support the server, controlling a bank of videodisc players and a switcher (Figure 19.3). The server would receive requests for images over the Ethernet from client applications. It would locate the material on one of the videodiscs and connect that machine to a dedicated channel on the campus cable system. Then it would send notification to the client to capture the image on the local workstation.

In order to perform these functions, a software system was required that could process these incoming requests. It would control the switcher, tuner, and videodisc devices, and communicate with the clients. *Galatea* is the system that was subsequently developed.

The Galatea Network Video Device Control System

The main design objective for Galatea was that any client application should have access to the resources of many video services such as the one at the Rotch Library. But handling negotiation with many video servers would be a burden to the client application. Therefore, a "local" Galatea server runs on the same workstation as the client application program and handles requests from the client program. If this server manages local video resources, it can use them to process requests directly. Or it can contact other servers and pass along client requests. The client application needs only to contact the local Galatea server; any remote access needs are forwarded automatically to these other servers.

Every Galatea server is identical. There are not "local" and "remote" versions of the server software. Each server is capable of controlling local resources, servicing requests from client applications, and forwarding requests to other servers. In fact, the manner in which a Galatea server contacts another Galatea server is by pretending to be a client application. There is no special protocol between Galatea servers for forwarding requests. It is therefore possible to "chain" servers. One Galatea server can contact another Galatea server, which can contact yet another server. In addition, a single Galatea server can contact several remote servers, so the chain of servers actually becomes a tree. In this way a client application can gain access to a broad set of resources without managing complicated information.

NETWORK TRANSPARENCY

The client application is passed a list of available videodiscs and can make requests for actions on any of these resources. This list is compiled from all the available servers. The client application is never informed by the Galatea server about the *locations* of the available videodiscs. If the desired videodisc is local, the local Galatea server will handle the request; otherwise the request will be forwarded to the appropriate remote server. The client need never know where the material is coming from.

Each server uses a local "configuration file" to determine what materials it is controlling locally and what remote servers it should contact when it starts. The

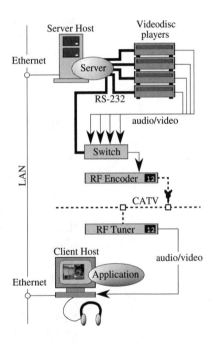

Figure 19.3 Analog Video Server Configuration. This schematic shows how the Rotch Visual Collection of slides is delivered to remote applications all over the MIT campus. A central Galatea server manages four copies of the videodisc library to improve response time. The audiovisual output of the Galatea server is broadcast on a reserved channel of MIT's cable television (CATV) network. Control information takes a different path from the video information, using the local area network (LAN) to transport the Galatea protocol.

person who builds the configuration file can assign arbitrary "volume names" to each videodisc. When the application is passed these names from the Galatea server, it displays them, so that the user can select which videodisc to use.

Optimized Image Delivery

Galatea was designed to use multiple copies of the same videodisc efficiently. When the system starts up, if the server finds the same name listed more than once, it records the listings as multiple copies of the same volume even if they reside on different servers. When a piece of information is needed, it does not matter which copy is used, only that one is available. The client specifies to Galatea which volume it wishes to control, not which copy of the videodisc. The Galatea server then finds an appropriate copy of the videodisc with which to respond to the request.

The most significant advantage of using volumes instead of explicit videodiscs is in searching for videodisc frames. When a client application requests a search for an individual videodisc frame on a volume, a videodisc player may take up to five seconds to find the frame, depending on how much of the videodisc it needs to traverse. When multiple copies are available in a volume, Galatea can query each player that contains a copy of the videodisc in order to determine which player is closest to the requested frame. The Galatea server will then use that videodisc player in processing the client's request.

This method provides substantial improvement in applications that use a large number of still frames. Programs often request up to forty single frames in rapid sequence, in order to display them in response to a user request. The use of two copies of a videodisc, instead of a single copy, greatly reduces the time required to view the forty frames.

The other advantage of multiple copies of a volume is dependability. When providing service to an entire campus, continuing availability of information is very important, so Galatea is designed to compensate for equipment failures.

Abstracting Device Control

Hiding the details of device control from the client application is another important goal for Galatea. Client applications should not be responsible for tracking the locations, quantities, or brand names of the videodisc players available. The Galatea server is responsible for concealing these characteristics. It builds an internal table which contains information about all of the videodisc resources available. This table is used in handling client requests, and only part of it is passed to the client. The client receives the names of the volumes available and the characteristics of each volume. There are limited differences among the devices that Galatea was intended to control, so the client can use a generic set of commands that Galatea interprets for the individual devices.

Galatea has "device control modules" for videodisc players, one for each make and model of each type of device. When the client request is executed, the Galatea server uses the functions that are appropriate for the particular kind of videodisc player. By taking this responsibility, the Galatea server eliminates the need for changing the client application when new types of videodisc players are introduced to the environment. The Galatea server needs to be changed—but that is only one program, whereas there may be many client applications that would otherwise need modification. This Galatea server functionality implies that the client application can be written in a "device-independent" manner, ignoring the particular videodisc player models available.

Record-Playback Devices

The largest class of devices controlled by Galatea are the *record-playback devices* which includes videodisc players. These machines offer a relatively consistent set of functions, primarily concerned with searching for frames, playing video forward and backward at different speeds, and switching audio channels on or off (Figure 19.4).

Different machines offer different capabilities in terms of speed and search functions: some can play only at fixed speeds, others play at continuously variable speeds within a certain range. Galatea receives requests from applications that involve continuously variable speeds. If necessary, it will quantize such a request to one of the fixed speeds supported by a given machine.

From this illustration of the difficulties in developing a device-independent interface, we can see that there is no easy way to accommodate differences across the range of devices. Either the server can send the client precise distinctions among the devices, which puts the burden of handling them on the application programmer, or the server can "interpret" the client request, which means that the client may be limited in how it takes advantage of special device functions.

Figure 19.4   A Galatea client application. This is a video controller called "gctl" distributed with the Galatea software. The custom spring-loaded scrollbar affects the rate of playback of the current video device. The middle position pauses the device, while positions to the left and right cause it to speed up in forward and reverse. This was designed to emulate the physical "joystick" controllers found in many commercial video editing systems. There is also a set of indicator "lights" showing the currently selected channels (video, left audio, and right audio) and a list of available video volumes (if more than one is present).

Complex Requests

In some instances Galatea provides support for more complex operations. A *segment* of video is a set of frames bounded by a start and an end frame. Not only can Galatea play segments in forward or reverse at a specified speed, but it can also manage *lists* of segments, playing whole sequences.

Similarly, a *dub* operation can be invoked, which plays a segment on one videodisc while recording it on another and thereby produces a new copy of the segment. Such an operation entails a whole sequence of commands, some of which must be initiated by the client application. Before a record operation can take place, for example, the application must request an allocation of recordable frames to make certain there is room for the new material.

Live Video Sources

Although most of the Galatea system is concerned with controlling videodiscs in a sophisticated manner, it is often necessary to view "uncontrolled" sources, such as broadcast television or camera output. For these cases Galatea creates an uncontrolled input volume. A client application can request to view such a volume, but no other controls are available.

Video Switchers

With more than one video source to control, Galatea must provide switching services. Switches control the distribution of the video from a record-playback device to the display device.

In the Rotch Visual Library system, for example, four videodisc players are connected to the input channels of a video/audio switch. The output channel of the switch is connected to the CATV cable. The switcher as well as the videodisc players can be software controlled, the principal function being to connect one of its input channels to one of its output channels.

Virtual Switchers

The communication between Galatea servers was modeled after the operation of physical video switches. With the idea of hiding the actual location of video materials, the goal is to create a large *virtual switcher* which links the resources of the various physical switching devices.

To accomplish this aim, Galatea is equipped with *virtual inputs* and *virtual outputs* in addition to whatever *physical* inputs and *physical* outputs it may have under its control. The virtual inputs and outputs can be joined to other servers or to display devices (including the workstation video input). The connection between servers is made by linking a virtual output from one server to a virtual input of the other server. Thus, any other servers appear to Galatea as switchers; requests for service are delivered as if to another physical switching device.

The client, when connecting to the Galatea server, identifies for the server the virtual output to which it should be connected. The Galatea server then passes to the client the list of volumes that can be routed through the virtual switch to that virtual output. When the client makes a request to view a particular volume, the server manipulates the physical switches in the "virtual switch" in order to route an appropriate videodisc player to the client. The volume table in the server keeps track of which videodisc players are connected to which inputs of the virtual switch. Since the list of volumes passed to the client contains videodiscs from multiple servers, a request for a volume can cause the Galatea server to choose a videodisc player on a remote server, thus causing physical switching on multiple servers.

LIFE (AND DEATH) ON A NETWORK

One of the problems in designing a distributed system is coping with distributed technical difficulties. The Galatea server had to be designed in such a way that the failure of one server on the network did not cause the remainder to lock up; additional server-to-server protocol was needed. Although a Galatea server emulates a client when connecting to another "remote" server, there is one request that only a server can make of another server: that is a "registration request," which identifies the client as a server. This registration allows more effective interserver communication.

Normal Shutdown

The first situation in which the information in a server's register is used is when it is being shut down normally. When a Galatea server is notified by the operating system that the computer is being shut down, the server sends a short message to all servers in its register. These client servers, which were previously connected to this server, now disconnect and rebuild their volume tables without references to the now unavailable videodisc resources.

System Failure

If the Galatea server is brought down because the computer crashed or was shut off without warning, this clean disconnect procedure will not take place, as the Galatea server has no chance to send out the notification messages. The same is true when the network between two servers fails, as the remote server is not informed of the network failure.

Network Failure

When a Galatea server is halted and cannot send out shutdown notification, the client servers will eventually detect the failure when requests to the now nonexistent server fail to evoke a response. When such a failure is detected, the client server will rebuild its volume table just as if the notification had occurred. Note that each client server must discover this failure mode separately, whereas in the first case, the terminating server notifies all of its client servers at the same time.

In either case, when the failed server restarts it invokes a notification procedure, which informs all of its previous client servers that its services are once more available. The client servers then reconnect to the remote server, rebuilding their volume tables to contain the videodisc resources from that remote server.

If the network between two servers is the unit that fails, the remote server does not send out a notification that it is available again, since the state of the network is not known to the server. Instead, the client servers periodically poll the remote server to determine if it is available. The poll elicits a response only when the remote server is running and the network between the two servers is fully functional. When a server gets a poll message, it responds by sending back a notification, just like the notification it sends when it is restarted. The poller reconnects to the remote server and rebuilds its volume table accordingly.

Sharing Resources

A further task of Galatea is to allow efficient but consistent sharing of videodisc resources. When one client makes a request of the Galatea server, that client expects to receive video information relating to its own request, not the request of another client request. For example, the clients could be sharing both the videodisc players and the cable television channel used to distribute the video signals.

Two mechanisms are in place to allow sharing of resources without conflicts. The first is mainly for the use of single-frame search applications. When a frame is requested, the server finds the frame, performs the appropriate switching to route the video to the client workstation, then notifies the client that the frame is available. The server waits for the client to respond that it is done with the frame. Until the client so responds, the server will not answer the request of any other client. However, the server will only wait about five seconds for the client's response. This restriction prevents one client from totally dominating the server. Usually the client digitizes the delivered video frame in less than one second, so a five-second delivery window is more than sufficient.

This form of conflict protection guarantees that single requests do not get confused. Sometimes, however, a client needs to request a sequence of operations in order to set up the videodisc appropriately. In this case, the client can prevent the server from responding to other clients' requests by "locking" the server. The client can then set various parameters on a videodisc player, get delivery of the desired frame, and digitize it. The client can even repeat this process a few times. A more complicated delivery is possible than is available with the normal conflict protection mechanism. Server locks are also restricted in time, but usually last at least thirty seconds in order to allow complex setup procedures.

SUMMARY

G. Davenport and W. Mackay, "Virtual Video Editing in Interactive Multimedia Applications," in *Communications of the ACM*, July 1989.

R. Schneeman, "Porting Multimedia Applications to the Open System Environment," in *IEEE Software*, Vol. 9, No. 6, November 1992, pp. 39–47.

This chapter has described in some detail the workings of a complex video server for distributing analog signals over a cable television system. The Galatea software has brought to light a number of issues that will continue to remain relevant to the delivery of video services, whether in analog or digital format. The AthenaMuse authoring system is layered upon the Galatea software, as are some exploratory video editing and viewing systems being developed by Media Lab researchers (see Davenport). Galatea is also being used outside of MIT at dozens of sites, including the National Institute of Standards and Technology (see Schneeman). The source code to Galatea has been made available for unrestricted use in the hope that others may benefit from this work. Galatea version 2.5 is available to Internet sites using anonymous ftp, from *media-lab.media.mit.edu*.

20. Broadband Network Computing

Contributed by: JOSÉ DIAZ-GONZALEZ

This book is based on the idea that computers will assume a major role as a communication medium. Multimedia technology holds an important place in this vision, but network distribution is equally critical. In this chapter we review the key issues in broadband (high-speed) network computing and assess the progress toward making distributed multimedia communications a reality.

In order to achieve a broadband network computing environment that can support multimedia applications, substantial improvements must be made in a number of critical technologies:

- Real-time network protocols for continuous media;

- Real-time operating systems and distributed network services;

- High-performance object stores;

- Multimedia object interoperability;

- Multimedia application development environments.

The last of these areas is treated elsewhere in this book. The first four are addressed in the following sections.

NETWORK PROTOCOLS FOR CONTINUOUS MEDIA

There are two basic types of communications networks: circuit switched and packet switched. Circuit switching is used today in the public telephone network, as well as in private voice and video networks. Packet switching is commonly used in computer networks. With circuit switched networks, an actual physical connection (the circuit) is temporarily allocated to communicating entities for the duration of a communications session. This approach has been preferred for continuous media, such as audio and video, because with dedicated resources there is no delay in transmission.

With packet switched networks, the information to be transmitted is partitioned into packets of various sizes. These are routed through the network without locking resources—the packets may even travel by different pathways to reach their destination. This approach allows more people to use limited network resources.

Packet switched networks have been employed primarily for computer applications, such as remote terminal access, file transfers, electronic mail, and the like.

For these purposes, reliability is far more important than timing; a few lost bits can have a profound impact on numeric data or a computer program, whereas delivery delay will generally not be noticed. With video and audio data the opposite is true; delay in delivery stands out far more prominently than lost bits.

		Layer	Function
application services are provided by the upper layer infrastructure	7	application	responsible for managing the communications between applications
	6	presentation	responsible for adding structure to the units of data that are exchanged
	5	session	responsible for adding control mechanisms to the data exchange
end-to-end services are provided by the lower layer infrastructure	4	transport	responsible for reliability and multiplexing of data transfer across the network
	3	network	responsible for data transfer across the network
	2	data link	responsible for transmission, framing, and error control over a single communications link
	1	physical	responsible for the electro-mechanical interface to the communications media

Figure 20.1   The seven layers of the OSI network model

From the perspective of multimedia computing, the challenge is to design a network technology that can satisfy the requirements of both classes of material. The current trend is toward packet switched networks that are modified to support time-critical delivery constraints. A network is a complicated set of services and processes that govern the many details of packaging and routing information. Collectively, the specification of these services is referred to as a network protocol.

Network protocols are structured in layers. Each layer handles some aspect of communicating information from one point to another. When a network transaction is initiated, each layer receives information from the layer above. It adds its own information and passes the package to the layer below. At the lowest level, the final result is transmitted over the physical network to the recipient node. It may be passed to one or more *intermediate nodes* along the way, which will unbundle enough of the package to route the message to the next point. When it reaches its final destination, it is unpackaged and passed through the layers in reverse order. The discussion in this section outlines protocol issues at the different layers of a network architecture, with the OSI Reference Model (OSIRM) as the framework for the discussion. Figure 20.1 outlines the seven layers of the model and their respective functions.

The Lower Layers

At the lower levels there are two principal characteristics of a network architecture that relate to distributing multimedia. The first is *bandwidth availability*, which determines how fast data can be moved from one point to another. The second is *bandwidth allocation*, which determines how the bandwidth can be shared among a number of users.

Bandwidth availability If a network is considered an information pipeline, bandwidth is analogous to the size of the pipe; it determines how fast data can be moved. Bandwidth is measured in bits per second—kilobits per second, (Kbps), megabits per second, (Mbps), or gigabits per second, (Gbps). Bandwidth is an important issue for multimedia service because of the quantity of data to be transferred (Figure 20.2). A forty-page text document contains roughly 1 Mbit of data; ten of these documents can be transmitted in one second over a 10 Mbps network (Ethernet, for example).

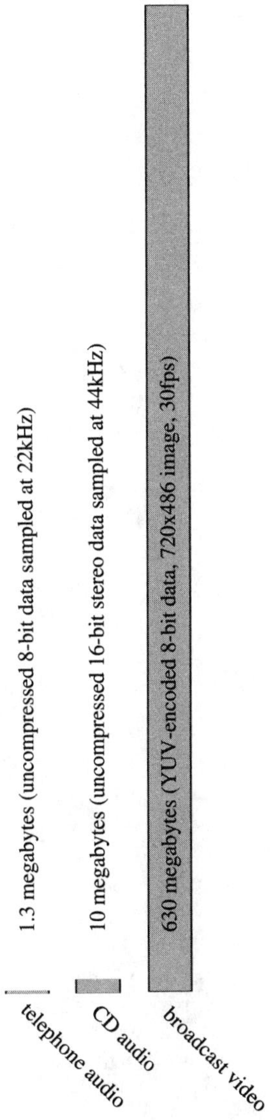

1.3 megabytes (uncompressed 8-bit data sampled at 22kHz)

10 megabytes (uncompressed 16-bit stereo data sampled at 44kHz)

630 megabytes (YUV-encoded 8-bit data, 720x486 image, 30fps)

telephone audio

CD audio

broadcast video

Figure 20.2 The digital storage capacity required to hold one minute of typical continuous media sources

On the other hand, one second of uncompressed digital video contains about 220 Mbits of data (640 by 480 raster, 24 bits deep, 30 frames per second). The 10 Mbps network that so easily transmitted text documents for many people fails by an order of magnitude for even a single video user. Note that video compression reduces this data rate considerably and makes it possible to consider a practical multimedia network. A number of network architectures offer bandwidths suitable for distributed multimedia. Networks of roughly 100 Mbps are available now (FDDI, ISDN), while still larger networks—the so-called gigabit optical networks—are under development.

	Physical	**Data Link**	**Topology**
FDDI	Copper or multi-mode fiber 100 Mbps	Timed token ring variable size frames (max 4500 bytes/frame)	Shared, dual counter-rotating rings
DQDB	Wire or fiber 45 Mbps (DS3)	Distributed queue access to timed slots	Shared, dual or looped bus
ISDN	Twisted pair 2 channels at 64 Kbps and 1 at 16 Kbps	Time Division Multiplexing (TDM)	Circuit-switching mesh
B-ISDN, ATM LAN	Optical fiber 155 Mbps to 644 Mbps	Asynchronous Transfer Mode (ATM)	Packet-switching mesh

A short-term approach to providing ATM technology is to graft the data link model and switching technology for ATM onto the physical layer encoding scheme used in FDDI.

With respect to bandwidth availability, two further points are worth noting. First, the network configurations described above do not treat the problem of how the network bandwidth is handled when it reaches the desktop. Bus speeds and I/O throughput at the workstation itself are also part of the link between the data source and the user's screen. Two approaches are being explored: faster bus and I/O hardware, and "desktop LANs" that would eliminate the workstation bus altogether and replace it with an internal packet switch linking the motherboard and peripheral subsystems.

Secondly, compression technologies for image and video radically reduce the amount of data transmitted and consequently lower the bandwidth needed for an application. The current generation of compression technologies includes the ISO's JPEG and MPEG standards for still and motion images respectively, and Intel's proprietary DVI technology. These are all based on Discrete Cosine Transform (DCT) algorithms.

JPEG is ISO JTC1/SC2/WG10; MPEG is ISO 11172 (JTC1/SC2/WG11).

Dynamic Bandwidth Allocation Multimedia information is "bursty"— some parts of a transmission require enormous bandwidth, while others require very little (as in a document that combines video and text). If a network user locks up bandwidth based on the highest possible level of use, much of that resource will be sitting idle while other users may be waiting to use the network. Some network architectures are able to allocate bandwidth dynamically so that it is consumed by a user only as needed. This more efficient use of a limited resource will be increasingly important in multimedia networking.

Fast, fixed-size, packet-switched transfer models (also known as cell switching) offer this type of bandwidth allocation flexibility. The Asynchronous Transfer Mode (ATM), advocated in the Broadband

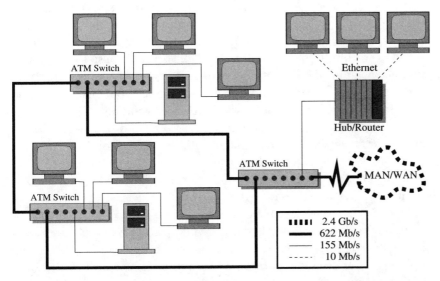

Figure 20.3   Future ATM LAN configuration. The ATM LAN is attractive both for its scalable bandwidth connections and its potential to seamlessly integrate public and private networks. Individual workstations, file servers, and hubs tying together existing LANs will connect to small switches in department-sized clusters (multiples of 8) at 155 Mbps over multi-mode fiber or data-grade unshielded twisted pair (UTP-5). The switches will probably be linked on a building-wide basis using 622 Mbps connections over single-mode fiber. Someday switches may be able to tie into public gigabit networks running at up to 2.4 Gbps over single-mode fiber.

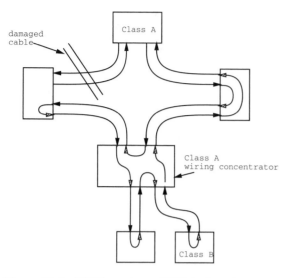

Figure 20.4 FDDI topology. FDDI is based on dual counter-rotating token rings looping through each network node. Class A devices have access to two independent segments in case one fails. Class B devices rely on a single segment.

SONET is a physical layer encoding scheme designed for optical fiber networks. Initially it will operate at OC-3 and OC-12 bit rates (155 Mbps and 644 Mbps).

Integrated Services Digital Network (B-ISDN), represents the best-known instance of the cell-switching model. While B-ISDN is being developed by telephone companies for large public networks, several computer companies and network equipment vendors are driving the deployment of ATM technology in the local area network (LAN) environment (Figure 20.3). ATM LANs are being used to connect high-performance multimedia workstations in communication-intensive settings, where ATM's bandwidth reservation characteristics are critical to maintaining simultaneous data, voice, and video transmissions.

ATM can be contrasted with the conventional Time Division Multiplexing (TDM) approach (used in narrow-band ISDN). With TDM, information is fitted into predefined time slots of fixed bit capacity. Each communication "circuit" is handled in terms of these time slots; everything is routed according to the time slot it occupies. The time slot is not easily adapted dynamically; each circuit uses a fixed amount of resources regardless of whether or not its time slots are filled. For instance, while FDDI satisfies the bandwidth availability requirements of multimedia applications, its shared media nature limits access to the ring(s) to the station in possession of the token (Figure 20.4). This type of contention makes it difficult for applications to receive performance guarantees when transporting continuous media such as audio and video.

With the ATM approach, the information is put into fixed-size packets (53 bytes) that can be intermixed anywhere inside the large payload frame provided by the Synchronous Optical NETwork (SONET). Each packet carries a "circuit identifier" and is switched according to the circuit identifier it carries, not according to the time slot in which it is found. This easily accommodates variations in packet frequency, but has the disadvantage that carrying and checking the circuit identifiers slows transmission. By contrast, with the use of multistage switching fabrics, the fixed-size cell of ATM helps speed up the switching process; only the header needs to be examined, and the cell becomes almost self-routable through the switch stages (Figure 20.5).

The Upper Layers

Whatever the network configuration at the lower layers, there are many issues to be resolved at the higher-level protocol layers as well. To support multimedia traffic, extensive changes are needed on the "end-to-end" layers of the OSI model: the transport, session, presentation, and application layers.

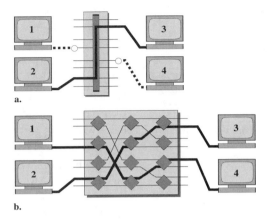

Transport Layer First, at the transport layer, mechanisms for specifying the grade of service for an isochronous (time-critical) connection are needed. Network management systems will use this information to determine the appropriate allocation of network resources needed to guarantee the level of service requested and to avoid network congestion.

Use of transport protocol priorities allows graceful degradation of a service, provided that the multimedia data is encoded with one of the hierarchical coding schemes that separate low-frequency and high-frequency information. In this approach the low-frequency data gives the general structure of an image, while the high-frequency data provides the fine-grained detail. Packets containing the low-frequency information would be assigned high priority for on-time delivery, while the high-frequency information would be ranked somewhat lower. Under these circumstances, it would be possible to drop packets containing the higher frequencies and still maintain respectable quality of service (see Karlsson).

Figure 20.5 Cell-Switching Architecture. In (a), each port is connected to a shared data bus. Information flowing between nodes 1 and 4 is momentarily suspended while another data transfer is in progress. Delay is minimized by fine-grained cell switching, but total throughput is limited to the speed of the bus. In (b), a multi-stage switching matrix allows all connections to proceed simultaneously. The parallelism of the architecture minimizes potential points of conflict, making it easier to scale up the number of connections. However, it also makes it more difficult to implement *multicasting*, whereby a single input cell is distributed to any combination of outputs.

Session Layer In cases where multimedia information does not come as a single stream (as when the video comes from a video server and the accompanying audio comes from a separate audio server) the session layer will have the unenviable task of synchronizing these simultaneous, parallel connections. The session layer will have to generalize current approaches to synchronization based on the insertion of "cue points" or markers in each of the individual data streams (see Shepard). The problem is complicated by the requirement in interactive video applications that the user be able to jump backward and forward through the combined data stream.

G. Karlsson and M. Vetterli, "Sub-band Coding of Video for Packet Networks," in *Optical Engineering*, Vol. 27, No. 7, July 1988, pp. 574–586.

D. Shephard and M. Salmony, "Extending OSI to Support Synchronization Required by Multimedia Applications," in *Computer Communications*, Vol. 13, No. 7, September 1990, pp. 399–406.

M. Rose, *The Open Book: A Practical Perspective on OSI*, Prentice-Hall, Englewood Cliffs NJ, 1989.

Presentation Layer   The presentation layer has been characterized as the layer where format conversion and data encoding should be performed. *Abstract Syntax Notation 1* (ASN.1) is the language used to specify the data types contained in messages sent across the network (see Rose). The encoding rules in ASN.1 would have to be extended to deal with new data types, such as standard compressed representations of digital video and audio. In addition, the presentation layer entities will have a role in negotiating service quality across the network. For it is at this layer that compression levels will be negotiated among the applications when the connection is established—since the presentation layer entities will have to determine the appropriate levels of compression needed to make efficient use of the bandwidth that can be obtained for their connection by the transport layer.

Application Layer   Application layer protocols provide connections for user-level information or data structures. Some of the most important protocols in this layer are the ISO X.400 (message-handling services) and ISO X.500 (global name resolution or *directory* services). While the protocols themselves are likely to remain stable, the type of data needed to be handled by these systems—as in the case of multimedia mail—will have to be extended. In addition, new protocols will be required to handle applications supporting the real-time sharing of information across networks, as in the case of multimedia conferencing. A number of institutions are addressing these issues (see Leiner). In Europe, ESPRIT has recently funded a project called OSI '95, chartered to develop an experimental distributed multimedia infrastructure. The lessons learned from applications developed with this infrastructure are expected to drive the next round of OSI networking standards. In addition, researchers at several U.S. institutions are addressing similar problems, using as their testbeds the emerging gigabit *National Research and Education Network (NREN)*, as well as other independent industrial and academic prototype networks.

B. Leiner (editor), *Critical Issues in High Bandwidth Networking*, Gigabit Working Group, RFC1077, November 1988.

REAL-TIME OPERATING SYSTEMS AND NETWORK SERVICES

With operating systems, as with networks, support for multimedia data introduces problems of timing. Time-sharing operating systems such as UNIX do not guarantee time-accurate performance. With stand-alone multimedia systems such as Intel's *Digital Video Interactive (DVI)*,

Phillips' *Compact Disc Interactive (CD-I)*, and Apple's *QuickTime* running under MacOS, the operating system's scheduler and file system can be modified to deal with the structure and timing requirements of multimedia applications. There is no need to worry about interoperability with real-time servers across the network, nor about compatibility and interference with existing services. The stand-alone approach does not, however, answer the needs of a multitasking or distributed computing environment.

In the past, the operating system community has dealt with new hardware and I/O devices by moving from a monolithic architecture to a simpler *system kernel* approach. The *kernel* of a computer operating system is the central piece of software, generally memory resident, that provides the most basic resource-management facilities in a multitasking environment, such as process scheduling, memory management, and I/O control. New devices and capabilities such as network interfaces can be added to the kernel incrementally.

When these systems were first developed, the goal was to make the basic operating system software small enough to use in single-processor architectures with limited amounts of memory.

UNIX was one of the earliest operating systems designed in this fashion. Early on, the minicomputer and workstation industries exploited these advantages in UNIX to make their applications usable in machines with less than one megabyte of main memory and only a few megabytes of disk space.

In most current operating systems, especially in UNIX, the kernel has grown more complex as new features and services have been added. At the same time, the growth of multiprocessor architectures and distributed systems are increasing pressure on the old designs. Consequently, new operating system designs are being developed that will address the needs of multimedia applications and the new distributed computing environments. With this in mind, let us analyze the type of functionality that users will come to expect from future operating systems, as distributed multimedia applications become pervasive in the information industry.

In the networked computing environment, resources needed for a multimedia application will normally be distributed across the network. They will be accessed through some form of the client/server model currently in vogue. In some instances audio and video information will be delivered to a client system through a single network connection. This would be the case when browsing a DVI or MPEG file, for example, where the video and audio data are merged. In other instances, the different media may arrive through separate network con-

Most computer workstations are shipped today with variants of the UNIX operating system, so we will use this system as our reference.

nections as streams originating in different points of the network. In the first example above, the operating system must parse the multimedia stream and place audio and video data into separate buffers where they can be handled by special-purpose processors. In the second example, the operating system must be able to keep up with multiple real-time network connections.

To complicate matters, the operating system supporting multimedia applications must be able to communicate with other systems about the priority of various activities. Task priority is one of the key mechanisms for achieving real-time performance in a multitasking operating system. In a client/server environment, priority must be negotiated among different systems across the network. In the case of file servers, negotiation implies a movement away from stateless servers, such as NFS, to servers that maintain a notion of the real-time requirements of the clients while a request is serviced.

J. K. Ousterhout, A. R. Cherenson, F. Douglis, M. N. Nelson, and B. B. Welch, "The Sprite Network Operating System," in *Computer*, Vol. 21, No. 2, February 1988, pp. 23–26.

A. S. Tanenbaum and R. van Renesse, "Distributed Operating Systems," in *ACM Computing Surveys*, Vol. 17, No. 4, December 1985, pp. 419–470.

In order to maintain the performance characteristics needed by multimedia clients, the operating system should be able to move its own processes across the network to workstations or servers that may be lightly loaded. Capabilities similar to these, but for non-real-time applications, are provided in experimental distributed operating systems such as Sprite (see Ousterhout) and Amoeba (see Tanenbaum). In the area of process migration and location transparency it is difficult to share data among operating system kernels executing on processors across the network. A distributed programming language supporting shared kernel data structures might provide a simple solution to this problem.

Finally, it must be stressed that extensions to handle continuous data in workstation operating systems must coexist with applications that might not need this extra functionality in the kernel. What is needed is a real-time extension to the philosophy of building operating systems based on the use of microkernels, pioneered by *Mach* (see Rashid) and *Chorus* (see Guillemont). The microkernel provides core functions, while specialized services are performed by subsystems that run in user space and communicate with the microkernel through *Inter-Process Communications (IPC)* ports. Under this approach a real-time microkernel scheduler would be able to circumvent the deficiencies of the UNIX scheduler, and different file-system architectures could be implemented as subsystems with specific performance expectations.

R. Rashid, R. Baron, A. Forin, D. Golub, M. Jones, D. Julin, D. Orr, and R. Sanzi, "Mach: A Foundation for Open Systems," in *Proceedings of the Second Workshop on Workstation Operating Systems (WWOS-II)*, pp. 109–113.

While the services needed to support real-time client/server multimedia applications seem daunting, the first steps are being taken. For years users of the different network operating system products have experienced interoperability problems when trying to communicate across product lines. This difficulty was generally due to the fact that most vendors use their own proprietary implementations of network protocols and file systems. With the continuous push for standardization and open systems, most of these vendors have announced their support for the *Distributed Computing Environment (DCE)* from the Open Software Foundation (OSF) (Figure 20.6). While the DCE does not provide any inherent support for distributed multimedia, it does offer a widely supported base platform to which the features can be added in an evolutionary manner (Figure 20.7).

M. Guillemont, "Microkernel Design Yields Real Time in a Distributed Environment," in *Computer Technology Review*, Vol. X, No. 16, January 1991, pp. 13–19.

HIGH-PERFORMANCE OBJECT STORES

Object-oriented programming techniques are well suited to implementing distributed multimedia applications. They simplify development and isolate technology-specific details of different media classes. But this approach depends on a high-performance object store that

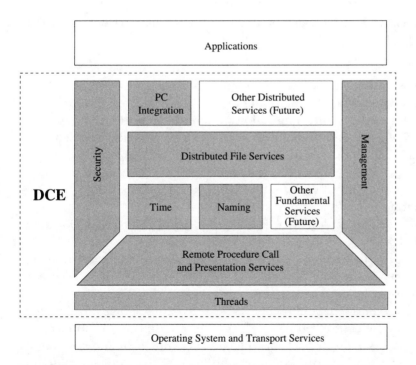

Figure 20.6   The Distributed Computing Environment (DCE) Architecture, as defined by the Open Software Foundation (OSF)

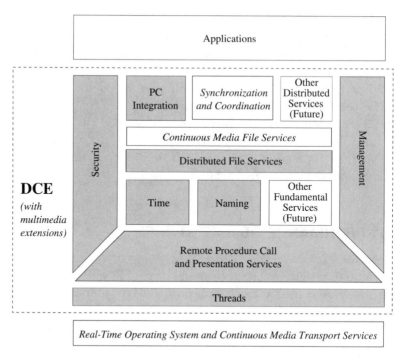

Figure 20.7   Suggested additions to the DCE architecture (in italics) needed to accommodate distributed multimedia applications

must satisfy a number of requirements. Size is an issue. Current relational database systems were designed primarily to support record-oriented data-processing applications, where the individual data units are quite small. Video or audio segments can be stored in the fields of a traditional database record, but most current implementations of large untyped fields—also known as *binary large objects (blobs)*—are limited to several kilobytes of data (~32 Kbytes), which is too small for practical applications of digital audio and video.

The size of multimedia data objects requires different block sizes and clustering strategies in the underlying data store. What is needed are ingenious access methods and storage layouts that can handle the addition and retrieval of massive pieces of information without compromising the performance of the whole system.

Hierarchical encoding schemes for video are a strategy for handling network congestion problems during the transmission of information from the server to a distant client. For implementation of such a scheme, the data store would have to manage the storage of different levels of the hierarchy and be able to respond to requests to deliver different levels of detail. With conventional databases, transactions are closed: when a request is received, all of the relevant data are delivered to the client in one transmission. This strategy may not be appropriate with large video objects. Rather, the database should understand how to transmit a large object in pieces, within the time constraints requested by the client. Also, the user may want to receive only a portion of a large object—several minutes out of a long video program. The database should understand how to handle these variations as well.

In addition to the need for storing and delivering very large binary objects, the multimedia object store must support simultaneous retrieval of audio and video elements by a number of users, while enforcing hard real-time constraints on parallel data accesses. Parallel access is needed to support applications where the video and audio are not stored together in the same storage device, but distributed across the network. It will also come into play where the different frames of a single video sequence are distributed among several storage devices operating in parallel, using the technique known as "striping" (see Cabrera).

L. F. Cabrera and D. D. E. Long, "Exploiting Multiple I/O Streams to Provide High Data Rates," in *Proceedings of the USENIX Summer Conference*, Nashville TN, 1991.

And because of expected changes in multimedia storage technology over the next few years, the multimedia object store must also be able to deal with multiple types of storage devices. Large-scale distributed systems are already outfitting the data-storage components with modularized device drivers to handle different types of optical juke-boxes and the like. With a distributed object store, access to media objects can be improved by replicating resources and moving them to the places where they are most needed. Such service will depend heavily on the naming and reliability capabilities of the operating system.

Addressing these issues constitutes a significant step forward in the management of multimedia applications. As mentioned earlier, most current multimedia applications are being designed for a stand-alone environment, where sharing of data does not occur. This situation will have to change as distributed multimedia applications become widespread across institutions and multimedia information becomes another valuable institutional asset.

MULTIMEDIA OBJECT INTEROPERABILITY

The multimedia interoperability layer will provide a homogeneous interface between applications and services. It will allow seamless integration of replicated servers for system reliability and normal growth, and will provide a mechanism to allow evolution of the hardware infrastructure underlying the system without damaging the information at the higher layers.

In addition, the interoperability layer will serve as an intelligent trader of services, negotiating between client applications and competing service providers. This negotiation process should not only take into consideration traditional concerns such as access charges, security, and trademark rights, but also more specific *Grade of Service (GOS)* requirements, such as real-time performance, bandwidth availability, video and audio quality, and the like.

For example, an application may request from the interoperability trader a video or audio object in a given format. The trader will attempt to locate a copy of the requested object in the appropriate format through an object store request. Once a copy is found in a storage server, the trader will find alternate paths between the client and the server selected. In order to decide on the most appropriate path, the trader will interrogate management agents located in the switches forming the nodes of the path, to determine whether the service request can satisfy the quality parameters requested by the user.

A similar negotiation will take place in binding clients to real-time services such as digital video protocol conversion. For example, if no copy of a video object is found in the appropriate format, the trader will perform a service request for a protocol conversion service and will negotiate changes to the quality of service sought between the requesting client and the protocol conversion service. Once the quality of service is negotiated, the trader will attempt to find a path from the storage server to the conversion server, and from there to the actual client. Some of these trading functions are starting to appear in the commercial world under the umbrella of distributed object management. In December 1991 the *Object Management Group (OMG)* released the first version of the specifications for the Common Object Request Broker Architecture (CORBA). CORBA's objective is to provide a standard interface that can be used by application vendors to describe the interfaces and services provided by object servers (Figure 20.8).

The Object Management Group is a non-profit organization chartered to establish interoperability standards for object-oriented programming.

One of the pieces of information a client must provide when requesting the service of a remote object is a *context*, a sequence of strings that the object request broker (ORB) uses in binding client to server. The context will be used by sophisticated ORB implementations to make binding decisions that take into consideration bandwidth availability and real-time capacity of servers. Once the interoperability layer is defined, the multimedia application development envi-

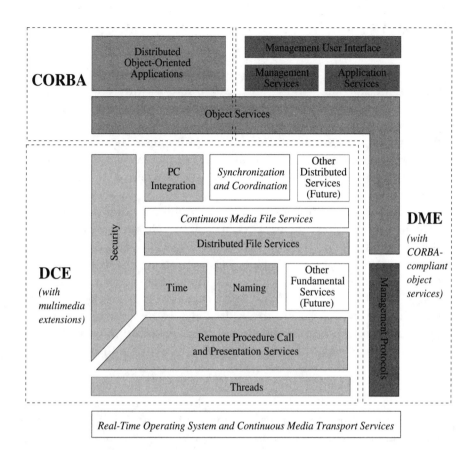

Figure 20.8   Open Systems Standards. Two industry consortia dedicated to open systems technology, the Open Software Foundation (OSF) and the Object Management Group (OMG), are specifying complementary standard software interfaces. The OSF's DCE will provide the lowest-level distributed services. The OSF's Distributed Management Environment (DME) will provide the framework for system and network administration. The OMG's Common Object Request Broker Architecture (CORBA) specifies how distributed objects can interoperate. The figure shows one vision of how these standards can fit together.

ronment—or *Service Creation Environment,* as it is known in telecommunications parlance—can be modified to take advantage of these network capabilities. Here the challenge is to make available these sophisticated services without dragging the author into a mire of complexity.

SUMMARY

Today multimedia applications are being developed primarily for stand-alone systems, where one user interacts with one computer, drawing from materials stored on a local device, such as a CD-ROM or videodisc player. The advances in technology discussed in this chapter suggest a fundamentally different type of application, wherein many users will communicate with one another over a network of computers, drawing upon comparatively vast resources distributed across the network.

Information providers will be able to "publish on demand" directly to consumers, using the network to solve their problems of media storage, delivery, and billing. Corporations will be able to link together employees in remote sites to form "virtual workgroups," using the network for conferencing and screen-sharing facilities. Shared "virtual realities" will become more and more convincing, allowing people to meet in information spaces that exist only on the network. These applications become possible once multimedia computing grows beyond the stand-alone environment and becomes part of a distributed network environment.

There is a simplistic view in some quarters of the telecommunications industry that the solution for distributed multimedia services lies in high-speed fiber-optic transmission coupled with fast cell switching. Unfortunately, basic data transport and switching capabilities are only the tip of a rather large iceberg. As discussed in this chapter, there are a host of complex software issues to be addressed, including network protocols for continuous media, real-time operating systems and network services, high performance object stores, and multimedia object interoperability.

This wide-angle view of the issues and technical underpinnings of broadband network computing may suggest that distributed multimedia services will not be in common use for quite some time. This is indeed the case; the first tentative models addressing some of these issues are only now beginning to appear in research laboratories. But this is a picture painted "in the large," describing what is needed to support large-scale multimedia applications for hundreds or thousands of users. In the shorter term, applications will begin to exercise intermediate versions of these facilities. It will be on the basis of these experiences that larger-scale systems will be implemented.

21. PackageSpec: The AthenaMuse Data Specification Environment

AthenaMuse was developed in two parts—a data specification environment and an object-oriented programming language. The subject of this chapter is the data specification environment, called PackageSpec. The object-oriented scripting language (EventScript) is described in the next chapter.

A data specification environment provides an author with predefined classes of objects. These can be "snapped together" as prefabricated parts, to build a variety of structures, in this case multimedia documents. The approach reduces the need for procedural programming, makes production easier and faster, and results in more flexible products.

Authors can supply values for some of the object attributes to change their appearance and to some extent their behavior. The data specification environment does not allow new classes of objects to be defined. There is no way to change the fundamental structure of the objects, and no provision is made for defining complex procedural characteristics. As a result, the definition of the objects is entirely in terms of data entries rather than procedures. The burden of complexity is reduced for the author, and the resulting material is easier to modify. However, there are limitations on what can be created, since everything is made from the same set of parts.

The quality of a data specification environment is determined by how easily the parts can be fitted together and modified to create the

For more information on the PackageSpec language, see the *AthenaMuse Data Description Language: Reference Manual,* by Matthew Hodges, Russell Sasnett, and Evelyn Schlusselberg, MIT Center for Educational Computing Initiatives, 1992.

267

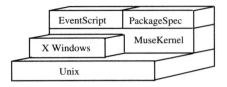

Figure 21.1   AthenaMuse Architecture

documents or applications that are needed. The particular set of objects provided in PackageSpec has some advantages over other sets of building blocks, as discussed in Chapter 5. It produces a relatively wide range of document types, but has serious limitations as a general system.

EventScript, the second part of the AthenaMuse system, provides a *procedural encoding* environment, where objects and behaviors are defined in terms of procedures. EventScript addresses some of the limitations of the PackageSpec architecture by providing a way to add customized behavior to PackageSpec objects and a way to access external data management and computational resources of the system (see Chapter 22).

The two components of AthenaMuse are layered on top of UNIX and the X Window System, as shown in Figure 21.1. The AthenaMuse run-time kernel serves both components. Objects defined in the two domains can be attached and can communicate with one another.

PACKAGESPEC

There are five basic types of objects that an author works with in the PackageSpec environment. These objects are called *packages, display elements, screens, dimensions,* and *maps.*

Packages   The basic "container" in PackageSpec is called a *Package.* Packages generally contain materials that function together as a unit; for example, a video and its subtitles or a picture and its caption.

Packages can be linked to form more complicated documents or information networks. Packages can be "active" or "inactive," so they do not all appear at the same time. One package can activate, deactivate, or cause a change of state in another package. Whole applications can be defined in terms of packages and transitions from one to another; this is the fundamental structure of any "hypermedia" system, and it is a very simple way to define a multimedia document or application.

Elements   The packages contain display materials defined as *Elements* (or Display Elements). These can be text, graphics, audio, video, still images, buttons, slidebars, or any of several other basic presentation elements. The various classes of display elements are described in more detail below.

Screens   When a package is activated, it "projects" its display elements onto a *Screen* or set of screens. Each screen maintains a reference to an X Window, which displays the package contents to the user. Each package identifies a set of screens it intends to use. Many packages may use the same screen, just as many films may be projected on the same screen in a cinema.

Dimensions   Dimensions define the shape and size of a package. If the package has shape and size, then the display elements can be assigned to different locations within it and displayed according to the viewer's current position within the package.

Suppose a package contains a video segment and some subtitles as its display elements. The subtitles should not appear all at once when the package becomes activated—they should be synchronized with the speaker in the video. Packages use the dimensions, the spatial construct, to define this relationship. When it is created, the package is given a dimension of time to organize the video and subtitles. Each package may be given one or more dimensions, which determine its "shape and size." Packages containing video generally have a dimension called *Time* or *FrameNumber*, long enough to accommodate the video sequence.

Maps   Next, the various display elements are mapped onto the package space, in effect defining where in the package each display element is located. These definitions are made with *Map* objects. Maps indicate when a display element will appear, when it will disappear, and in some cases how the data are to be "spread" over the package space.

In the video with subtitles example, the video element is mapped over the whole duration of *Time*. Each of the subtitles is mapped only to a small segment of *Time*, as shown in Figure 21.2.

The package has a notion of a "current position" within its space, which determines the frame of video that is displayed and the subtitle that will appear. The current position can be driven or jumped to any point in the range of the package. As the current position changes, the display elements are constantly updated.

The spatial construct in PackageSpec is quite powerful. It can be used to choreograph complex interactions very efficiently. Some authoring systems (for example, MacroMind Director) include a notion of time as a "hard-wired" aspect of each document. In AthenaMuse, the dimensions are completely under the control of the author. They can be used to model time and synchronize events in a temporal docu-

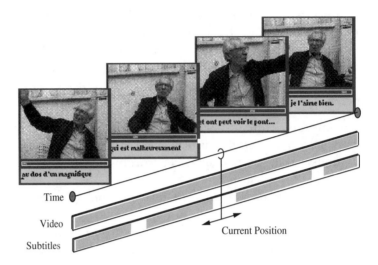

Figure 21.2   Video and corresponding subtitles mapped to a dimension of Time. In this example, there are two streams of subtitles and one stream of video. The current position along the dimension of Time determines which materials will be displayed.

ment, or they can be combined to construct a physical space or an abstract "state space."

Dimensions lay out the field of possibilities for change within a package. The spatial structure will vary according to the particular requirements of the package. Whatever dimensionality is assigned to the package, its state can be manipulated through a consistent set of action statements:

```
set_position      rset_position     reset_position
set_rate          rset_rate         reset_rate
set_range         rset_range        reset_range
activate          activate_set      activate_reset
switch_to         expire            quit
send_message
```

DISPLAY ELEMENTS

AthenaMuse provides a limited set of display elements that can be mapped into the package space. Each display element declares its type; this associates it with an appropriate set of display routines. Each type of display material has different attributes; these are recognized and processed by the different display routines.

Some of the attributes are media specific. Audio and video have an inherent temporal nature which text does not have, audio has multiple channels, and so on. Other attributes are hardware specific. Video display hardware offers a range of different capabilities for still and motion images. In AthenaMuse, these image classes are handled as two distinct display elements in order to take advantage of hardware capabilities.

The display elements contain maps in a hierarchical relationship. Maps contain the specific attributes of the display elements—size, color, file names, frame numbers, and the like. The maps associate these attributes with regions in the package space. Thus, in some cases, as with video and subtitles, the display element may change its appearance depending on the position within the package space from which it is viewed.

AthenaMuse supports the following classes of display elements:

Video   a sequence of images stored on videodisc;

Still Image   a sequence of video images which differs from motion video in that it can be scaled—a temporary artifact of the display hardware;

Pixmap   a sequence of images stored in binary format files on the computer;

Composite   an experiment in handling arrays of images, where the individual elements are stored as sequential frames on videodisc;

Text   based on the X Toolkit Text Widget, with the capability to associate character positions with regions in the package space;

Widgets   buttons and scrollbars, using X Toolkit Widgets embedded in AthenaMuse "wrappers";

Action   used to associate an action with a region of package space—nothing is displayed;

Package   a mechanism used to nest packages hierarchically, where the child package is activated or deactivated based on the current state of the parent package.

EXAMPLES

The following examples show the raw data description language for PackageSpec definitions. These definitions are normally not seen by the developer using the MuseBuilder and other high-level document editors.

Example 1.   Goodbye World

Goodbye World simply puts a button on the screen, which exits the application if pressed. Figure 21.3 shows the screen and the schematic representation of the document.

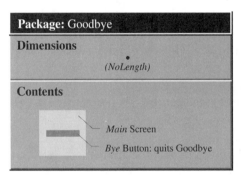 

Figure 21.3   Goodbye package

```
#  goodbye.m

#  First define a screen named Main:   parent is X Display's Root Window;
#  position 0, 0; 200 by 200 pixels; border width 8, color gray (45);
#  background color light gray (50).

screenset
{
    ("Main" window "RootWindow" 0 0 200 200 8 45 50)
}
```

```
#  Next define a package named "Goodbye": projects on screen "Main", active
#  on startup.  One dimension is required, set here to no length.

package "Goodbye"
{
    screen_name "Main"
    active
    dimension "NoLength" { min 0 max 0 initial 0 range 0 boundary limit }

#  One content element is included, called "Controls", containing one
button

    element "Controls"
    {
        type tkwidget
        screen_name "Main"
        active
        map button
        {
            pos_in 0
            pos_out 0
            label "Goodbye World"
            # x     y   w h fg bk brdcolor brdwidth
            ( 30   90   5 2 35 50     35        1     )
            font "times-bold18"
            function quit
        }
    }
}
```

Example 2.   A Video Controller

The second example shows a simple video controller. It has buttons to
play the video forward at 30 frames per second and to stop. It has a
scrollbar that can drag the video forward and backward and show the
passage of time as the video plays.

This example shows how video can be mapped onto a package's
space, then controlled indirectly by manipulating the "key dimension"
to which it is linked. In this case the dimension is affected independently by the timer and the scrollbar. Regardless of what causes the dimension to change its position, the video will be updated each time to
the appropriate frame.

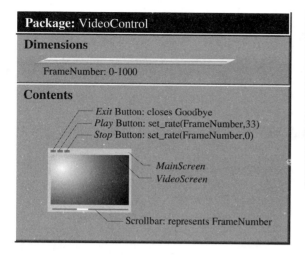

Figure 21.4   VideoControl package

```
#  video controller.m

#  Two screens are defined.  MainScreen will be used as the name of the set.
#  Its parent is the X RootWindow.  VideoScreen will show the video.  Its
#  parent is MainScreen.  The numbers specify placement (relative to parent),
#  border width and color, and background color.

screenset
{
    ( "MainScreen" window "RootWindow"  0  0 680 550 0 0 50 )
    ( "VideoScreen" video "MainScreen" 16 40 640 480 0 0 50 )
}


package "VideoControl"
{
    screen_name "MainScreen"
    active

#  The dimension has a timer associated with it.  Pace is the timer
#  function, called on an interval specified by rate (rate of 0 means
#  it is turned off for the moment).  When the Play button is pressed
#  the rate will be set to 33 milliseconds.  Then Pace will move the
#  current position of the dimension 1 step forward every 33
#  milliseconds (30 frames per second).  The Stop button resets the
#  rate to 0.

    dimension "FrameNumber"
```

```
   {
       min 0 max 1000 initial 0 range 0 boundary limit
       timer_fn pace
       parameter "VideoControl" 1
       rate 0
    }

   element "controls"
   {
       type tkwidget
       screen_name "MainScreen"
       active
       map button
       {
           pos_in 0
           pos_out 1000
           label "Exit"
           # x   y   w h  f bk bd bw
           ( 16 10 5 2 35 50 35 1 )
           font "*times-bold-r-normal—18-*"
           function quit
        }
       map button
       {
           pos_in 0
           pos_out 1000
           label "Play"
           # x   y   w h  f bk bd bw
           ( 66 10 5 2 35 50 35 1 )
           font "*times-bold-r-normal—18-*"
           function set_rate ("VideoControl" 33)
        }
       map button
       {
           pos_in 0
           pos_out 1000
           label "Stop"
           # x    y   w h  f bk bd bw
           ( 120 10 5 2 35 50 35 1 )
           font "*times-bold-r-normal—18-*"
           function set_rate ("VideoControl" 0)
        }

#      The scrollbar is set to represent dimension FrameNumber
#      in package VideoControl.  It represents the current position
#      of that dimension.  The width of the scrollbar represents
#      100 units of the dimension's length.  This statement
#      establishes a two-way constraint that causes the scrollbar
#      to move as time passes and lets the user drag the video
```

```
#      forward and backward

       map tkscroll
       {
          pos_in     0
          pos_out    1000
          orientation       horizontal
          # x    y    w  h  f bk bd bw
          ( 16 525 640 15 35 50 35  2)
          represents  "VideoControl" "FrameNumber" position 100
       }
}

# The video element maps frames 500 to 1500 on "VideoDisc" to
# positions 0 to 1000 on dimension FrameNumber.

   element "video"
   {
      type video
      active
      screen_name "VideoScreen"
      map video
      {
         pos_in 0
         pos_out 1000
         label "VideoDisc"
         in 500
         out 1500
         key_dimension 0
      }
   }
}
```

Example 3.   A Student Notebook

This example shows the user notebook from the *ChronoScope* application described in Chapter 6. At the outset the book has one hundred blank pages. The user can add images and text to each page to create a personal notebook. The book package is activated from the main menu of the *ChronoScope*. It can be opened and closed as needed.

This example shows communication with EventScript objects through the send_message action. In this instance there are two EventScript objects, which create new PackageSpec objects (text and still images) and insert them into the book package dynamically.

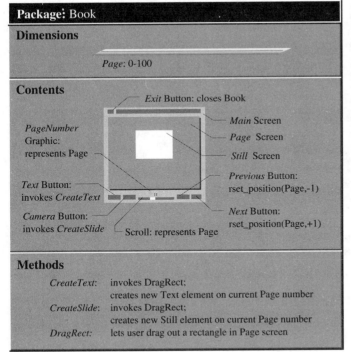

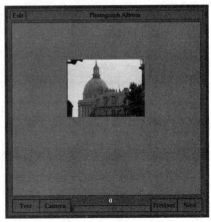

Figure 21.5   Book package

```
#  book.m

screenset
{
    ( "Main" window "RootWindow" 665 390 589 605 9 49 47 )
    ( "Page" window "Main" 11 40 560 505 2 44 51 )
    ( "Still" still "Page" 163 108 240 177 0 44 51 )
}

#  The book package defines a space of 100 pages, which are all blank
#  except for one still image on page 0.
#  Book uses some EventScript objects to add text and images to its pages.
#  It sends an initialization message to BookSlideMaker each time
#  it is opened (activated).

package "Book"
{
    screen_name "Main"
    active
    on_open send_message "BookSlideMaker: Initialize"
    dimension "page" { min 0 max 100 initial 0 range 0 boundary limit }
```

```
element "controls"
{
    type tkwidget
    screen_name "Main"
    active
```

The first button has no function. It serves as a title.
The numbers in parentheses specify the placement and
color of the button (x, y, width, height, foreground,
background, border color, and border width).

```
    map button
    {
        pos_in 0
        pos_out 100
        (56 6 522 26 41 48 39 1)
        label "Photograph Album"
        font "*times-bold-r-normal—18-*"
        resize 0
    }
```

The Next and Previous buttons use the rset_position
function (relative set_position) to step the page number
forward and back one unit.

```
    map button
    {
        pos_in 0
        pos_out 100
        (504 558 70 35 41 48 42 2)
        label "Next"
        font "*times-bold-r-normal—18-*"
        resize 0
        function rset_position ("Book" 1  )
    }
    map button
    {
        pos_in 0
        pos_out 100
        (423 558 78 35 41 48 42 2)
        label "Previous"
        font "*times-bold-r-normal—18-*"
        resize 0
        function rset_position ("Book" -1  )
    }
```

The Exit button causes the book package to expire, but
does not stop Muse. The main Orsay packages would still

```
#     be active while the book is open; the book could be
#     reopened from another package.

      map button
      {
          pos_in 0
          pos_out 100
          (8 6 43 26 41 48 39 1)
          label "Exit"
          font "*times-bold-r-normal—18-*"
          resize 0
          function expire ("Book" 0)
      }
```

```
#     The Text button causes a new text object to be created
#     and added to the current page of the book.  The button
#     sends a message to the EventScript object called
#     TextMaker, telling it to CreateText for package 'Book'.

      map button
      {
          pos_in 0
          pos_out 100
          (11 558 77 35 41 48 42 2)
          label "Text"
          font "*times-bold-r-normal—18-*"
          resize 0
          function send_message "TextMaker: CreateText Book"
      }
```

```
#     The Camera button works the same way as the Text button,
#     sending a message to the EventScript object responsible
#     for creating new still images.

      map button
      {
          pos_in 0
          pos_out 100
          (90 558 91 35 41 48 42 2)
          label "Camera"
          font "*times-bold-r-normal—18-*"
          resize 0
          function send_message "BookSlideMaker: CreateSlide Book Orsay:Side2"
      }
      map tkscroll
      {
          pos_in 0
          pos_out 100
          (185 577 234 16 35 48 42 2)
```

```
         orientation horizontal
         represents "Book" "page" position 100
      }
   }

#  PageNumber is a dynamic graphic text label.  It is bound to
#  the current position of dimension 'page' in package 'book'.
#  Whenever the page dimension changes, this element is updated
#  and prints the new page number on the screen.

   element "PageNumber"
   {
      type graphic
      screen_name "Main"
      active
      map label
      {
         pos_in 0
         pos_out 100
         label set_label_equal("Book,page,position")
         x1 300
         y1 570
         foreground 1
         font "*times-bold-r-normal—18-*"
         erase 1
      }
   }

#  The following element places frame 1 of Orsay:Side2 as a still
#  image on the first page of the book.

   element "still"
   {
      type still
      screen_name "Still"
      active
      map still
      {
         pos_in 0
         pos_out 0
         in 550
         out 550
         key_dimension 0
         label "Orsay:Side2"
      }
   }
}
```

22.　The EventScript Object System

When we faced the matter of building interactive editing facilities for AthenaMuse documents, we saw two alternatives: to add generic editing features to the run-time environment, or to create a set of independent special-purpose editors. Ultimately we decided on a completely different approach, which was to add an interpreted object language component to our basic document structure. We gave this layer access to the essential document manipulation procedures inside the AthenaMuse run-time system. Thus, editors could be written in AthenaMuse itself.

This solution appears to have a number of benefits. Editors become much easier to create and customize from within the document framework. Since *specification* and *programming* are separate activities, document construction can be broken into stages, possibly performed by different people. For example, a designer can use a point-and-click data editor to create a user interface, while a programmer implements the underlying functionality. Nontechnical users are able to grow into the system gradually, learning the programming side only as the need arises.

The EventScript object system was designed as an extension mechanism for AthenaMuse. It is an interpreted object programming environment that helps smooth the transition between the high-level PackageSpec layer and low-level resources such as C, UNIX, and the X

For more information on the EventScript language, see the *AthenaMuse EventScript: User Manual,* by V. Judson Harward, Evelyn Schlusselberg, and John Tedrow, MIT Center for Educational Computing Initiatives, 1992.

Window System. EventScript occupies the middle ground between PackageSpec and C, simplifying access to both layers while interfering with neither. The object orientation of the language makes it ideal for building abstractions around the core AthenaMuse entities, and for hiding the complexities of operating system interfaces.

EventScript objects are an optional part of an AthenaMuse document. They are necessary only when an author wants to perform a complex procedure not covered by the set of built-in *actions*, or to create an information editor that can synthesize new PackageSpec objects at run-time.

In this chapter we describe the basic concepts embodied in the EventScript object system, along with the fundamental language constructs and the behavior of the run-time system. Along the way we explore the pros and cons of various features, and evaluate in hindsight the wisdom of some of our design decisions.

EVENTSCRIPT OBJECTS

An EventScript object is a software entity characterized by a specific set of attributes and behaviors. An object's attributes are captured in *variables* that detail its current state. Behavior is described using simple procedural scripts, with each capability handled by a separate *method*. Objects interact with one another by sending *messages* back and forth. An object treats the receipt of a message as an *event*, and determines the appropriate method for handling it based on the content of the message.

The syntax used to describe an EventScript object is as follows:

```
object objectname
   [ uses "obj1" [, "obj2" [, ... ]] ]
{
   var var1 [, var2 [, ... ] ];
   ...

   on eventname [ param1 [, param2 [, ... ]] ]
   {
      statement;
      ...
   }
   ...
}
```

Here is an example of an object declaration:

```
object Total
{
    var sum;

    on add number
    {
        put (sum + number) into sum;
    }
}
```

Significant design features of the EventScript objects are outlined in the following paragraphs.

Object Cloning

In most object systems, objects are defined in terms of *classes*. A class description defines all of the attributes and behaviors expected for objects of a particular type. The class description is then used to create the individual objects, which are referred to as *instances* of the class.

In EventScript any object can be used as a *template* for new copies simply by *cloning* it. Templates are ordinary objects, with no special protocol for creating or initializing new instances. Instead, authors either can customize a template to their liking and then clone several copies, or they can initialize the individual clones one at a time after creation.

At the time of cloning, each clone is an exact copy of its template, including, if desired, the current values of all its variables. The clone has an independent copy of each variable in the template, but shares access to a single copy of the methods that remain stored in the template. Unfortunately, method sharing leads to hidden dependencies between theoretically independent templates and clones. We decided that the cost of copying methods would be excessive for large numbers of objects.

Objects are cloned with the C function *CloneObj()*:

```
Cfunc CloneObj(template_name, clone_name, copy_state);
```

The template object named *template_name* is located, and an exact duplicate of it named *clone_name* is created. If the *copy_state* flag is true, the values of all variables in the clone will be the same as those in the template; otherwise, all variables will be initialized to zero. Immediately after cloning, the system generates an optional *NewClone* message and sends it to the newly-cloned object. This message can be used to establish instance-specific initial values at the time of object creation.

Each clone stores the name of its parent, and each template keeps a list of its children. Any object can be cloned, even one that was created as a clone itself. Objects can find out about themselves and their environment via built-in C functions:

```
Cfunc theObj() returns Cstr;
— returns name of current object (self)

Cfunc IsClone(Cstr) returns Cint;
— returns True if given object is a clone

Cfunc ParentObj(Cstr) returns Cstr;
— returns name of parent object, if cloned

Cfunc HasChildren(Cstr) returns Cint;
— returns True if given object has been cloned
```

There are also utility functions, as for destroying objects or for sending a message to all clones of a given object. Since the current implementation of objects allows for method sharing, a template object cannot be destroyed if it has any children.

```
Cfunc DestroyObj(Cstr) returns Cint;
— destroys named object, returns error code

Cfunc SendToChildren(Cstr,Cstr);
— sends message string to all children of named object
```

Object Reference

Because EventScript was designed for naive users, we did not want authors to have to deal with pointers, addresses, memory management, and other problems that keep professional programmers awake nights. We decided that objects would be identified by a unique name. If two objects are declared with the same name, the system simply replaces the first one with the most recent declaration. The same holds true for environment variables and methods, and for object variables and methods.

One consequence of the decision to remove pointer syntax from the language is that objects cannot directly "contain" other objects. Most other object languages allow variables to hold complex object structures or indirect references to them. In EventScript an object variable can only contain the *name* of another object as a reference. This eventually forces some unusual programmer gymnastics in order to guarantee unique object names. For example, a programmer creating a linked list of objects must store object names in each node; and each node must be guaranteed a unique name, such as "MyListNode.1," "MyListNode.2," and so forth.

Variables

Variables hold simple values, primarily strings or numbers. They can be attached either to object or to the environment. All variables are untyped; internally the values are stored as character strings, integers, or floating-point numbers. Any variable can be modified with the *put* construct, which evaluates an expression and places the result into the named variable.

The internal representation of a variable may change during execution. In the context of a character string expression, a number may be promoted automatically to a string. In an arithmetic context, variables are converted to a more efficient numeric representation. The same policy applies to function calls, where the system takes care of any conversions needed to invoke a procedure with the correct parameter types. The author is usually not concerned with these details, although internal conversions may be forced, as in the following examples:

```
put (a+0) into a;
put (a+0.0) into a;
put (a & "") into a;
```

There are four kinds of variables: *ordinary, temporary, shared,* and *active*. Ordinary variables are the default variety attached to objects, and the only kind of environment variables. Ordinary variables maintain their values between method and function invocations.

Temporary variables occur in the context of a method or function definition; they are automatically created during parsing whenever an undeclared variable is encountered. This convention was borrowed from the BASIC language. Unfortunately, it can create hard-to-find bugs when the author misspells an object variable name and the system quietly turns it into a new temporary variable. In future versions of EventScript, authors will be able to set a flag in the interpreter to disallow the automatic creation of undeclared temporary variables.

```
object Test
{
    var myValue;

    on test
    {
       put 17 into MyValue;
       - note misspelling of myValue;
       - creates unwanted temporary var 'MyValue'
    }
}
```

In the case of a shared variable, the template object and all its clones access a single copy of the variable. Thus the author can maintain a memory common to a "class" of objects as a whole (analogous to *class variables* in other languages). An *active* variable is used to implement *active value* semantics, whereby the variable sends its owner a message whenever its value changes (see Stefik).

Active values are typically used when authors need to create continuously updated graphical representations of some data item. An *active* variable guarantees that all such changes will be shown automatically. Objects can arrange to receive a special "ValueChanged" message whenever a shared or active value changes state. Shared values are implicitly active; this method makes it easy to notify all objects of a given type about important changes in shared variables.

M. Stefik, D. Bobrow, and K. Kahn, "Integrating Access-Oriented Programming into a Multiparadigm Environment," in *IEEE Software*, Vol. 3, No. 1, January 1986.

```
object Thermometer
{
    active temperature;

    on ValueChanged name
    {
       if(name = "temperature")
       {
          - this section executes on every state change
          draw gauge with current temperature
       }
    }
}
```

Methods and Messages

All of the "work" in EventScript is done by the object methods (also called *handlers*), which are really just procedures owned by particular objects. Methods are invoked in response to messages sent to objects. A message in EventScript is an ordinary character string, whose first word is the *selector* naming the desired method. Subsequent words in the message string are parameters of the chosen method. Since any string can be used as a message, authors can easily construct messages at runtime using the built-in string operations.

method syntax:

```
on Message [Arg1 [,Arg2 [, ...]] ]
{
    statements ...
}
```

message syntax:

```
send "Message [Arg1 [Arg2 [...]] ]" to "objectname";
```

messaging example:

```
send "test one two three" to "TestObject";

object TestObject
{
    on test p1,p2,p3
    {
        p1 is 'one', p2 is 'two', p3 is 'three'
    }
}
```

When an object receives a message, the system checks whether the recipient owns a matching method. If not, the system backtracks through the list of "used" objects to see if any of them owns such a method. If found, the method is "borrowed" and executed within the context of the current object (the message recipient). If no such method exists, the system ignores it, but prints out a warning message.

Objects can completely *override* methods that would normally be borrowed from a "used" object by providing their own method with the same name. In this case, the borrowed method will never be called. An alternative is to perform a *partial override:* the used object's method is still invoked, but the recipient adds some processing of its own along the way. Partial overrides are accomplished with the *forward* statement, which causes the system to find and invoke every similarly named method in all of the "used" objects before returning.

```
— an example of forwarding

object A
{
    var a;

    on init
    {
        put 0 into a;
    }
}

object B
    uses A
{
    var b;

    on init
    {
        forward; — let component 'A' initialize
        put 0 into b;
        — now both a and b are 0
    }
}
```

THE OBJECT ENVIRONMENT

Objects in EventScript exist within an *environment*. The environment it-self can be given attributes and behaviors accessible to all the objects in the environment.

```
environment envname
    [ uses "envfile1" [, "envfile2" [, ...]] ]
{
    function prototypes ...
        Cfunc aFunction(Cint) returns Cint;

    global variables ...
        var aGlobal;
```

```
global methods ...
    on OpenEnv
    {
       - method description
    }

object definitions ...
}
```

The environment plays an important role in linking EventScript to the X Windows System and to other compiled C functions. It can contain *function prototypes* describing C-language function interfaces and external variables that these functions may use. The prototypes let EventScript know the number and type of parameters expected by a C function, and what type of value it returns (if any). The same syntax is used to declare external variables. EventScript objects can call any of these functions or access any of the variables declared in this way, thereby providing an easy way to access any compiled function linked to the program space.

```
- Cflt describes a floating-point C variable;
- Cint an integer; and Cstr a string.

Cfunc sqrt(Cflt) returns Cflt;
Cfunc atoi(Cstr) returns Cint;
Cint errno; - a global integer defined in C code
```

Also, the environment itself can be the target of *system* messages generated by the AthenaMuse kernel. Some system messages inform specially named objects about important events, such as error conditions. Other system messages are synthesized dynamically in response to X Window System events and delivered to designated "event handler" objects. Although any object can send messages to any other object, only the system can invoke the environment's event handlers.

Handling X Events Special support is provided for registering an EventScript object to handle events for a given X Window. Any X Window System occurrences in the window, such as mouse movement or button events, will automatically be translated into EventScript messages, and delivered to the registered object.

```
Cfunc RegisterWindow(Cstr,Cint);
- binds given X window ID and named object.
```

```
— as in this example:
RegisterWindow("ObjectA", WindowID);
```

The registered object uses special method names to select the events it is interested in receiving. Here are the formats of some X-specific message handlers:

```
on ButtonPressed which,x,y { }
on ButtonReleased which,x,y { }
on KeyPressed ascii,code,string { }
on ExposeWindow { }
on EnterWindow mode,detail,subwindow { }
on LeaveWindow mode,detail,subwindow { }
on MouseMoved x,y,keymask { }
on LeftDownMotion x,y,keymask { }
on RightDownMotion x,y,keymask { }
on MiddleDownMotion x,y,keymask { }
etc.
```

EventScript also provides a number of interface functions that map into X requests. For example:

```
 — pass a window ID to these X interface functions:
MapWindow(Cint); — make the window visible
UnmapWindow(Cint); — hide the window
RaiseWindow(Cint); — bring the window to the front
LowerWindow(Cint); — push the window to the back
ClearWindow(Cint); — clear to background color
etc., etc.
```

Because EventScript was developed with version 10 of the X Window System, it does not support the concept of multiple X displays. Information about the display is held in system globals, accessible from object scripts that need to call X functions directly:

```
Cint myDisplay;
Cint myScreen;
Cint myColormap;
```

External Function Calls

EventScript can invoke correctly any C function that accepts parameters and returns values in any of the following atomic data types: *char, char*, int, long, float, double.* Complex types such as pointers to structures are not supported, unless the pointer can be treated by EventScript as an "opaque type" (never dereferenced). If a particular function requires such complex types, the author needs to create a *wrapper* function that accepts only atomic types, translates them into the more complex types, and then calls the desired function.

Today many operating systems support *dynamic linking*, whereby new functions can be loaded into a running program. At GTE Laboratories we modified EventScript to support dynamic linking under SunOS 4.1. This feature lets authors load and invoke their own compiled C functions from EventScript, without having to link them into the Athena-Muse program.

Functions may return values to EventScript in one of two ways: by ordinary "return" statements, and by modifying any string parameters in place. In the latter case, EventScript will notice that the string values have been modified by the function, and it will copy them back into the relevant EventScript variables. Strings are defined as character arrays of length 255; longer strings may be created by C functions, with pointers to them passed back and forth in EventScript as integers.

PackageSpec Interface

EventScript environments may be loaded into AthenaMuse applications with the *scriptfile* declaration. Refer to Chapter 21 for details of the AthenaMuse data definition language. Objects may be attached to AthenaMuse elements by specifying a special *script* attribute.

```
# example: attaching a script to an AthenaMuse element

element "Picture"
{
    type still
    screen_name "Frame"
    active
    script "VideoButtonObject"

    map still
    {
        pos_in 0
        pos_out 54000
        in 9247
        key_dimension 0
    }
}
```

In this example the element contains a single map that places a still video image (frame 9247) onto the screen (really just an X window) named "Frame." When the package containing this element is activated, the EventScript template object "VideoButtonObject" will be cloned with a unique name and attached to the map. Any selected X events that occur on the screen, such as the user pressing a mouse button, will be reported in messages to the clone of VideoButtonObject.

If there were several maps in the above element, a different copy of VideoButtonObject would be cloned and attached to each one. At GTE Laboratories, AthenaMuse has been enhanced to allow named objects to be attached directly to individual maps rather than to the parent element. The common problem of authors having to create a large number of single-map elements, when each map requires a different template object, is thereby avoided.

Objects bound to AthenaMuse elements often need access to internal AthenaMuse data structures. Authors may need to discover the AthenaMuse package where the object exists, or to invoke one of the built-in AthenaMuse actions such as *set_position*. When objects are being attached to an element at run-time, each new clone will receive a *SetPkgInfo* message immediately after the *NewClone* message. The *SetPkgInfo* handler receives parameters telling it the package, element, screen, map, and widget identifiers relevant for the AthenaMuse object to which it is attached. These identifiers, or IDs, can then be used as parameters to "glue" functions that manipulate AthenaMuse data structures.

AthenaMuse authors can specify an optional initialization message to be sent to clones immediately after the *SetPkgInfo* message. This is accomplished with the following syntax:

```
optional initialization syntax for object scripts:

script "TemplateName: selector [Arg1 [Arg2 [...]] ]"

example:
script "VideoButtonObject: SetIconFrame 1293"
```

AthenaMuse, using the built-in *send_message* action, can generate EventScript messages in three ways. Authors can cause a message to be sent whenever a button widget is pressed:

syntax for a send_message action:

```
map button
{
   ...
   function send_message "ObjectName: selector [Arg1 [Arg2 [...]] ]"
}
```

example:

```
send_message "VideoButtonObject: PlayVideoSegment 12000 12100"
```

An EventScript object can be registered to receive notification whenever a package changes position in its dimension space:

```
package "ColorPalette"
{
   screen_name "Main"
   dimension "grayscale"
   {
      min 0
      max 31
      initial 0
      boundary limit
      on_change send_message "ColorObject: NewColor"
   }
   ...
}
```

Finally, objects can be notified whenever a particular package is opened ("activated") or closed ("expired").

```
package "ColorPalette"
{
   ...
   on_open send_message "MainObject: OpenPackage"
   ...
}
```

There are also several administrative tasks in the AthenaMuse environment that can be delegated to special objects, such as overseeing the loading and unloading of new information from the parsers. Generally an object is registered for such tasks via a C function; thereafter the registered object receives status messages from the runtime system.

SUMMARY

As with any scripting language, EventScript seeks to make an effective compromise between ease of use and power. Making a language easy to use opens the door to the nonspecialist. The authoring system has greater impact because more people can use it. At the same time, the ability to support complexity lends strength to the authoring system in that it broadens the range of applications that can be created.

In the wider view of things, we do not view procedural programming as easy for nonspecialists. Crossing the boundary from data specification to procedural coding is a major transition in difficulty and leaves many people behind.

Nonetheless, we can say that some of the features of EventScript were designed for ease of use. The first of these is characteristic of scripting languages in general; the code is interpreted at run-time rather than compiled. The modification cycle is therefore greatly simplified, a feature that is extremely important to nonspecialists. The simple connection to the compiled program space through the *Cfunc* declarations has proved highly effective.

The object model of EventScript was chosen for both ease of use and power. The level of complexity in object programming can vary widely, from extremely simple models that are easily planned and implemented to extremely subtle complexes whose interactions and behaviors may be difficult to comprehend. With its forwarding mechanism for partial behavior overwrite, shared variables, active values, and multiple inheritance, EventScript offers a great deal of expressive power.

H. Lieberman, "Using Prototypical Objects to Implement Shared Behavior in Object-Oriented Systems," in *Proc. of 1986 Conf. on Object-Oriented Programming Systems, Languages, and Applications (OOPSLA),* ACM Press, New York NY, pp. 214–223.

One of the simplifying features of EventScript is its cloning model of inheritance, which eliminates the common confusion between class definition and instance (see Lieberman). It also increases the dynamic character of the language in the same way that the interpreter does—new species of objects can be created while the program is running, whereas the conventional class/instance approach allows only new instances of pre-defined classes.

This type of simplification can backfire. One of the "obvious" simplifications turned out to be a liability, that of undeclared-variable creation. Failing to declare a variable is a common error in beginner programming. Therefore, if the variables need not be declared explicitly before being used, one would expect matters to be simpler for the nonspecialist. It turns out, however, that programmers tend to misspell variable names at least as frequently as they fail to declare them, and tracing a program failure to a spurious variable is far more difficult than responding to a complaint from the interpreter for having failed to declare one.

These are consequences that cannot always be anticipated. Event-Script, like its counterpart, PackageSpec, was developed as an experiment. It showed some good features and some poor ones. Above all, it offered insight into how to combine data specification with scripting, and in turn scripts with compiled program segments. It is largely through this integration that one can address the broader issues of reconciling ease of use with powerful programming.

Afterword

When first introduced, the computer was a tool for manipulating numbers. Now it is evolving into a multipurpose tool for communication and the expression of ideas. The computer has grown beyond its numeric foundations to incorporate text, color graphics, digital audio, and motion video. Each of these media adds to the expressive power of the machine, but at the same time heightens its complexity and increases the challenge of providing easy access to its resources.

In this book we have presented an in-depth look at our experiences designing multimedia systems and applications for the MIT community. In addition we have tried to present a coherent framework for thinking about the emerging role of these technologies in business and academic settings. Perhaps our greatest contribution here has been to address the most fundamental question about multimedia: "what is it good for?"

As new technologies emerge, new fields of possibility open up. Often the potential of these developments greatly exceeds our ability to imagine new uses for them. Who could have foreseen the creation of the multimedia applications described in these pages upon viewing the first photographs or motion pictures? As the computer's expressive powers begin to unfold, we must continue searching for the fundamental forms that will enable us to make the most effective use of this new medium.

Index

COMPLIMENTARY VIDEOTAPE

The authors would like to know more about you. Please take a moment to answer the questions below. Cut out or make a copy of this page, fill in your responses, and return it to us along with your name and address. We will send you a videotape highlighting applications described in the book, with commentary by the authors.

Thank you for your interest.

Matthew Hodges and Russell Sasnett

1 Which chapters did you find most useful? _____

2 Would you like more technical information? _____

3 Do you need more detailed strategic information about multimedia? _____

4 Would you find case studies of business applications useful? _____

In what areas? _____

5 Is your company engaged in re-engineering its communication processes? _____

Internally? _____   With customers? _____   With suppliers? _____

6 Other comments or questions:

Name _____

Title _____   Company _____

Address _____

City _____   State/Country _____

Postal Code _____   Telephone _____

Electronic Mail _____   Fax _____

This videotape has been produced courtesy of Convergent Media Systems Corporation, 25 Porter Road, Littleton, MA 01460 USA, and Vision Arts Incorporated.

Return to: Vision Arts, 9 Selden Street, Waban, MA 02168 USA

Include $4.95 for postage and handling. Make checks payable to Vision Arts.